高等学校法学双语系列教材

华东政法学院课程和教材建设委员会

主　任　何勤华
副主任　杜志淳　王立民　顾功耘　叶　青
委　员　刘宪权　张梓太　王虎华　杨正鸣　宣文俊
　　　　　王嘉禔　张明军　岳川夫　徐永康　穆国舫
　　　　　苏惠渔　游　伟　肖建国　刘丹华　殷啸虎
　　　　　林燕萍　何　萍

The Fight against Money Laundering
A Comparative Perspective

反洗钱：比较法的视角

何 萍（He Ping）著

北京大学出版社
PEKING UNIVERSITY PRESS

图书在版编目(CIP)数据

反洗钱:比较法的视角 = The Fight against Money Laundering: A Comparative Perspective/何萍著. —北京:北京大学出版社,2006.8
(高等学校法学双语系列教材)
ISBN 978 - 7 - 301 - 10987 - 8

Ⅰ.反… Ⅱ.何… Ⅲ.金融－刑事犯罪－对比研究－世界－双语教学－高等学校－教材－英、汉 Ⅳ.D912.280.4

中国版本图书馆 CIP 数据核字(2006)第 096431 号

书　　　名:反洗钱:比较法的视角
　　　　　　The Fight against Money Laundering: A Comparative Perspective
著作责任者:何萍(He Ping)　著
责 任 编 辑:丁传斌　王业龙
标 准 书 号:ISBN 978 - 7 - 301 - 10987 - 8/D·1549
出 版 发 行:北京大学出版社
地　　　址:北京市海淀区成府路 205 号　100871
网　　　址:http://www.pup.cn
电　　　话:邮购部 62752015　发行部 62750672　编辑部 62752027
　　　　　　出版部 62754962
电 子 邮 箱:law@ pup.pku.edu.cn
印　刷　者:三河市北燕印装有限公司
经　销　者:新华书店
　　　　　　730 毫米×980 毫米　16 开本　19.75 印张　354 千字
　　　　　　2006 年 8 月第 1 版　2011 年 1 月第 3 次印刷
定　　　价:28.00 元

未经许可,不得以任何方式复制或抄袭本书之部分或全部内容。
版权所有,侵权必究
举报电话:010 - 62752024　电子信箱:fd@ pup.pku.edu.cn

Abbreviation

APG	Asia/Pacific Group on Money Laundering
AWF	Analytic Work File
BIS	Bank of International Settlement
CDPC	European Committee on Crime Problems
CFATF	Caribbean Financial Action Task Force
CHERC	China-Holland Education and Research Center
CJHA	Cooperation in Justice and Home Affairs
EC	European Community
ECHR	European Convention for the Protection of Human Rights and Fundamental Freedoms
ECSC	European Coal and Steel Community
ECUPL	East China University of Politics and Law
EDU	Europol Drugs Unit
EEC	European Economic Community
EJN	European Judicial Network
ELN	Europol Liaison Network
EU	European Union
EUR	Erasmus University Rotterdam
Eu-ratom	European Atomic Energy Community
Europol	European Police Office
FATF	Financial Action Task Force on Money Laundering
FinCEN	Financial Crimes Enforcement Network
FIU	Financial Intelligence Unit
GDP	Gross Domestic Product
ICPO	International Criminal Police Organization
ISD	Investment Services Directive

IT	Information Technology
KYC	Know Your Customer
NCCT	Non-Cooperative Countries and Territories
NPC	National's People's Congress
OAS	Organization of American States
OECD	Organization for Economic Cooperation and Development
OLAF	EU's Anti-Fraud Organization
PRC	People's Republic of China
RMB	Ren Min Bi (Chinese Currency)
SAFE	State Administration of Foreign Exchange
SIS	Schengen Information System
UK	United Kingdom
UN	United Nations
USA	United States of America
US $	United States Dollars
Vol.	Volume

Preface

In February 2001 I was luckily selected by the Chairman of CHERC (China-Holland Education and Research Centre), Prof. Willem Lammerts van Bueren, to have the chance to be included in a two-month Master Class in Erasmus University Rotterdam in July-August 2001. During the two months, I attended all the wonderful lectures organized by CHERC and showed great interest in the research topic with regard to money laundering. Under the guidance and supervision of Prof. Hans de Doelder, the then dean of the law faculty, and Dr. Vincent Mul, an expert in the field of anti-money laundering, I embarked on a preliminary research work. With the approval from Prof. De Doelder of my proposal, I was encouraged to pursue a further research. Therefore, conducting Ph. D. research abroad, a long-cherished dream turned out to be a reality for me in the beginning of the New Millennium.

In the last four years, I traveled back and forth between China and Holland. Every year I spent several months in Rotterdam, a fascinating place boasting a fascinating people. Rotterdam was my second home, where I nourished a new hope of my career. No doubt, life style of doing Ph. D. research abroad was boring and hard, but it was also rewarding and encouraging. Collecting material, seeking advice, reading and writing ceaselessly, I was deeply absorbed in my research topic.

Little by little, step by step, slowly but steadily, considerable progress has been made in my chosen area. In the process, I had four English articles published in the *Journal of Money Laundering Control* in the United Kingdom. They were "*Chinese Criminal Law Concerning Money Laundering*", "*The Chinese Financial Institution Campaign against Money Laundering*", "*Banking Secrecy and Money Laundering*", and "*New Trends in Money Laundering—From the Real World to Cyberspace*". Additionally, I saw several of my Chinese articles printed in China's journals, such as *Law* and *Juristic Review*. All of these are essential parts of my dissertation.

After I submitted my dissertation to my supervisor, Prof. De Doelder, he thought highly of my work. "You have done a wonderful job", "You are one of my best Ph. D. students" are some examples of his compliments. Dr. Mul made the following comments on my dissertation, "Your book is complete, up to date, very well documented, and has a high level of intellectual analysis. Further, you have put much your own opinion and criticism in it."

Looking back on the last four years, I would like to say:

To start this Ph. D. project was an act of courage.

To carry on the project in the face of difficulties was an act of perseverance.

The successful conclusion of the project was a combination of excellent guidance, zealous support and good luck.

During the course of my Ph. D. research project, I owed a lot to the following:

First and foremost, I greatly appreciate the encouragement, guidance and academic stimulus from my promoter Prof. De Doelder from the inception of this study to its completion. His instructions will stimulate me to make greater efforts forever.

Second, I would like to express my sincere gratitude to Dr. Mul for his guidance and invaluable comments that I have been able to incorporate into my work. Every bit of the progress that I have made during my Ph. D. research is closely related to his genuine help.

As mentioned above, Prof. Lammerts van Bueren is the initiator who made my Ph. D. research abroad possible. Allow me to show my heartfelt thanks to him. I am also very grateful to Mrs. Tseng Wei-jia, the managing director of CHERC, and Mr. Zhao Qi, the assistant of CHERC, for their organizing my several trips to Holland and providing me a lot of convenience.

My gratitude goes to Mrs. Zhu Li-fang, my dear colleague in East China University of Politics and Law, and my American friend Mr. Andrew C. Johnston, who gave me a lot of help in improving my English language and polishing my dissertation.

My thanks also go to my Dutch friends, Miss Cathelijne van der Schoot, Mr. Paul Verloop, Mr. Joost Verbaan, Mr. Haje Weisfelt, Mr. Ernst pols, Dr. Tom Blom, Dr. Arthur Hartmann and Mr. Robin Dijke, who made me feel at home during my stay in Holland.

Besides, I would also like to show my great thanks to my Finnish friend Mr. Timo Ahonen, who mailed some English material about my topic from remote Finland.

In addition, I am indeed obliged to my dear husband, Zhou Wei-ping, whose limitless devotion and support was a comfort helping me to complete this book. I am equally thankful to my kindly parents, He Mu-jun and Hu Yue-hui, for their encouragement and pride of their daughter. Moreover, I am thankful to my beloved son Zhou Yi-ren who was not able to receive my full attention in my absence.

Finally, successful conclusion of this Ph. D. project would not have been possible without the financial help of the "Hoogeschool-Fonds 1920". I owe a lot to this foundation. I truly doubt words can express my devout gratitude for their indispensable, generous support.

Prelude

```
The Speech of Prof. Hans De Doelder on defense day
```

My dear He Ping,

At this very moment (in 2004) you are Associate Professor in Criminal Law and Deputy Dean of Studies at East China University of Politics and Law. You have started your PhD project on money laundering at Erasmus University, Rotterdam in 2001. You have written dozens of Chinese papers in print in China's Journals, such as *Law* and *Juristic Review*. You also have published several English papers in the *Journal of Money Laundering Control* in the United Kingdom.

You were born in 1970. This means that you are 34 years old. That is rather young for having written so many articles, even in international journals. You have as a dean for Studies a responsible function within your University. And you have written your PhD thesis within three years!

I can see that the audience agrees with me saying that you have done a wonderful job. Your book is a high standard book about an international problem, not only to be solved at a national level, but indeed at an international level. International mutual cooperation is therefore necessary. From now on the cooperation between Chinese and EU-policemen, prosecutors and judiciary could be improved, because of the fact that they can learn from your book about the situation in the EU as well as in China.

You not only want to fight against money laundering, but also want to maintain the order of the society and to create a peaceful and stable living environment. So, not only law enforcement is important, but also the protection of human rights. Governments have the duty to take into account both sides. Although it is, in this world threatened by organized crime and terrorism, quite modern to only think of fighting criminals, it should be said that this world would not be getting safer, better and more justified by policing civilians too much. There has to be left room for living without being confronted with too much controls and law-enforcement agencies. That is the concept of freedom we want to keep in our society.

Dr. He Ping, you have written your thesis under my supervision, but Mrs. Tsjeng and Mr. Lammers van Bueren have helped you in an extraordinary way. Prof. Lammerts Van Bueren has selected you together with Dr. Van der Pijl in Shanghai, expecting that you could write a well-written thesis within a reasonable time. These three people symbolize the strong wish of the Erasmus University to cooperate with your home university. During the last years there has been an extraordinary cooperation between CHERC, the China-Holland Education and Research Center on the side of the Erasmus University and your University on the other side. We have made it possible by financing and giving supervision; you from your side have done the work. The first successful PhD student from your university we have had in our Dutch Law School, Prof. Liu Xian-quan is the dean of your faculty. The second student we had was your colleague Tang Bo, who also successfully did her PhD defense today. Of course we congratulate her with her result. And you are the third teacher having succeeded in getting the Rotterdam PhD-title.

I already mentioned CHERC. I want the underline here the extraordinary task they fulfill within our university. They spend the money given by the general board of our university and the High School Funds on a very sophisticated way, namely by spending it in very successful projects like this one. They give a very important emotional and mental support to the Chinese participators on this PhD program. I thank them in the person of Prof. Lammerts Van Bueren and Mrs. Tsjeng very much, and I also want to thank Dr. Van de Pijl for his mentioned financial and personal support.

One of the disadvantages of this successful day is that we have to say goodbye to you. You have been here for several times and have worked here, leaving your husband and son, in a sandwich like program: a few months here in Rotterdam, followed by a longer stay in your home city Shanghai. During your time here in Rotterdam I have tried to give you some assistance, but was not very available. Therefore I thank Dr. Vincent Mul and other members of my department very much that they were able and willing to help me by giving advise to you during the past years. And, by the way, of course, I am very proud to see three of my former PhD students (not only Dr. Mul, mentioned before), but also Prof. Schaap and Prof. Rogier as members of this committee. So you can expect having a same great future.

Saying good-bye will not be a definitive separation of our ways. My law School has decided to intensify the cooperation between our two institutions. We will receive delegations of your university and I look forward to visiting your University again and again to give some lectures. I already have visited Shanghai several times, and I have also made some interesting excursions in the neighborhood. I like your city very much.

My dear Mrs. He, I am going to finish. You have done a wonderful job; you have been very special in quick understanding the European and Dutch legislation. You have adjusted yourself to the Dutch way of living in a short time: you even like cheese. You are an example for a real world citizen. My congratulations for all these results!

Prof. Dr. Hans De Doelder
September 2, 2004

Contents

Introduction ·· 1

Chapter 1 General Remarks on Money Laundering ····································· 5
    1.1 Introduction ·· 5
    1.2 The Emergence and Status Quo of Money Laundering ················· 5
    1.3 The Definition of Money Laundering ·· 8
    1.4 The Characteristics of Money Laundering ··· 11
    1.5 The Significance of Preventing and Fighting against
        Money Laundering ··· 13
    1.6 Conclusions ·· 15

Chapter 2 Global Responses to Money Laundering ································· 16
    2.1 Introduction ·· 16
    2.2 The Basel Committee Statement ··· 17
    2.3 United Nations Convention against Illicit Traffic in Narcotic
        Drugs and Psychotropic Substances ··· 20
    2.4 United Nations Convention against Transnational
        Organized Crime ·· 32
    2.5 The Financial Action Task Force ··· 40
    2.6 Interpol ·· 59
    2.7 Conclusions ·· 67

Chapter 3 Western European Responses to Money Laundering ············ 69
    3.1 Introduction ·· 69
    3.2 The Council of Europe Recommendation ··· 71
    3.3 The Council of Europe Convention on Laundering, Search,
        Seizure and Confiscation of the Proceeds from Crime ··················· 75
    3.4 Council Directive of 10 June 1991 on Prevention of the Use of the
        Financial System for the Purpose of Money Laundering ··················· 83

3.5 Directive 2001/97/EC of the European Parliament and of the Council, Amending Council Directive 91/308/EEC on Prevention of the Use of the Financial System for the Purpose of Money Laundering 92
3.6 Europol 104
3.7 Eurojust 108
3.8 Conclusions 111

Chapter 4 Chinese Criminal Law Concerning Money Laundering 113
4.1 Introduction 113
4.2 Evolution of the Criminal Law 114
4.3 The Elements of Money Laundering Crime by Criminal Law 120
4.4 The Relationship between Money Laundering and Relevant Offences 128
4.5 The Punishment for Money Laundering Crime 129
4.6 Conclusions 133

Chapter 5 The Chinese Financial Institution Campaign against Money Laundering 134
5.1 Introduction 134
5.2 Background 134
5.3 Major Contents 136
5.4 Conclusions 147

Chapter 6 The Current Situation of Money Laundering Crime in China 150
6.1 Introduction 150
6.2 Predicate Offences 150
6.3 Other Factors Conducive to Money Laundering Crime 156
6.4 The Judicial Situation of Money Laundering Crime: Few Has Been Prosecuted Yet 162
6.5 The Endeavors to Be Made to Investigate Money Laundering Crime 166
6.6 Conclusions 170

Chapter 7 Comparison of Anti-money Laundering System between the EU and China 171
7.1 Introduction 171

7.2	Criminal Measures	172
7.3	Preventive Measures	180
7.4	Conclusions	195

Chapter 8 Several Special Issues ………………………………… 197
   8.1 Banking Secrecy and Money Laundering ……………………… 197
   8.2 Lawyers, Notaries, Accountants and Money Laundering ………… 210
   8.3 High Technology and Money Laundering
        —A New Trend in Money Laundering:
        From the Real World to Cyberspace ……………………… 222

Chapter 9 Summary and Conclusions ………………………………… 235
   9.1 The Issue of Money Laundering ………………………………… 235
   9.2 Common Efforts in the World ………………………………… 236
   9.3 China's Anti-money Laundering Efforts and the Gaps
        between the EU and China ………………………………… 240
   9.4 Banking Secrecy, Professional Privilege and High Technology ……… 243
   9.5 Final Remarks ………………………………………………… 245

Appendix ……………………………………………………………… 247
   Appendix 1 《中华人民共和国刑法修正案(六)》对洗钱罪的修改 ……… 247
   Appendix 2 Rules for Anti-money Laundering by Financial Institutions … 249
   Appendix 3 Administrative Rules for the Reporting of Large-Value and
               Suspicious RMB Payment Transactions ……………… 255
   Appendix 4 Administrative Rules for the Reporting by Financial
               Institutions of Large-Value and Suspicious Foreign Exchange
               Transactions ………………………………………… 261
   Appendix 5 The Forty Recommendations (2003) ……………………… 270
   Appendix 6 Council Directive on Prevention of the Use of the Financial
               System for the Purpose of Money Laundering (2001) ……… 289

Bibliography ……………………………………………………………… 297

Introduction

Purpose of this Project

Money laundering, the lifeline of international organized crimes, has posed a great threat to the international community. Money laundering undermines the integrity of financial institutions. Money laundering facilitates underlying crimes by allowing criminal funds to be reinvested. Money laundering has a corrosive influence on economic development and political stability. As it does serious harm to the society, the research on how we can set up a comprehensive system to effectively control this problem is of vital importance.

It has been noted that much response has been made at the international level during the last two decades. This book aims to look through the various efforts in combating money laundering, to find out how the measures against money laundering are getting from strength to strength and what are the currently international standards, which can be followed by individual countries.

Due to the short history of legal system in China and the backward economic base for a long time, the fight against money laundering in China is just at the initial stage. Money laundering crime was first provided under the "Decision on Suppressing Drug Dealing" in 1990. Afterwards, it was formulated under the 1997 Amendments to the Chinese Criminal Code. However, these articles haven't been invoked yet. That is to say, no one has been prosecuted for money laundering in China.

Besides, Chinese preventive measures against money laundering didn't emerge all along until January 2003, when three administrative rules were adopted. However, experience shows that it is easier to pass anti-money laundering policies, while it is much more difficult to implement them. Established laws and regulations are short-lived if they are not applied in practice. Therefore, China just has taken the first step of the fight against money laundering. It still has a long way to go. Many problems are still waiting to be overcome and solved.

This book is meant to be a study on the Chinese Criminal Code, the financial legislations on combating money laundering on the basis of international standards, to make some comparison between the EU countries and China, to analyze the advantages and disadvantages of China's suppressive and preventive measures, with a viewing to offering some useful advice to improve the comprehensive capability to prevent and retaliate money laundering.

Method of Research

Money laundering is a very complicated problem. The effective control on money laundering concerns criminal law, international law, financial law and other areas of law. Therefore, comprehensive interdisciplinary study will be carried out in this project. From the perspective of criminal law, constitutional elements of money laundering will be examined in detail, such as the scope of predicate offences, the mens rea of money laundering, the behavioral pattern of money laundering. Besides, confiscation system is an essential part of suppressive measures, which needs to be addressed. From the viewpoint of international law, international instruments aimed at combating money laundering will be introduced and analyzed. After all, international cooperation is indispensable for effective control of money laundering. Final success in the fight against money laundering requires a great emphasis on preventive measures. Therefore, financial regulations, as the "yellow warning", which are of considerable importance in the prevention of money laundering, will be examined as well.

Money laundering is not only a theoretical problem but also a practical issue. It is significant to integrate theory with practice. Theory is the guideline of practice, while practice promotes theory in return. Through judicial practice, we can find out the defects in the legislation and then can do better. The integration of theory and practice is also a significant way to be adopted.

Additionally, comparative study is the most important means in this book. Comparison is of vital importance in the process of understanding. Where there is comparison, there is difference. This book, by means of chronological observation of history, various anti-money laundering instruments will be addressed to see how the anti-money laundering measures evolve constantly. More importantly, by means of horizontal comparison of reality, different measures adopted by different regions in the world, in particular, such as the EU and China, will be compared and analyzed, to see what the similarities and differences are between the EU and China concerning the anti-money laundering measures so that China can learn from others' strong points to offset its weakness, and ultimately combat money laundering more effectively and efficiently.

Structure of the Study

This study is structured into nine chapters which can be divided into five large parts about the following issues: general remarks on money laundering, global responses, West European response, China's efforts, comparison between the EU and China, several special issues concerning anti-money laundering.

Chapter 1 provides general information about a global money laundering problem. It describes the emergence and status quo of money laundering. The definition and characteristics of money laundering is also given. Besides, it describes the significance of preventing and fighting against money laundering.

Chapter 2 reviews the global responses to money laundering. In this chapter, five international benchmarks are explored. They are: the Basel Committee Statement of Principles, the 1988 Vienna Convention, the 2000 Palermo Convention, the efforts conducted by the FATF, and the efforts made by the Interpol.

Chapter 3 addresses the West European Response to money laundering. In this chapter, two levels of efforts in the fight against money laundering are discussed. One level is within the Council of Europe. The 1980 Council of Europe Recommendation and the 1990 Strasbourg Convention are presented. The other level is within the European Union. The 1991 anti-money laundering directive and the 2001 Amendment to this Directive are explored in detail. In addition, the efforts taken by the Europol and Eurojust are introduced.

The next Chapters 4, 5, 6 contain observations on China's efforts in the fight against money laundering. Chapter 4 focuses on the Chinese Criminal law concerning money laundering. The constitutional elements of money laundering are addressed in detail. And the confiscation system is also analyzed. Chapter 5 focuses on administrative measures against money laundering in China. Three recent rules are discussed and commented on. Chapter 6 describes the judicial practice of money laundering in China, which points out that although money laundering is an actual problem in China, no money laundering cases are available in judicial practice. Therefore this chapter points out the endeavors to be made to investigate money laundering in China.

Chapter 7 provides the comparison between the EU and China concerning suppressive and preventive measures against money laundering. In this chapter, six issues are examined in detail, which include money laundering offence, confiscation system, coverage of anti-money laundering measures, customer identification, suspicious transactions reporting, awareness raising, training and supervision. By means of horizontal comparison, this chapter endeavors to find out what the existing problems are in the fight against money laundering in China and what China should learn from the EU countries so that China can improve its comprehensive competence in combating money laundering.

In Chapter 8, three special issues related to the fight against money laundering are addressed, that is banking secrecy, professional privilege and high technology. The fact is that the existence of banking secrecy and professional privilege provide a safe harbor for money launderers. And high technology is also exploited by money launderers to conduct sophisticated schemes. This chapter shows the conflict between combating money laundering and protecting individual interests, and the contradiction between the professional privilege and anti-money laundering obligation. This chapter also describes the high technology laundering, which is the new challenge we are confronted with. It attempts to offer the reasonable solutions to this sensitive problem.

Chapter 9 contains the conclusions of the study. It summarizes the study as a whole. It briefly addresses the issue of money laundering and common efforts against it. It summarizes the China's progress made so far in the fight against money laundering on the one side, and on the other side there are still significant deficiencies in some areas. It also points out the common endeavor direction that is indispensable in the fight against money laundering, that is the reasonable balance between fighting crime and protecting individual interests, and the necessary attention to the high technology laundering.

Chapter 1

General Remarks on Money Laundering

1.1 Introduction

This chapter will provide general information about a global money laundering problem. It first describes the emergence and status quo of money laundering. Then it discusses the definition and the characteristics of money laundering. Finally it attempts to provide an overall assessment of the significance of preventing and fighting against money laundering.

1.2 The Emergence and Status Quo of Money Laundering

The term of "money laundering" comes forth along with the ever-growing gravity of organized crime in the modern world. Money laundering activities aims at disguising or concealing illicit funds to make them appear legitimate. It should be acknowledged that this phenomenon is as old as civilization. However, in the past, complex schemes to hide the criminal origin of capital or assets were rare because organized crimes in ancient times were not very serious and the amount of proceeds generated from crime was not so great as today. Besides, the system of finance and taxation was not so rigid and transparent as it is at present.

The Fight against Money Laundering: A Comparative Perspective

In the modern world, organized criminal activities, such as drugs, smuggling, mafia and extortion, are getting extremely serious and generating tremendous profits. But criminals find it hard to squander, transfer and circulate the money in their economic activities because of the rigid systems of finance and taxation. "*It is no use making a large profit out of a criminal activity if that profit cannot be put to use.*"[1] Criminals need to disguise their money so they can use it freely. Thus money-laundering crime in the modern times came into existence.

With the advancement of modern technology and prosperity of economy, grand scale, extensive scope, and modernization of means of activities are the characteristics of organized crimes. Money laundering crime, simultaneously, is getting ever-increasingly grave and taking on the following aspects:

First, criminals frequently make use of financial institutions to conduct money-laundering activities. This is due to several reasons. Financial institutions can provide multiple services, such as deposit, loan, acceptance, discount, foreign exchange, settlement and the like. Financial institutions have diversified financial instruments and provide various ways for financial resources transition. With the global economy and integrated financial market, transferring funds across international borders is convenient and prompt. Moreover, the principle of banking secrecy exactly exists in almost every country. Owing to these characteristics, financial institutions are the most vulnerable sectors for money launderers. With the help of financial institutions, wittingly or unconsciously, criminals transfer capital through transferring accounts or remit funds into other countries, and eventually cover up or conceal the nature or source of the illegally obtained proceeds.

Second, more and more criminals take advantage of non-financial institutions to conduct money-laundering activities. Because of the fact that, from the beginning of the fight against money laundering, financial institutions are required to assume anti-money laundering obligations, such as customer identification, record keeping and suspicious transaction reporting, money-laundering activities now penetrate many other business industries, which can produce a large amount of currency. Criminals conceal the illegal origin by the way of purchasing cars, precious metals, valuable jewelry and antiques. Criminals also disguise the nature of proceeds by means of operating

---

[1] David McClean, *International Judicial Assistance*, Oxford, 1992, p.184.

restaurants, hotels, shops and casinos through which they integrate dirty money with legal earning. Therefore, financial institutions represented by banks are not the sole industry that is involved in money laundering scheme. In fact, apart from financial institutions, many other business industries are exploited by money launderers.

Third, it should be stressed that money laundering operations at present are quite sophisticated and they are frequently run by practitioners who are themselves very skilled or who hire skilled help. The continuous effects of combating money laundering have made the work of money launderers more difficult. To circumvent relevant counter-measures, money launderers have to develop more complex schemes. They turn to the expertise of lawyers, notaries, accountants and other professionals to start new methods for money laundering and minimize risks surrounding their criminal activities. Since the later 1990s, the phenomenon that lawyers, notaries, accountants and other professionals are involved in money laundering schemes is revealed continuously, which has attracted close attention of international communities.

Fourth, criminals are taking advantage of modern technology to update money-laundering schemes. With the continuous and intensive efforts of combating money laundering both at the national level and the international level, the traditional methods of money laundering are confronted with more and more difficulties. The development of high technology is a double-sided sword. It does raise the people's living standard on the one hand, and on the other hand, it also provides great opportunities for criminals. With the extensive use of personal computers and the emergence of web-based financial service, money launderers can circumvent the traditional methods of client identification and suspicious transaction reporting through the Internet. With the help of electronic money, Internet bank, Internet casinos and other neoformation, criminals try to swerve money-laundering activities form the real world to cyberspace.

Fifth, criminals prefer to carry out money laundering activities in developing countries, especially in those countries that experience the transition of economic system in recent years. There is no denying that money laundering activities originated from western developed countries, which are rampant places for drugs crimes and organized crimes. With the fight against money laundering deepening in the developed countries, the shift of laundering from developed countries to developing countries is noticeable. This tendency is also closely linked with the situation of developing countries. Developing countries "*have a strong need to attract resource from abroad in or-*

der to finance growth and development program, while their systems and institutions for checking criminal activities are often limited and insufficient."[2]

1.3 The Definition of Money Laundering

The term money laundering was first coined by American law enforcement officials and entered popular usage during the Watergate inquiry in the United States in the mid-1970s.[3] Although money laundering has been widely accepted as a term both at the international and the national level with the rampant emergence of drug dealing in the eighties of the twentieth century, the precise meaning varies from country to country or from region to region.

In theoretical circle, various definitions of money laundering have been given. "*Money laundering is an activity aimed at concealing the unlawful source of sums of money*"[4]. "*Money laundering is the process of converting or 'cleansing' property knowing that such property is derived from serious crime for the purpose of disguising its origin*"[5]. "*Money laundering is the conversion of illicit cash to another asset, the concealment of the true source of ownership of the illegally acquired proceeds, and the creation of the perception of legitimacy of source and ownership.*"[6] However, among these expressions, several important issues are not definite. What does "unlawful source of sums of money" mean? Does it mean only money (cash) or mean the broad meaning of property, movable or immovable, corporeal or incorporeal, tangible or intangible, which derived from crimes? And what does "serious crime" mean? That is, how wide should be the scope of the predicate offences? Moreover, what is the definite meaning of laundering? Does it only mean concealing, converting, transferring or

---

[2] Ernesto U. Savona, *Responding to Money Laundering, International Perspectives*, Harwood Academic Publishers, 1997, p.6.

[3] See William C. Gilmore, *Dirty Money, The Evolution of money Laundering Counter-measures*, Council of Europe Press, 1995, p.23.

[4] Ernesto U. Savona, *Responding to Money Laundering, International Perspectives*, Harwood Academic Publishers, 1997, pp.3,6.

[5] Tom Sherman, International Efforts to Combat Money Laundering: The Role of the Financial Action Task Force, Money Laundering, *Hume Paper on Public Policy*, Vol.1 No.2, Edinburgh University Press, 1993, p.13.

[6] William C. Gilmore, *International Efforts to Combat Money Laundering*, Cambridge International Document Series, Volume 4, 1992, p.X.

also include acquisition, possession or use of property, knowing, at the time of receipt, that such property is the proceeds of crime?

After the terrorist attack in New York and Washington on 11 September 2001, much more attention was paid to money laundering given its connection to terrorist activities and a subtle change in the definition of money laundering began to be observed. Money laundering is no longer seen as just the laundering of criminal proceeds, but as the means by which terrorists hide their revenue generating processes and gain access to their funds. That is to say, not only the criminal origin of the money, but a criminal purpose as well is included in the definition of money laundering. Money laundering now is defined as *"moving funds through financial institutions or accounts to disguise its origin and/or purpose"*[7].

In legal documents, there are a variety of expressions.

Under the United Nations Convention Against Illicit Traffic in Narcotic Drugs and Psychotropic Substances (hereafter referred to as the 1988 Vienna United Nations Convention), money-laundering crime only covers drug-related money laundering. In the 1990 Convention on Laundering, Search, Seizure and Confiscation of the Proceeds from Crime Strasbourg Convention (hereafter referred to as the 1990 Strasbourg Convention), laundering offence is not restricted to drug-related laundering. Instead it extends to any predicate offence. And also the 1990 Strasbourg Convention permits the criminalisation of negligent laundering. In the 1990 Recommendations of Financial Action Task Force, it provides possible extension of corporate criminal liability, which reads, " *Where possible, corporations themselves—not only their employees—should be subject to criminal liability.* "[8] Besides, the Strasbourg Convention, and the 2000 United Nations Convention against Transactional Organized Crime (hereafter referred to as the 2000 Palermo United Nations Convention), both provide that money-laundering offence may not apply to the persons who committed the predicate offence.

From the overview of various expressions, it is obvious that many problems concerning money-laundering crime need to be discussed to get unanimous. Should mon-

---

[7] Jackie Johnson, 11 September 2001: Will it Make a Difference to the Global Anti-Money Laundering Movement? *Journal of Money Laundering Control*, Vol. 6 No. 1, p. 10.

[8] *The FATF Recommendations on Money Laundering (1990), Recommendation 7.*

ey laundering only be regarded as drug-money laundering or should the definition be expanded to non-drug related money laundering? Should money laundering only be viewed as an offense in cases where the offender actually knew that he was dealing with the funds from crimes or should it also regarded as an offense in cases where the offender ought to have assumed that the property was illegal proceeds? Should money laundering be considered only as fencing, which means a sort of favor or should it become an independent and autonomous crime?

It should be made plain that the term money laundering in this book is not simply from its definition given by scholars, neither from legal documents, but from the most general criminological aspect. The most general meaning of money laundering contains the following elements: First, money laundering depends upon the existence of an underlying crime that has generated proceeds, whether it is a drug-related crime or not. Second, money launderers already know or ought to have assumed that they are dealing with the property from a crime, "*property shall means assets of every kind, whether corporeal or incorporeal, movable or immovable, tangible or intangible, and legal documents or instruments evidencing title to, or interest in, such assets.*"[9] Third, a money launderer could be an individual or an organization, whether he is the owner of the dirty money or not. Fourth, the behavioral patterns of money laundering could include the conversion or transfer of the property, the concealment or disguise of the true nature, source of the property, the acquisition, possession or use of the property.

As current anti-money laundering legislation all emphasize that money-laundering crime has an implied or specific predicate offence that generates financial reward, while terrorism may not result in profits but will use funds may be legally or illegally earned, the act that terrorists hide the revenue generating process and gain access to their funds can not be considered "money laundering" but "terrorism financing".

---

[9] *United Nations Convention against Transnational Organization Crime*, Article 2 (d). *United Nations Convention Against Illicit Traffic in Narcotic Drugs and Psychotropic Substances*, Article 1 (17).

1.4 The Characteristics of Money Laundering

Money laundering is a secret crime, which is often masked in terms of legal activities. Due to the dark figure of money laundering, no one knows precisely how much money is accumulated and laundered every year in the world. The United Nations estimated drug trafficking proceeds worldwide at $ 300 billion in 1987. The Financial Action Task Force also estimated that sales of cocaine, heroin and cannabis amount to approximately $ 122 billion per year in the United States and Europe, of which 50 to 70% or as much as $ 85 billion per year could be available for laundering and investment.[10] In 1992, one US law enforcement agency estimated the total figure for US drug and non-drug-related money laundering at $ 300 billion annually.[11] In 1996, the United Nations estimated that US $ 1 billion daily was involved in money laundering. The Commercial Crime Bureau of the international Chamber of Commerce believes this figure to be greatly understated.[12] With regard to terrorism alone, the amount of money involved is surprisingly large. As Deputy Secretary of the Treasury Dam testified: *"Since September 11, the United States and other countries have frozen more than $ 80 million in terrorist-related assets."*[13] However making statements about the seriousness of a problem and demonstrating its real size are two different issues. Therefore some people warn against politically motivated inflated estimates and stress the necessity for a methodologically responsible empirical research of this phenomenon.[14] Irrespective of what the exact figures are, the extent of the illegitimate proceeds of crime is clearly growing.

---

[10] See *Financial Action Task on Money Laundering Report of 6 February 1990.*

[11] See *US Treasury Dept Financial Crimes Enforcement Network Assessment of US Money Laundering: Submission to the Financial Action Task Force 2 (1994).*

[12] See International Chamber of Commerce, Guide to the Prevention of Money Laundering, *Journal of Commerce*, 4, June 1998.

[13] *Financial War on Terrorism and Implementation of Money-Laundering Provisions in the USA Patriot Act: Hearing of the Senate Banking, Housing and Urban Affairs Comm.* 107th Cong.

[14] See Petrus C. Van Duyne, Money-Laundering: Estimates in Fog, *The Journal of Asset Protection and Financial Crime*, Vol. 2 No. 1, 1994, pp. 58—59.

Money Laundering is a transnational crime[15]. With the development of high technology and prosperity of economy, staff flowing, funds moving, service providing and changing are getting ever-greater globalization. However, economic globalization is a two-side sword. It is promoting the legitimate economy and at the same time is utilized by money launderers. The globalization of money laundering can be felt that money launderers are always distributed in different countries and the proceeds are often sent from one country to another, especially to those regions entitled as "secrecy heaven". The internationalism of money laundering is confirmed in the investigation of the Operation Green Ice in 1992. The result was arrest of more than 200 people in six countries and the seizure of nearly US $ 42 million in alleged illegal drug profits worldwide.[16] In the transnational money laundering case adjudicated by Hong Kong court in 1995, criminals laundered $ 93 million of proceeds through 362 accounts, covering the USA, Thailand, Singapore, Australia, Switzerland, Hong Kong and Taiwan.[17]

Money laundering is a complicated crime. Money laundering is a process, rather than a single act, aiming at covering up or concealing the nature or source of the proceeds illegally obtained from crimes. One complete process of money laundering includes three stages:[18]

—Placement stage: where cash derived directly from criminal activity is first placed either in a financial institution or used to purchase assets.

—Layering stage: the stage at which there is the first attempt at concealment or disguise of the source of the ownership of the funds.

—Integration stage: where the money is integrated into the legitimate economic and financial system and is assimilated with all other assts in the system.

---

[15] According to the United Nations Convention against Transnational Organized Crime, "Transnational crime" includes the following situations: a. It is committed in more than one states; b. It is committed in one state but a substantial part of its preparation, planning, direction or control takes place in another country; c. It is committed in one state but involves an organized criminal group that engages in criminal activities in more than one state and; d. It is committed in one state but has substantial effects in another state. And the United Nations Convention against Transnational Organized Crime considers money laundering crime is a transnational crime.

[16] See William C. Gilmore, Money Laundering: The International Aspect, Money Laundering, *Hume Papers on Public Policy*, Vol. 1 No. 2, 1993, p. 2.

[17] See Xing Dao Daily, 31 October 1995.

[18] See William C. Gilmore, *Dirty Money, The Evolution of Money Laundering Counter-measures*, Council of Europe Press, 1995, p. 37.

Money laundering is a professional crime. As money-laundering schemes always involve complicated financial system and legal system both at the national level and the international level, not ordinary criminals but professional criminals are competent for such complicated activities. Criminals who haven't competent knowledge turn to the lawyers, notaries, accountants and other professionals to aid them. Besides, with the development of the Internet and the emergence of electronic business, criminals fully exploit these high technologies that offer money launderers a more extensive space. At present, money-laundering crime has developed a highly complex and professional industry, which is difficult for ordinary criminals to commit.

Money laundering is a crime, which has no direct victims. Money laundering is quite different from such traditional crimes as robbery, fraud, larceny, homicide, rape and the like. It is difficult to perceive the harm resulting from money laundering activity because it has neither direct victims nor noticeable consequence. Few people will report a case to the security authorities. For this reason, it is not easy to detect money-laundering crime in both developing countries, which lack perfect preventive system, and developed countries, which have taken many steps responding to money laundering. For example, though money-laundering crime exists indeed in China, nobody has been prosecuted up to the present in judicial practice. Even in developed countries, the dark figure of money laundering crime also is very high.

1.5 The Significance of Preventing and Fighting against Money Laundering

Some people consider that money has no smell and it is not necessary to make a distinction between clean money and dirty money. Money is only money.[19] Even if the funds are illegally derived from criminal activities, it is not harmful but helpful for developing countries to attract foreign capital from abroad.[20] There is no denying the fact that disparities in economic development between different parts in the world re-

---

[19] Tom Sherman, International Efforts to Combat Money Laundering: The Role of the Financial Action Task Force, Money Laundering, *Hume Papers on Public Policy*, Vol. 1 No. 2, Edinburgh University Press, 1993, p. 16.

[20] See Gao ming-xuan, Zhao bingzhi, *Collected Review of Criminal Law*, Law Press, 1999, p. 301.

sult in differences in the ability and determination to respond to money laundering. The fight against money laundering is closely linked with the objective of promoting economic development and combating poverty.[21]

In fact, developing countries perhaps can get short-term economic interest as a result of indulging money-laundering crime. In the long run, the loss is greater than the gain because the potential damage to the whole society is considerable. Money laundering can undermine the integrity of financial institutions and thus undermine public confidence in the financial system. Money laundering can facilitate underlying crime to self-finance, diversify and grow by allowing criminal funds to be reinvested. Money laundering can also have a corrosive influence on economic development and political stability. More specifically, the significance of fighting against money laundering is as follows:

First, effective check on money laundering affects the incidence of other crimes, especially affects those crimes seeking for huge profits. Economic crimes are banned in legislation and severe punishments are imposed on them in judicial practice. However so many criminals risk the danger in desperation to commit economic crimes and the fight against economic crimes hasn't lead to a satisfying result. One of the most important reasons is the temptation of high profits. Making it more difficult for criminals to keep the proceeds of their crime, and making the enjoyment of those proceeds more dangerous, can eliminate the main incentive for profit wrongdoings.

Second, action against money laundering does not consist solely in the repression of crime, but ensure the integrity of financial system. It is a fact that setting up the preventive system against money laundering may result in increasing the costs of commercial banks and the reduction of deposit. For this reason, commercial financial institutions maybe do not have much interest in the fight against money laundering on the basis of their short interests. However, in the long run, the establishment of a preventive system against money laundering will contribute to the security of financial institutions and the long-term interests of a country, and ultimately will be helpful to maintain the order of the society and to create a peaceful and stable environment.

Third, effective control on money laundering will contribute to a favorable figure

---

[21] See Ernesto U. Savona, *Responding to money laundering*, *International perspectives*, Harwood Academic Publishers, 1997, p.6.

of a country. Money laundering is an international problem affecting individual countries. "*The response to it must embrace as many countries as possible. The more widespread the action against money laundering, the more effective it will be.*"[22] Activities by any country to seek short-term gains can impose high costs on all. China, as a country that has played an ever-growing important role both in economic and political stage, should pay indispensable attention to prevent money laundering by means of setting up a comprehensive preventive system. If China doesn't cooperate with other countries to fight against money laundering, criminals will try to find their way into China. Thus other countries will make futile effort in the fight against money laundering and the image of China will suffer.

1.6　Conclusions

Money-laundering crime in the modern world is a twin brother of the organized crimes, such as drug-related crime, smuggling, terrorism and the like. With the growing gravity of organized crimes, money laundering is getting more rampant with various new forms. At present, money laundering is an international crime, which has developed into a greatly complex and professional industry. Money laundering poses significant risks to society. Money laundering activity disguises the original source of dirty money and impedes the investigation exercised by judicial authority. Money laundering damages the credibility of public confidence in the financial system in general and banks in particular. Money laundering sabotages the fair and competitive order of market economy and tends to lead to financial crisis. Furthermore there is the risk that further criminal activities can be developed by allowing criminal funds to be reinvested. Therefore, every country should make great efforts to fight against money-laundering crime, not only for attacking criminal activities, but also for defending the transparency of economic system, and ultimately to maintain the order of the society and to create a peaceful and stable living environment.

---

[22] Tom Sherman, International Efforts to Combat Money Laundering: The Role of the Financial Action Task Force, Money Laundering, *Hume Paper on Public Policy*, Vol. 1 No. 2, Edinburgh University Press, 1993, p. 20.

Chapter 2

Global Responses to Money Laundering

2.1 Introduction

Since 1980s, money laundering, as a transnational crime, attracted much attention of international communities. How to combat money laundering more efficiently and effectively has becoming a hot topic in both legal research and financial circles. An essential means of raising standards and awareness is the effort made at an international level to create benchmarks by which national legislation can be judged. In this chapter, five international benchmarks which are worthy of particular mention are explored below. First it introduces the Basel Committee Statement of Principles which exerted a pioneer function in the fight against money laundering. It then shows the efforts made by the United Nations, that is the 1988 Vienna Convention and the 2000 Palermo Convention, though they don't specially aim at the fight against money laundering, both of them paid much attention to this problem. This chapter also examines the wonderful job conducted by the FATF, the international body which concentrates solely upon the fight against money laundering. Last, this chapter draws on the efforts made by the Interpol, the largest international police organization in the world.

2.2 The Basel Committee Statement

2.2.1 Background

The Basel Committee on Banking Regulation and Supervisory Practices (hereinafter referred to as the Basel Committee) comprises representatives of the central banks and supervisory authorities of the Group of Ten Nations[23], which meet semi-annually to discuss banking supervision. Generally, the Committee concerns its supervisory responsibilities in matters such as the capital adequacy, solvency, liquidity and foreign exchange operations of financial institutions.[24]

In late 1980s, the Basel Committee became aware of the fact that criminals and their associates used financial systems to make payments and transfers of funds from one account to another; to hide the source and beneficial ownership of money; and to provide storage for banknotes through a safe-deposit facility.[25] That is to say, banks and other financial institutions are unwittingly exploited to assist criminals to commit money-laundering crime. Although the primary function of banking supervision is to maintain the overall financial stability and soundness of banks rather than to ensure that individual transactions conducted by bank customers are legitimate, all members of the committee firmly believe that supervisors cannot be indifferent to the use made of banks by criminals. Because such indifference may cause banks to suffer losses through fraud or to erode public confidence and undermine the stability of the banking system[26]. For these reasons, the Basel Committee maintains that ethical standards of professional conduct among banks and other financial institutions are essential. And one way to promote this objective is to obtain international agreement to a statement of

---

[23] The so-called "G10 Nations" include Belgium, Canada, France, Germany, Italy, Japan, Netherlands, Sweden, Switzerland, United Kingdom, United States and Luxembourg. See International Efforts to combat money laundering, *Cambridge International Documents Series*, Volume 4, p. 274.

[24] See Kern Alexander, The International Anti-Money-Laundering Regime: The Role of the Financial Action Task Force, *Journal of Money Laundering Control*, Vol. 4 No. 3, p. 236.

[25] See *Basle Committee on Banking Regulations and Supervisory Practices December* 1988 *Statement on Prevention of Criminal Use of the Banking System for the Purpose of Money-Laundering*, Preamble, http://www.camlmac.gov.cn/com/info.do? action = detail&id = 52, 20 June 2006.

[26] Ibid., p. 274.

principle, to which financial institutions should be expected to adhere.[27] Thus, in December 1988, the Basel Committee on Banking Regulations and Supervisory Practices adopted a Statement of Principles, which covered customer identification, compliance with law and cooperation with law enforcement authorities for banks to implement.

2.2.2　Customer Identification

The statement requires banks to take these measures: making reasonable efforts to determine the true identity of all customers requesting the institution's services; instituting effective procedures for obtaining identification from new customers; refusing to conduct business with customers who fail to provide evidence of their identity; paying particular attention to identify the ownership of all accounts and those using safe-custody facilities.[28]

2.2.3　Compliance with Laws

Banks' management should ensure that business is conducted in conformity with high ethical standards and that laws and regulations pertaining to financial transactions are adhered to. Banks should not set out to offer services or provide active assistance in transactions which they have good reason to suppose are associated with money-laundering activities.[29]

2.2.4　Cooperation with Law Enforcement Authorities

Within any constraints imposed by rules relating to customer confidentiality, banks should cooperate fully with national law enforcement authorities. Banks should avoid providing support or assistance to customers seeking to deceive law enforcement agencies through the provision of altered, incomplete or misleading information. Where there are reasonable grounds for suspecting money laundering, take appropriate measures that are consistent with the law, for example, to deny assistance, sever

---

[27]　Ibid.
[28]　Ibid., p.276.
[29]　Ibid., p.277.

relations with the customer and close or freeze accounts.[30]

2.2.5 Policies, Procedures and Training

All banks should formally adopt policies consistent with the principles set out in the Statement and should ensure that all members of their staff concerned are informed of the bank's policy in this regard. Attention should be given to staff training in matters covered by the Statement. Banks should implement specific procedures for customer identification and for retaining internal records of transactions. Arrangement for internal audit may need to be extended in order to establish an effective means of testing for general compliance with the Statement.[31]

2.2.6 Evaluation

Just as mentioned in the preamble to the text, "*the Statement is not a legal document*" and it has no binding legal effect on the Group of Ten Nations. The Statement, however, does serve as a form of soft law by reinforcing the notion, introduced by the Council of Europe Recommendation of 1980, that financial institutions are the linchpin to effective money-laundering prevention and detection.[32] In contrast with the Council of Europe Recommendation, it has been far more influential at the practical level. Under the influence of this Statement, "*various formulas have been used to make its principles an obligation, notably a formal agreement among banks that commits them explicitly (Austria, Italy, Switzerland), a formal indication by bank regulators that failure to comply with these principles could lead to administrative sanctions (France, United Kingdom), or legally binding texts with a reference to these principles (Luxemburg).*"[33] In addition, shortly after the appearance of the Statement of Principles, practical measures have already been taken in many countries, such as the appointment of a compliance officer in each bank, in charge of the application of the

---

[30] Ibid.
[31] Ibid.
[32] See Kern Alexander, The International Anti-Money-Laundering Regime: The Role of the Financial Action Task Force, *Journal of Money Laundering Control*, Vol. 4 No. 3, p. 237.
[33] Financial Action Task Force on Money Laundering Report of 6 February 1990, Programs Already in Place to Combat Money Laundering, International Efforts to combat money laundering, *Cambridge International Documents Series*, Volume 4, p. 11.

internal programs against money laundering. Many countries have set detailed guidelines for banks, making the Principles precise and practical obligations.[34]

The Statement of Principles not only has profound impacts on members of Basel Committee, but also has far-reaching influence beyond its scope. Just as expected in the preamble: "*with a view to its acceptance worldwide, the Committee would also commend the Statement to supervisory authorities in other countries.*" For example, Australia, Austria, Spain are not members of the Basel Committee, the bank regulators and supervisors of these three countries however express that they consider this Statement as also applicable to their supervised banking systems.[35] In addition, the State of Principles has been endorsed by the Offshore Group of Banking Supervisors, which consists of 19 members including major financial centers such as Hong Kong and Singapore as well as the principle offshore banking and financial service "heavens" in the Caribbean and elsewhere.[36]

More importantly, the Statement of Principles provides important references for forthcoming international anti-money laundering documents. Its main contents such as identifying customer, avoiding transaction with suspected money laundering, cooperation with law enforcement agencies can easily found in FATF Recommendations, EC Directive and other relevant documents in this area. Although these documents without doubt are more comprehensive and perfect in contrast with the Statement of Principle, the pioneer function of the Statement of Principles is indubitable.

2.3　United Nations Convention against Illicit Traffic in Narcotic Drugs and Psychotropic Substances

2.3.1　Background

The close attention paid to the problem of money laundering by the United Nations resulted from the concern of ever-growing gravity of illicit traffic in narcotic

---

[34] Ibid.
[35] Ibid.
[36] See William C. Gilmore, *Dirty Money, The Evolution of Money Laundering Counter-measures*, Council of Europe Press, 1995, p. 104.

drugs and psychotropic substances. In fact, due to the special characteristics of these matters, international initiatives to regulate drug abuse and illicit trafficking date back to the International Opium Convention of 1912 and the 1931 Convention Limiting the Manufacture and Regulating the Distribution of Narcotic Drug.[37] Prior to 1988 there were another two important international treaties, which strove to provide international controls over narcotic drugs and psychotropic substances. The first one was the 1961 UN Single Convention on Narcotic Drugs, as amended by the 1972 Protocol, and the second one is the 1971 UN Convention on Psychotropic Substance. These international treaties ever made a positive contribution to controlling the production of drugs and to preventing their diversion into the illicit market place. However, with the magnitude and extent of illicit traffic and its grave consequence, these treaties gradually became inadequate. It was widely accepted that this would need to reinforce and supplement the measures provided in these two treaties.

In 1984, the UN General Assembly requested that the UN Economic and Social Council instruct the Commission on Narcotic Drugs in preparing a draft convention as a matter of priority. In 1986 the Commission adopted a resolution in which it identified 14 elements for inclusion in a draft convention. After a lengthy process of negotiation, United Nations Convention against Illicit Traffic in Narcotic Drugs and Psychotropic Substances (hereinafter referred to as the 1988 Vienna UN Convention) opened for signature in Vienna, the Capital of Austria in December 1988, and entered into force in November 1990.[38] The purpose of this Convention is to "*promote co-operation among the Parties so that they may address more effectively the various aspects of illicit traffic in narcotic drugs and psychotropic substances having an international dimension*", and it urges the parties to "*take necessary measures, including legislative and administrative measures, in conformity with the fundamental provisions of their respective domestic legislative systems*"[39]. Up to the present, there are more than 100 countries signed this Convention.

The United Nations Convention improves upon the above-mentioned multilateral

---

[37] See William C. Gilmore, *Dirty Money, The Evolution of Money Laundering Counter-measures*, Council of Europe Press, 1995, p. 61.

[38] Ibid., p. 63.

[39] *United Nations Convention Against Illicit Traffic in Narcotic Drugs and Psychotropic Substances*, Article 2.

agreements, that is, the 1961 UN Single Convention on Narcotic Drugs, and the 1971 UN Convention on Psychotropic Substance. These two agreements did not provide for confiscation of proceeds derived from drug trafficking, although they contained the provisions on confiscation of narcotic drugs and psychotropic substances, materials and equipment or other instrumentalities used in or intended for use in offences[40]. As a matter of fact, confiscating proceeds can play a significant role in the fight against transnational drug trafficking since it is an indisputable truth that sudden huge profit drives criminal activities. For this reason, one of the main objectives of the United Nations Convention is to "*deprive persons engaged in illicit traffic of the proceeds of their criminal activities and thereby eliminate their main incentive for so doing*"[41].

Another issue closely linked with the criminal proceeds is the problem of money laundering. "*Drug trafficking, like many other forms of criminal activity, is highly cash intensive. Indeed, In the case of heroin and cocaine, the physical volume of notes received from street dealing is much larger than the volume of the drugs themselves*".[42] It is hard for drug traffickers to squander, transfer and circulate the dirty money in economic activities because of the rigid systems of finance and taxation. Thus the drug traffickers have an urgent need to disguise their money so that they can use it freely. It is obvious that laundering of proceeds from drug trafficking provides criminals both substantial and spiritual support. It is for this reason that the money laundering crime was specified in the United Nations Convention, although laundering offence is not as a special terminology put forward in the Convention at that time.

In addition, a range of important mechanisms designed to promote international cooperation have been established in the United Nations Convention. The Convention utilizes the following modalities of inter-state cooperation: recognition of foreign penal judgments (e.g. the recognition of orders of forfeiture); the freezing and seizing of assets; extradition; and mutual legal assistance. Although additional bilateral or mul-

---

[40] See *The Single Convention on Narcotic Drugs, 1961*, Article 37; *The 1971 Convention on Psychotropic Substance*, Article 22.

[41] *United Nations Convention Against Illicit Traffic in Narcotic Drugs and Psychotropic Substances*, Preamble.

[42] William C. Gilmore, International Efforts to Combat Money Laundering, *Cambridge International documents Series*, Volume 4, Grotius Publications Limited, 1992, p. x.

tilateral agreements are necessary to make the United Nations Convention more effective, it is still considered that these mechanisms can play a significant role in the fight against drug offences and the accompanying money laundering crime.

2.3.2 Money Laundering Crime

The 1988 Vienna UN Convention for the first time addressed the issue that money laundering should be criminalized at international level. Article 3(1)(a) sets forth an obligation for signatory states to criminalize a comprehensive list of activities related to drug trafficking—from production, cultivation, distribution and possession to the organization, management and financing of trafficking operation. Article 3(1)(b) then imposes an obligation on signatory parties to criminalize drug-related money laundering. Under Article 3(1)(b), the crime of money laundering is:

"(i) *The conversion or transfer of property, knowing that such property is derived from any offence or offences established in accordance with subparagraph (a) of this paragraph, or from an act of participation in such offence or offences, for the purpose of concealing or disguising the illicit origin of the property or of assisting any person who is involved in the commission of such an offence or offences to evade the legal consequences of his actions;*

(ii) The concealment or disguise of the true nature, source, location, disposition, movement, right with respect to, or ownership of property, knowing that such property is derived from an offence or offences established in accordance with subparagraph (a) of this paragraph or from an act of participation in such an offence or offences."

In addition, Article 3(1)(c) of this Convention requires signatory states to criminalize the following acts under its domestic law, subject to its constitutional principles and the basic concepts of its legal system:

"(i) *The acquisition, possession or use of property, knowing, at the time of receipt, that such property was derived from an offence or offences established in accordance with subparagraph (a) of this paragraph or from an act of participation in such offence or offences;*

..."

(iv) Participation in, association or conspiracy to commit, attempts to commit and aiding, abetting, facilitating and counseling the commission of any of the offences established in accordance with this article."

Moreover, Article 3(3) addresses the important issue concerning the appropriate burden of proof in relation to these offences, which provides that knowledge, intent or purpose required as an element of an offence may be inferred from objective factual circumstance. "*The purpose of this paragraph is to state that the inclusion of those elements in the description of the offences is not intended to change in any way the level or form of proof required by a Party's domestic law. Thus the paragraph affirms the possibility of proving these elements circumstantially.*"[43] The Convention also obliges signatory parties to make all of the above offences liable to sanctions, which take into account the grave nature of these offences. These sanctions may include imprisonment, other forms of deprivation of liberty, pecuniary sanctions and confiscation.[44]

The characteristics of money laundering offence specified in the 1988 Vienna UN Convention can be summarized as follows. First, as the title indicates, the United Nations Convention focuses basically on various crimes associated with drug trafficking. For this reason, the term "money laundering" is not used in the text of the Convention. Rather, money-laundering activity is contained in the fairly lengthy and comprehensive list of activities of illicit traffic in narcotic drugs and psychotropic substances, which have a major international impact. Secondly, due to its narrow objective that strives to make the fight against drug trafficking more effectively, the 1988 Vienna UN Convention only covers drug-related money laundering. "*It falls short of other initiatives that cover violent crimes, terrorist acts, organized crime and other non-drug-related offences that generate large profits.*"[45] Such initiatives can be found later in the Council of Europe Convention, Recommendations of FATF, the EC Directive and many domestic criminal laws. Thirdly, the 1988 Vienna UN Convention provides both mandatory and permissive obligations to signatory states in regard to criminalizing

---

[43]   William C. Gilmore, International Efforts to Combat Money Laundering, *Cambridge International documents Series*, Volume 4, Grotius Publications Limited, 1992, p. 105.

[44]   See *United Nations Convention Against Illicit Traffic in Narcotic Drugs and Psychotropic Substances*, Article 3 (4)(a).

[45]   Ernesto U. Savona, *Responding to Money Laundering, International Perspectives*, Harwood Academic Publishers, 1997, p. 123.

money-laundering activity. More specifically, Article 3(1)(b) includes a mandatory obligation on signatory parties to enact legislation criminalizing money laundering. If domestic laws are not compatible with this obligation, enacting or changing relevant domestic laws will be necessary. While Article 3(1)(c) lists the permissive categories of offences. Criminalisation of those acts under Article 3(1)(c) should be subject to each party's constitutional principles and the basic concepts of its legal system, namely it is an optional obligation. The Convention leaves the signatory parties with the discretion on whether criminalize those activities under Article 3(1)(c) or not.

2.3.3 Confiscation

Another important issue addressed by the 1988 Vienna UN Convention relates to confiscation of proceeds derived from, and instrumentalities used in drug trafficking. Confiscation measures are of vital importance in the fight against profit wrongdoings. It not only can prevent criminals from unjust enrichment but also can eliminate the main incentive for drug trafficking and money laundering. Under Article 5, two sets of obligations concerning confiscation measures are embraced. One is about the measures to be taken at the national level and the other one is about the necessary mechanisms to give effect to international cooperation.

At national level, each party shall adopt necessary measures to enable confiscation of: "(a) *proceeds derived from offences established in accordance with article 3, paragraph 1 (that is all drug trafficking and money laundering offences therein described), or property the value of which corresponds to that of such proceeds*; (b) *Narcotic drugs and psychotropic substances, materials and equipment or other instrumentalities used in or intended for use in any manner in drug trafficking and money laundering offences.*"[46] In order to make the confiscation measures run smoothly, this Convention requires each party to take the necessary measures to allow their competent authorities to identify, trace, seize or freeze proceeds, property, instrumentalities or any other thing as the necessary preliminary steps toward the eventual forfeiture of that

---

[46] *United Nations Convention against Illicit Traffic in Narcotic Drugs and Psychotropic Substances*, Article 5(1).

property.[47] Moreover this Convention obligates each party to empower its court or other authorities to order that bank, financial or commercial records be made available or be seized. A party shall not decline to act on the grounds of bank secrecy.[48] This stipulation is due to the reason that "*existing bank secrecy laws are being used in many instances to obstruct cooperation and the provision of information needed for the investigation of allegations of drug-related offences.*"[49] This provision and a similar provision in Article 7(5) are intended to prevent banking secrecy laws from obstructing either forfeiture proceedings or the investigation and prosecution of trafficking offences and money laundering crime. The lifting of banking secrecy is one of the most important measures in combating drug trafficking and money laundering offences in the Convention.

At international level, the article requires each party to assist other parties upon request in identifying, tracing, seizing, freezing or forfeiting proceeds, property, instrumentalities or any other things within its territory.[50] This stipulation reflects the fact that measures only to be taken at the domestic law are unlikely to be fully effective in combating drug trafficking and money laundering offences due to their transnational features.

It is commendable that the 1988 Vienna UN Convention establishes a system of confiscated assets sharing. Article 5 (5) b provides, "*When acting on the request of another party in accordance with this article, a party may give special consideration to concluding agreements on*:

> (i) *Contributing the value of such proceeds and property, or funds derived from the sale of such proceeds or property, or a substantial part thereof, to intergovernmental bodies specializing in the fight against illicit traffic in and abuse of narcotic drugs and psychotropic substances;*
>
> (ii) *Sharing with other parties, on a regular or case-by-case basis, such proceeds or property, or funds derived from the sale of such proceeds or property,*

---

[47] Ibid., Article 5 (2).
[48] Ibid., Article 5 (3).
[49] William C. Gilmore, *Dirty Money, The Evolution of Money Laundering Counter-measures*, Council of Europe Press, 1995, p. 69.
[50] See *United Nations Convention against Illicit Traffic in Narcotic Drugs and Psychotropic Substances*, Article 5 (4).

in accordance with its domestic law, administrative procedures or bilateral or multilateral agreements entered into for this purpose."

The purpose of this provision is to give incentive to agencies responsible for seizing and freezing assets and to enhance international confiscation cooperation. However, we should not lose sight of the fact that this provision is double-sided. Just as some experts remarked, "*such a profit motive may create a de facto policy of giving priority in international cooperation and enforcement to those crimes involving the greatest sums of money susceptible to seizure. Consequently, serious crimes that do not involve the potential for confiscation of assets (e. g. hijacking, taking of hostages, and terrorism) may become secondary in certain international cooperation and enforcement efforts.*"[51]

In view of the fact that proceeds derived from and instrumentalities used in illegal trafficking could escape forfeiture simply because their form had been changed or they had been commingled with property,[52] Article 5 (6) addresses this issue: If proceeds have been transformed or converted into other property, such property shall be subject to restraint or confiscation. If proceeds have been intermingled with legitimate assets, only an amount equal to the intermingled assets may be confiscated. In addition, income or other benefits derived form illegally obtained proceeds or property shall also be forfeitable.

Pursuant to Article 5 (7), parties may reverse the burden of proof regarding the lawful origin of alleged proceeds or other property liable to confiscation, subject to a party's principles of domestic law. In addition, Article 5 (8) states that the provisions of the article shall not affect the rights of bona fide third parties. However, the article does not attempt to define those rights. "*The rights of bona fide third parties are defined by the domestic law of each party. Thus this paragraph simply states that it was not the intention of the negotiators to inadvertently change the rights bona fide third parties have under the domestic law of a party.*"[53]

From the above overview of the Article of confiscation, which is of great signifi-

---

[51] Ernesto U. Savona, *Responding to Money Laundering*, *International Perspectives*, Harwood Academic Publishers, 1997, p. 171.

[52] See William C. Gilmore, International Efforts to Combat Money Laundering, *Cambridge International documents Series*, Volume 4, Grotius Publications Limited, 1992, p. 118.

[53] Ibid., p. 119.

cance in the fight against drug trafficking and the accompanying money laundering offence, it is easy to see that this article is highly innovative: First, this article extends the scope of confiscation, in contrast with the former international agreements. More specifically, Article 37 of the Single Convention on Narcotic drugs states: "*any drugs, substances and equipment used in or intended for the commission of any of the offences, referred to in article 36, shall be liable to seizure and confiscation.*" Article 22 (3) of the Convention on Psychotropic Substances contains a similar provision on the seizure and confiscation of psychotropic substances and equipment. While under the 1988 Vienna UN Convention, all proceeds derived from drug trafficking and money laundering offences as well as drugs themselves, materials, equipment or other instrumentalities shall be confiscated. Second, in respect of the means of confiscation, this article stipulates substitute confiscation and value confiscation so that proceeds or instrumentalities could not escape confiscation despite the fact that their form had been changed or they had been commingled with other property. Third, it merits attention that this article establishes confiscated assets sharing system to give a motivation to responsible agencies in the fight against drug trafficking and money laundering offences. For these reasons, this highly complex and innovative Article has attracted great praise from commentators: "*The provisions ... can be properly viewed as a major breakthrough in attacking the benefits derived from drug trafficking activities and are a forceful endorsement of the notion that attacking the profit motive is essential if the struggle against drug trafficking is to be effective.*"[54]

2.3.4 International Cooperation

Article 7 of the 1988 Vienna UN Convention is a miniature mutual legal assistance treaty. It requires the parties to provide "*the widest measure of mutual legal assistance in investigations, prosecutions, and judicial proceedings in relation to criminal offences established in accordance with article 3, paragraph 1*". The mutual legal assistance to be provided are as follows: "*taking evidence or statements from persons; effecting service of judicial documents; executing searches and seizures; examining objects

---

[54] William C. Gilmore, *Dirty Money, The Evolution of Money Laundering Counter-measures*, Council of Europe Press, 1995, p.74.

and sites; *providing information and evidentiary items*; *providing originals or certified copies of relevant documents and records, including bank, financial, corporate or business records*; *identifying or tracing proceeds, property, instrumentalities or other things for evidentiary purposes.* "[55] However, the list is not intended to restrict a Party's domestic practice of providing mutual legal assistance, since paragraph 3 of this Article provides that other forms of mutual legal assistance may be provided if permitted by the domestic law of a party. It is of value to note that requests for assistance could not be refused on the ground of bank secrecy[56]. This article is intended to "*apply not only to a request made according to the procedure set forth in the article, but also to modify any existing or future legal assistance treaties. Thus, bank secrecy laws alone cannot be imposed to block assistance*"[57].

In addition, it is worth mentioning that the procedure for mutual assistance in the administration of justice is separately stipulated in Article 9 which is entitled "*Other Forms of Cooperation and Training*". This article requires parties to cooperate closely with one another to enhance the effectiveness of law enforcement action. These activities include as follows: establish and maintain channels of communication to facilitate the secure and rapid exchange of information; conduct enquiries concerning the identity, whereabouts and activities of suspected person and the movements of proceeds, property or drugs; in appropriate cases and if not contrary to domestic law, establish joint teams and promote the exchange of personnel and other experts, including the posting of liaison officers.[58] This article also requires parties to initiate, develop or improve specific training programs for its law enforcement and other personnel and to use regional and international conferences and seminars to promote cooperation and stimulate discussion on problems of mutual concern.[59] It is in evidence that this article extends international cooperation to the area of administration of justice to prevent and combat transnational crimes and goes beyond traditional mutual le-

---

[55] *United Nations Convention against Illicit Traffic in Narcotic Drugs and Psychotropic Substances*, Article 7 (2).

[56] Ibid., Article 7 (5).

[57] William C. Gilmore, International Efforts to Combat Money Laundering, *Cambridge International documents Series*, Volume 4, Grotius Publications Limited, 1992, p.130.

[58] See *United Nations Convention against Illicit Traffic in Narcotic Drugs and Psychotropic Substances*, Article 9 (1).

[59] Ibid., Article 9 (2), (3).

gal assistance model which focuses on criminal matters.

From the brief overview of international cooperation stipulated by the 1988 Vienna UN Convention, it did provide a mechanism of all-sided mutual assistance, ranging from mutual legal assistance in investigations, prosecutions, and judicial proceedings in relation to criminal offences to administration of justice. However, these provisions are not as detailed as those in bilateral or regional agreements. The reasons are multi-folds. First, it is due to its global scope, 106 states that have different legal systems took part in drafting this convention. In order to maximize the number of signatures, compromise and flexibility are necessary. Second, this Convention is the first international instrument to suppress drug trafficking and money laundering offence. It is difficult to stipulate all of the substantive or procedural provisions in detail. For these obvious reasons, the Convention suggests iteratively that signatory parties conclude bilateral and multilateral agreements to carry out or enhance the effectiveness of relevant provisions.[60]

2.3.5 Evaluation

The 1988 Vienna UN Convention is one of the most important international instruments in the efforts to fight against money laundering offence. From its content, the following major breakthroughs have been reached in this convention. First, it for the first time creates the obligation for signatory states to criminalize the laundering of money from drug trafficking at international level. Second, this convention is aware the fact that an effective international anti-money-laundering regime is to take the profit out of crime and controlling money-laundering crime is an effective way to combat drug trafficking. Actually, implementing the United Nations Convention further proved the fact that combating money laundering is also of great significance to combat organized crime, terrorism and other non-drug-related offences that generate large profits. Third, it also promotes international cooperation by requiring signatory states to provide the widest measure of mutual legal assistance in criminal matters and administration of justice as well.

From its sphere of influence, just as mentioned above, 106 states took part in

---

[60] Ibid., Article 6(11), 7(20), 10(3).

drafting this convention and by September of 1994, it had attracted 101 states plus the European Communities as parties. In addition to the major drug consumer nations in North America and Western Europe, the Convention is signed by key transit states in the Caribbean and Central America. More significantly, a growing number of drug producing nations have accepted its obligations. These include Afghanistan, Bolivia, Colombia, India, Iran, Mexico, Myanmar, Nepal and Pakistan.[61] For its global influence, it is hard to over-praise that the Convention is the foundation of the international legal regime in the anti-money laundering field.

Under the influence of the Convention, plenty of countries amended their criminal law to criminalize money-laundering activity and lift the banking secrecy to trace and forfeiture proceeds derived from crimes[62]. And also many bilateral and multilateral treaties, agreements or arrangements have been reached to enhance inter-states cooperation. In addition, this instrument has had a major influence on subsequent efforts in anti-money laundering. For example, the first of FATF 40 Recommendations contained in the 1990 Report was that *"each country should, without further delay, take steps to fully implement the Vienna Convention, and proceed to ratify it"*. The 1990 Council of European Convention also takes the Convention for reference to make the Convention more effective on the one side and improves the Convention on several issues on the other side.

However, the Convention is not an instrument specially aimed at the fight against money laundering but aimed at the fight against drug trafficking. The definition of money laundering offence under this convention is merely limited to drug-related offences. In fact, money laundering extends far beyond drug proceeds. Although drug trafficking accounts for a significant portion of the illegally generated proceeds, non drug-related money laundering is on the rise. In addition, due to its global scope, many of the substantive and procedural provisions under the Convention are not pro-

---

[61] See William C. Gilmore, *Dirty Money, The Evolution of Money Laundering Counter-measures*, Council of Europe Press, 1995, p. 64.

[62] China is one of those countries. Chinese government ratified the Convention on 4 September 1989. And on 28 December 1990 the Standing Committee of the National People's Congress enacted a regulation entitled Decision Suppressing Drug Dealing, of which Article 4 defined the act of money laundering. Another example, according to Second Commission Report to the European Parliament and the Council on the implement of the Money Laundering Directive, all of the Member States have sighed and ratified the Vienna Convention and implementation of the relevant anti-money laundering articles is complete.

vided in detail. For this reason, the 1988 Vienna UN Convention alone is far from enough to control money-laundering crime, although it indeed has a profound and significant influence in combating money laundering in international community.

2.4 United Nations Convention against Transnational Organized Crime

2.4.1 Background

The globalization of economic system is one of the distinguished characteristics in the modern world. The developments in transportation and communications technologies have created enormous opportunities for legitimate commercial activities, but they have also created significant new opportunities for organized crimes. Transnational organized crime is gradually becoming the most serious challenge which we are confronted with. Whether to effectively control the transnational organized crime directly affects the development and prosperity of the economy, the peace and security of the world.

The work of the United Nations to strengthen international cooperation to combat organized crime dates back to the last three decades. However, they focused on a special area, such as drug crime, aircraft crime, or they limited international legal assistance, especially procedure cooperation at international level. As the transnational organized crime has become much more serious, efforts of the international community to develop international instruments against transnational organized crime have to be made.

The idea of preparing a United Nations Convention against Transnational Organized Crime was first formally raised at the World Ministerial Conference on Organized Transnational Crime held in Naples on 23 November 1994. In this Conference, the Naples Political Declaration and Global Action Plan against Organized Transnational Crime were adopted. On 9 December 1998, the General Assembly established an open-ended intergovernmental Ad Hoc Committee for the purpose of elaborating a comprehensive Convention against Organized Crime. In its resolution 54/126 of December 1999, the General Assembly requested that the Ad Hoc Committee accelerate and complete its work by the year 2000. The Ad Hoc Committee approved the Convention in July 2000. On 15 November, the General Assembly formally adopted the instruments, United Nations Convention against Transnational Organized Crime (hereafter referred to as 2000 Palermo UN Convention), which was opened for signature in Palermo in December 2000.[63]

2.4.2 Criminalisation of Money Laundering

The purpose of the 2000 Palermo UN Convention is international cooperation. Article 1 of the Convention gives the purpose as "... *to promote cooperation to prevent and combat transnational organized crime more effectively*". To that end, the Convention deals with the fight against organized crime in general and establishes four specific crimes, that is participation in organized criminal groups, money laundering, corruption and obstruction of justice, which are commonly used in support of transnational organized crime activities.

Article 6 rules the criminalisation of the laundering of proceeds of crime, which reads, "*Every State Party shall adopt, in accordance with fundamental principles of its domestic law, such legislative and other measures as may be necessary to establish as criminal offences, when committed intentionally*:

(a) (i) *The conversion or transfer of property, knowing that such property is the proceeds of crime, for the purpose of concealing or disguising the illicit origin of the property or of helping any person who is involved in the commission of the predicate offence to evade the legal consequences of his or her action;*

(ii) *The concealment or disguise of the true nature, source, location, disposition, movement or ownership of or rights with respect to property, knowing that such property is the proceeds of crime;*

(b) *Subject to the basic concepts of its legal system*:

(i) *The acquisition, possession or use of property, knowing, at the time of receipt, that such property is the proceeds of crime;*

(ii) *Participation in, association with or conspiracy to commit, attempts to*

---

[63] See *The Convention: A Brief Historical Background*, http://www.unodc.org/palermo/convhist.htm, 22 Jul. 2003.

commit and aiding, abetting, facilitating and counseling the commission of any of the offences established in accordance with this article. "[64]

In order to eliminate differences among national systems and set standards for domestic laws, the Convention requires that each State Party shall seek the widest range of predicate offences. Specifically, predicate offences shall include all serious crimes, which mean those offences punishable by a maximum deprivation of liberty of at least four years or a more serious penalty, and the offences established in accordance with article 5 (participation in organized criminal groups), article 8 (corruption) and article 23 (obstruction of justice) of the Convention.[65]

Besides, according to the Convention, predicate offences shall also include offences committed both within and outside the jurisdiction of the State Party in question. However, "*offences committed outside the jurisdiction of the State Party shall constitute predicate offences only when the relevant conduct is a criminal offence under the domestic law of the State where it is committed and would be a criminal offence under the domestic law of the State Party implementing or applying this article had it been committed there.* "[66]

Similar to the 1988 Vienna UN Convention, the 2000 Palermo UN Convention also provides that knowledge, intent or purpose as an element of an offence may be inferred from objective factual circumstances.[67] And property also shall mean assets of every kind, whether corporeal or incorporeal, movable or immovable, tangible or intangible, and legal documents or instruments evidencing title to, or interest in, such assets.[68] In addition, the Convention provides that money laundering crimes do not apply to the persons who committed the predicate offence,[69] if required by fundamental principles of the domestic law of a State Party, which can be found in the 1990 Strasbourg Convention.

It should be noted that liability of legal persons, may be criminal, civil or administrative, is ruled under the 2000 Palermo UN Convention. Article 10 reads,

---

[64] *United Nations Convention against Transnational Organized Crime*, Article 6-2.
[65] Ibid., Article 6-2 (a), (b).
[66] Ibid., Article 6-2 (c).
[67] Ibid., Article 6-2 (f).
[68] Ibid., Article 2 (d).
[69] Ibid., Article 6-2 (e).

"*Each State Party shall adopt such measures as may be necessary, consistent with its legal principles, to establish the liability of legal persons for participation in serious crimes involving an organized criminal group and for the offences established in accordance with article 5 (participation in an organized criminal group), 6 (money laundering), 8 (corruption), and 23 (obstruction of justice) of his Convention.*" For the first time in an international convention, companies and corporations become liable for taking part in money-laundering activities. These business entities are to be punished appropriately and suffer substantial economic penalties.

2.4.3 Measures to Combat Money Laundering

The 2000 Palermo UN Convention absorbed the principles and measures provided in the 1988 Basel Committee Statement, the 40 Recommendations of the Financial Action Task Force and the EC Directive, and provided a set of measures in order to combat money laundering efficiently and effectively. Article 7 provided these measures:

——Institute a comprehensive domestic regulatory and supervisory regime for banks and non-bank financial institutions and other bodies particularly susceptible to money-laundering, such as the requirements for customer identification, record-keeping and the reporting of suspicious transactions, in order to detect and deter all forms of money laundering;

——Establish a financial intelligence unit to serve as a national center for the collection, analysis and dissemination of information regarding potential money-laundering, in order to ensure the administrative, regulatory, law enforcement and other authorities have the ability to cooperate and exchange information at the national and international levels;

——Implement feasible measures to detect and monitor the movement of cash and appropriate negotiable instruments across their borders. Such measure may include a requirement that individuals and businesses report the cross-border transfer of substantial quantities of cash and appropriate negotiable instruments.

Besides, States Parties are called upon to use as a guideline the relevant initiatives of regional, interregional and multilateral organizations against money-laundering and to endeavor to develop and promote global, regional, sub-regional and bilateral cooperation among judicial, law enforcement and financial regulatory authorities in order to combat money-laundering.

2.4.4 Other Measures Contributing to Preventing and Suppressing Money Laundering

Apart from above-mentioned measures, other provisions in the 2000 Palermo UN Convention also contribute to preventing and suppressing money laundering crime.

2.4.4.1 Confiscation and Seizure

Articles 12—14 provide for the confiscation and disposal of money or property, which is either proceeds of crime or has been used in crime. Provisions for international cooperation in seizure and forfeiture cases are included. Under Article 14, seized proceeds would normally be disposed of by the state which recovers them, but may also be shared with other countries for the purposes of paying compensation or restitution to victims or other purposes, or contributed to intergovernmental bodies working against transnational organized crime.

2.4.4.2 Obligations for International Cooperation

Cooperation under the Convention includes extradition and mutual legal assistance and other more specific measures, such as law-enforcement cooperation and collection and exchange of information. To keep criminals suspects from fleeing prosecution in one country to reach freedom in another, the Convention aims to tighten up extradition proceeding. State Parties are asked to recognize crimes covered by the Convention as extraditable, when no extradition treaty exists with the nation where the suspect is located; speed up extradition procedures; conclude bilateral and multilateral agreements to make extradition more effective. To tighten the net around organized criminal suspect, who have fled to foreign soil, State Parties should cooperate by legally assisting one another, collecting evidence and exchanging pertinent information. Legal assistance include: carrying out searches and seizure; providing originals or certified copies of relevant documents and records, including bank, financial, corporate or business records; permitting testimony or other assistance to be given via video link or other modern means of communications; granting witness safe conduct when testifying in a second country; and granting immunity from prosecution or giving reduced penalties to people who cooperate substantially with law enforcement investigating an offence and entering into like arrangement with witnesses from one nation whose testimony is needed in another.[70]

It should be acknowledged that these provisions are similar to traditional provisions already in place in many regional or bilateral agreements. The major significance of these provisions is that a large number of countries ratify the Convention, making legal assistance and extradition available much wider.

2.4.4.3 Prevention

Article 31 calls on States Parties to develop and evaluate national projects and to establish and promote best practices and policies aimed at the prevention of transnational organized crime. Many of them conduce to preventing money-laundering crime. Under the Convention, State Parties are urged to:[71]

—Tighten cooperation between law enforcement agencies or prosecutors and relevant private entities, including industry;

—Promote codes of conduct for relevant professions, in particular lawyers, notaries public, tax consultants and accountants;

—Prevent the misuse by organized criminal group of tender procedure conducted by public authorities and of subsidies and licenses granted by public authorities for commercial activity.

In addition, under this Convention, State Parties are required to stop criminals from misusing companies or corporations by:[72]

—Setting up public records on companies or corporations as well as persons involved in their establishment, management and funding;

—Using court orders or other means to keep people convicted of offences covered by this Convention for a reasonable period of time from acting as directors of companies or corporations;

—Setting up national registers of people disqualified as directors of compa-

---

[70] See *After Palermo: An Overview of what the Lonvertion and Protocols Hope to Accomplisk*, http://www.unodc.org/adhoc/palermo/sum1.html, 25 July, 2003.

[71] See *United Nations Convention against Transnational Organized Crime*, Article 31-2(a)(b)(c).

[72] See *United Nations Convention against Transnational Organized Crime*, Article 31-2(d).

nies or corporations;

—Exchanging information contained in the records with the competent authorities of other State Parties.

2.4.5 Comparison between the 1988 Vienna UN Convention and the 2000 Palermo UN Convention

It is apparent that the provisions of money laundering offence in the 2000 Palermo UN Convention are distinct from those under the 1988 Vienna UN Convention.

Firstly, money laundering offence is considered as one of the offences of drug trafficking in the 1988 Vienna UN Convention, while it is an independent crime in the 2000 Palermo UN Convention.

Secondly, the predicate offence under the 1988 Vienna UN Convention only refers to drug trafficking, while under the 2000 Palermo UN Convention, predicate offences include all serious crimes and the offences established in this Convention, namely participation in organized criminal groups, corruption and obstruction of justice. This change fully absorbed the contents provided in the 1990 Strasbourg Convention and the 40 Recommendations of the FATF and is the first time to expand the definition of money laundering in the United Nations convention.

Thirdly, a subtle change can be found on the way of jurisdiction between the 1988 Vienna UN Convention and the 2000 Palermo UN Convention. Under the 1988 Vienna Convention, traditional ways of jurisdiction are stimulated, namely territorial jurisdiction, personal jurisdiction.[73] Although it does not exclude the exercises of any criminal jurisdiction established by a party in accordance with its domestic law,[74] it does not require its parties to adopt legislative provisions in such circumstances that the predicate offence was committed extraterritorially. Under the 2000 Palermo UN Convention, no matter where the predicate offences commit, within or outside the jurisdiction, the State Party is warranted to deal with the money laundering crime. It is clear that the 2000 Palermo UN Convention is intended to cover extraterritorial of-

---

[73] See *United Nations Convention against Illicit Traffic in Narcotic Drugs and Psychotropic Substances*, Article 4 (1), (2).

[74] Ibid., Article 4(3).

fences. However, offences committed outside the jurisdiction of the State Party shall constitute predicate offences only when the relevant conduct is a double criminality.

Fourthly, under the 1988 Vienna UN Convention, only nature persons will be punished for money laundering crime, while under the 2000 Palermo UN Convention, not only nature persons but also legal persons will be responsible for money laundering crime.

Finally, the main purpose of the 1988 Vienna UN Convention is to fight against drug trafficking. Accordingly the 1988 Vienna UN Convention failed to formulate special measures to combat money laundering, neither did it establish preventive measures concerning money-laundering activities. Under the 2000 Palermo UN Convention, it paid much attention to these contents. Article 7 required the adoption of other legal and administrative measures to regulate financial activities in such a way as to make concealing proceeds more difficult, to facilitate the detection, investigation and prosecution of money-laundering, and to provide international assistance or cooperation in appropriate cases. And Article 31 called on State Parties to establish and promote best practice and policies aimed at the prevention of the crimes provided in the Convention. Obviously, these provisions are of great significance in the prevention and suppression of money laundering crime.

2.4.6 Evaluation

The 2000 Palermo UN Convention is a legally binding instrument committing member states to taking a series of measures against transnational organized crime. It signifies the recognition of all the member states that transnational organized crime is a serious and growing problem, which can only be solved through close international cooperation.

In respect of its contents, the Convention deals with the fight against organized crime in general and some crimes that are commonly involved in transnational organized crime, such as money laundering, corruption and the obstruction of investigations or prosecutions. Fundamental provisions under this Convention include the creation of domestic criminal offences, the adoption of new, sweeping frameworks for mutual legal assistance, extradition, law-enforcement cooperation and technical assistance and training. With the adoption of the Convention, States Parties will be able to rely on one another in investigating, prosecuting and punishing crimes committed by organized criminal groups. This should make it much more difficult for offenders and organized criminal groups to take advantage of gaps in national law, jurisdictional problems or a lack of accurate information about the full scope of their activities.

This Convention strengthens the international cooperation mechanism and legal measures provided in the 1988 Vienna UN Convention and 1990 Strasbourg Convention, and extends well beyond the sphere of cooperation on drug trafficking and money laundering. It seeks to construct an international framework of legal instruments aimed at fighting against transnational organized crime, the most serious threats to human society.

The Convention adopts criminal, financial and administrative measure to control transnational organized crime and succeeds in transferring the single international criminal cooperation into the multiple and integrative cooperation mechanism. And also this Convention does not only focus on procedure cooperation mechanism, which is the traditional international cooperation, but also extends the international cooperation to a substantial sphere, such as the establishment of domestic criminal offence and the creation of legal persons' liability.

For its international and substantial nature, the 2000 Palermo UN Convention got more than 120 countries to sign it. Pino Arlacchi, Under-Secretary-General and Executive Director of the United Nations Office for Drug Control and Crime Prevention, said, "*never before had an international convention attracted so many signatures barely four weeks following its adoption by the Assembly.*"[75] It is no exaggeration to say that the 2000 Palermo UN Convention marks a milestone in the history of the fight against transnational organized crime.

2.5 The Financial Action Task Force

2.5.1 Background

The Financial Action Task Force (FATF) is an independent international body,

---

[75] See *More Than 120 Nations Sign New UN Convention on Transnational Organized Crime, as High-Level Meeting Concludes in Palermo*, http://www.unodc.org/palermo/1215a.doc, 25 July 2003.

whose Secretariat is located at the OECD (Organization for Economic Cooperation and Development). It is "*the only international body which specializes in and concentrates solely upon the fight against money laundering*"[76]. The establishment of the FATF dates back to the nineteen eighties. In July 1989, the heads of State or Government of the seven major industrial nations (Group of Seven or G-7)[77] and the President of the Commission of the European Communities met in Paris for fifteenth annual Economic Summit. In consideration of the serious drug problem, it was concluded that there was an "*urgent need for decisive action, both on a national and international basis*" to "*counter drug production, to reduce demand and to carry forward the fight against drug trafficking itself and the laundering of its proceeds*"[78]. Among their resolutions on drug issues, they decided to convene a financial action task force from Summit Participants and other countries interested in these problems, to assess the results of cooperation already undertaken and to consider additional preventive efforts in this field. They decided that France would call the first meeting of this Task Force, and that its report would be completed by April 1990.[79]

In its first year of operation, the Task Force expanded quickly from the G-7 nations to a group of 15 countries. Other eight countries consist of Sweden, Netherlands, Belgium, Luxemburg, Switzerland, Austria, Spain and Australia. The expansion of the Task Force was undertaken "*in order to enlarge its expertise and also to reflect the views of other countries particularly concerned by, or having particular experience in the fight against money laundering, at the national or international level*"[80]. With broadened influence of the FATF, more and more countries and organizations became members of FATF. By June 2003, the membership of FATF had comprised

---

[76] Tom Sherman, *International Efforts to Combat Money Laundering: The Role of the Financial Action Task Force*, Money Laundering, Edinburgh, 1993, p. 20.

[77] The Seven countries consist of United States, Japan, Germany, France, United Kingdom, Italy and Canada.

[78] Group of Seven Economic Declaration of 16 July 1989, *International Efforts to Combat Money Laundering*, Cambridge, 1992, p. 3.

[79] See *Financial Action Task Force on Money Laundering Report of 6 February 1990*.

[80] Ibid.

31 governments and two regional organizations.[81]

The FATF is not a permanent international body and it does not have an unlimited life span. In the second Report issued on 13 May 1991, the delegations agreed to "*continue FATF for a period for five years, with a decision to review progress after three years*"[82]. While during the 1993—1994 round, it was decided that the FATF should be maintained for a further five years,[83] that is to say the FATF would remain in being until 1998—1999. However, during the 1997—1998 round, it was recognized that although standards have improved enormously in the past few years, particularly within the FATF membership, the FATF should spread the anti-money laundering message to all continents and regions of the globe. For this reason, on 28 April 1998, the Minister of the FATF and the European Commissioner for Financial Services approved the FATF's strategy for the years 1999 through 2004.[84] Whether the FATF will continue to exist and to perform its function after this date depends on the agreement by the member governments. During the period of more than ten years, the FATF focused on the following major tasks:[85]

• Monitoring members' progress in applying measures to counter money laundering. All member countries have their implementation of the Forty Recommendations monitored through a two-pronged approach: an annual self-assessment exercise and the more detailed mutual evaluation procedure.

• Reviewing money laundering techniques and countermeasures. Money laundering is an evolving activity, the trends of which will continue to be monitored. FATF members gather information on money laundering trends so as ensure that the Forty Recommendations remain up to date and effective.

---

[81] The 31 member countries and governments are: Argentina; Australia; Austria; Belgium; Brazil; Canada; Denmark; Finland; France; Germany; Greece; Hong Kong, China; Ireland; Italy; Japan; Luxembourg; Mexico; the Kingdom of the Netherlands; New Zealand; Norway; Portugal; the Russian Federation; Singapore; South Africa; Spain; Sweden; Switzerland; Turkey; the United Kingdom and the United States. Two regional organizations are European Commission and Gulf-Cooperation Council. See *Financial Action Task Force on Money Laundering Report 2002—2003*, http://www.fatf-gafi.org/dateoecd/13/0/34328221.pdf.

[82] See *Financial Acton Task Force on Money Laundering Annual Report 1990—1991*, 13 May 1991.

[83] See *Financial Acton Task Force on Money Laundering Annual Report 1993—1994*, 16 June 1994, Summary.

[84] See *Financial Acton Task Force on Money Laundering Annual Report 1997—1998*, June 1998, Summary.

[85] See *Financial Action Task Force on Money Laundering Annual Report 1992—1993*, June 29, 1993 Summary p3. http://www.fatf-gafi.org/dataoecd/13/61/34325384.pdf, 20 June 2006.

- Spreading the anti-money laundering message to all continents and regions of the globe. FATF fosters the establishment of a worldwide anti-money laundering network based on appropriate expansion of its membership, the development of regional anti-money laundering bodies in the various parts of the world, close cooperation with relevant international organizations and designating non-cooperative countries and territories.

2.5.2 Recommendations

The most important achievements of the FATF efforts to combat money laundering are undoubtedly the issuance of the Forty Recommendations. The forty Recommendations were issued in April 1990, and were revised first in 1996 and in 2003 again to reflect changes in money laundering trends. Besides, after the terrorist attack on 11 September 2001, the FATF issued the *"Eight Special Recommendations on Terrorist Financing"*.

2.5.2.1 The 1990 Original 40 Recommendations

In view of the fact that *"Many of the current difficulties in international cooperation in drug money laundering cases are directly or indirectly linked with a strict application of bank secrecy rules, with the fact that, in many countries, money laundering is not today an offense, and with insufficiencies in multilateral cooperation and mutual legal assistance"*[86], the FATF Recommendations start with the overall general framework for its many specific proposals. That is, the Recommendations urge member countries to ratify the Vienna Convention, to ensure that financial institution secrecy laws do not inhibit implementation of the recommendations, and to promote multilateral cooperation and mutual legal assistance in investigations, prosecutions, and extraditions.[87] After that, the 1990 Forty Recommendations address the concrete Recommendations concerning three aspects: improvements in national legal systems, enhancement of the role of the financial system and strengthening international cooperation, to constitute *"a minimal standard in the fight against money laundering"*[88].

---

[86] *Financial Action Task Force on Money Laundering Report of February 1990*, III (A).

[87] See *Financial Action Task Force on Money Laundering Report of February 1990*, Recommendations 1, 2, 3.

[88] Ibid., Recommendations.

a. Improvements in national legal systems

In respect to legal improvements, *"there is a clear recognition that in the fight against money laundering major reliance must be placed on criminal justice mechanisms."*[89] Therefore, just as the 1988 UN Convention, the Recommendations require countries to criminalize drug-related money laundering, *"each country should take such measures, as may be necessary, including legislative ones, to enable it to criminalize drug money laundering as set forth in the Vienna Convention."*[90] Similarly, as provided in the 1988 Vienna Convention, Recommendation 6 stipulates that, *"the offence of money laundering should apply at least to knowing money laundering activity, including the concept that knowledge may be inferred from objective factual circumstances."* In addition, Recommendation 8 requires countries to adopt measures to permit the identification, freezing and seizure of assets related to money laundering, also as stipulated as the Vienna Convention.

However, two of the recommendations broadened the contents contained in the 1988 UN Convention. First, Recommendation 5 encourages the coverage of all serious crimes or all crimes that generate large proceeds. *"Each country should consider extending the offences of drug money laundering to any other crimes for which there is a link to narcotic; an alternative approach is to criminalize money laundering based on all serious offences, and/or on all offences that generate a significant amount of proceeds, or on certain serious offences."* Second, Recommendation 7 provides possible extension of corporate criminal liability, which reads, *"Where possible, corporations themselves—not only their employees—should be subject to criminal liability."*

b. Enhancement of the role of the financial system

Although criminal law can play an essential role in the fight against money laundering, preventive measures are no less important than repressive approaches to money laundering crime. This perception is fully embodied in the second element in the FATF program, namely enhancement of the role of the financial system. Recommendations 9 to 29 provide a set of strategies to engage the financial system in the effort to combat money laundering, which are built upon the precedent Basel Committee State-

---

[89] William C. Gilmore, *Dirty money, The Evolution of Money Laundering Counter-measures*, Council of Europe Press, 1995, p. 98.

[90] *Financial Action Task Force on Money Laundering Report of February 1990*, Recommendation 4.

ment, with more ambitious provisions, though. Among them are well-known strategies such as customer identification, recording keeping, suspicious transactions reporting, internal control and the like.

In respect of customer identification, although the Basel Committee Statement has already addressed this problem, the FATF Recommendations take a further step to require financial institutions to obtain information on the beneficial ownership of funds, which reads, "*Financial institutions should take reasonable measures to obtain information about the true identity of the persons on whose behalf an account is opened or a transaction is conducted if there are any doubts as to whether these clients or customers are not acting on their own behalf, in particular, in the case of domiciliary companies (i. e. institutions, corporations, foundations, trusts, etc., that do not conduct any commercial operation in the country where their registered office is located).*"[91]

The 40 Recommendations also go beyond the Basel Statement by emphasizing a new prevention measure, suspicious transaction reporting. The Recommendations instruct that, "*Financial institutions should pay special attention to all complex, unusual or large transactions, which have no apparent economic or visible lawful purpose. The background and purpose of such transactions should, as far as possible, be examined, the findings established in writing, and be available to help supervisors, auditors and law enforcement agencies.*"[92] If financial institutions suspect that funds are connected to criminal activity, "*they should be permitted or required to report promptly their suspicions to the competent authorities*"[93].

The contribution of customer identification and suspicious transaction reporting can only occur when the collected information is made available for law enforcement authorities. Therefore the 40 Recommendations address the issue of record keeping, which reads, "*Financial institutions should maintain, for at least five years, all necessary records on transaction, both domestic or international, to enable them to comply swiftly with information requests from the competent authorities. Financial institutions should keep records on customer identification (e. g. copies or records of official identi-*

---

[91] Ibid., Recommendation 13.
[92] Ibid., Recommendation 15.
[93] Ibid., Recommendation 16.

fication documents like passports, identity cards, driving licenses or similar documents), account files and business correspondence for at least five years after the account is closed. These documents should be available to domestic authorities, in the context of criminal prosecutions and investigations. "[94]

Besides these above-mentioned provisions, the 40 Recommendations also address the following issues, which are not included in the 1988 Basel Statement, such as dealing with the problem of countries with no or insufficient anti-money laundering measures (Recommendation 21 and 22), monitoring cross border flows of cash (Recommendation 23), and making suggestions as to the role of regulatory and other administrative authorities in order to ensure effective implementation (Recommendations 26 to 29).

c. Strengthening international cooperation

Due to its transnational characteristic of money laundering crime, money launderers can exploit differences between national jurisdictions and the existence of international boundaries. Therefore, enhanced international cooperation between enforcement agencies, financial institutions, and financial institution regulators and supervisors to facilitate the investigations and prosecution of money launderers, is critical. To promote international cooperation, Recommendations 30 to 40 address this problem, which consolidate the progress achieved in the 1988 UN Convention. First, the Recommendations encourage authorities to exchange information on currency flows and money-laundering techniques and on suspicious transactions or operations.[95] Second, the Recommendations suggest that international cooperation should be supported by bilateral and multilateral agreements based on generally shared legal concepts.[96] Last, the Recommendations encourage countries to take steps to improve mutual assistance on the following topics: cooperative investigations, mutual assistance in criminal matters, seizure and confiscation, coordination of prosecution actions and extradition.[97]

The 1990 Recommendations are viewed as the most important achievements contributed by the FATF, which cover the role of legal and financial systems in the fight

---

[94] Ibid., Recommendation 14.
[95] Ibid., Recommendations 30—32.
[96] Ibid., Recommendations 30—34.
[97] Ibid., Recommendations 36—40.

against money laundering, as well as the area of international cooperation. They provide a complete set of measures to build a coherent anti-money laundering system and are intended for universal application. Although they are only recommendations, this does not diminish their effectiveness. In fact, many of these Recommendations already have embodied in the provisions of existing bilateral or multilateral conventions or domestic legislations. All these measures provide an international framework for effective anti-money laundering action.

2.5.2.2 The 1996 Revised 40 Recommendations

Money laundering is an evolving phenomenon. Efforts to combat laundering, therefore, must be similarly dynamic. Since the 1990 Recommendations were first created, the global money-laundering problems have changed significantly. FATF has developed a certain number of Interpretative Notes[98] designed to clarify or further explain the Recommendations. To preserve their continued utility, the FATF therefore decided that its Recommendations should be revised. Under the US Presidency of the FATF in 1995/1996, some Recommendations were amended and new ones were introduced. The major changes were[99]:

• The extension of the money laundering predicate offences beyond narcotics trafficking, to include all serious crimes;[100]

• The application of the financial Recommendations to the bureaux de change and all other non-bank financial institutions;[101]

• The application of the financial Recommendations to the financial activities of non-financial businesses or professions;[102]

• The expansion of the Recommendation on customer identification, to take into account problems raised by the identification of legal entities;[103]

• The need to pay special attention to and if necessary take measures to pre-

---

[98] Interpretative Notes are elaborated by the FATF during the period 1990—1995, which are designed to clarify the application of specific Recommendations.
[99] A full description of the stocktaking review of the Forty Recommendations can be found at the FATF VII Annual Report, http://www.fatf-gafi-org/dataoecd/13/29/34326515.pdf, p6, 20 June 2006.
[100] See *The Forty FATF Recommendations on Money Laundering (1996)*, Recommendation 4.
[101] Ibid., Recommendation 8.
[102] Ibid., Recommendation 9.
[103] Ibid., Recommendation 10.

clude the use of new or developing technologies for money laundering purposes;[104]
- The mandatory reporting of suspicious transactions;[105]
- The monitoring of cross-border cash movements;[106]
- The particular attention required when dealing with shell corporations;[107]
- The encouragement of the use of "controlled deliveries" techniques.[108]

These revised recommendations of the Task Force are in full consideration of the development of money laundering activities, such as the wider scope of predicate offences, the extended coverage of non-bank financial institutions or non-financial businesses, adoption of new technologies and making use of shell corporations. These revised recommendations also set higher requirements of financial institutions and other relevant professions, such as identification of legal entities, mandatory reporting of suspicious transactions, monitoring of cross-border cash movements. The impacts of the revised recommendations are far-reaching. For example, the European Union perceived the pressure that the EC Directive is behind the Forty Recommendations and is no longer considered as an effective and sufficient instrument, therefore the amended directive came into being in 2001. Furthermore, these revised recommendations gained worldwide recognition as the international standards in the fight against money laundering. On June 10th, 1998, the Special Session of the United Nations General Assembly recalled that "*the Forty Recommendations of the Financial Action Task Force ... remained the standard by which anti-money laundering measures adopted by concerned states should be judged.*" The Special Session of the United Nations General Assembly also approved a political declaration to recommend the States that have not yet done so adopt by the year 2003 national money-laundering legislation and programs in accordance with the action plan against money laundering.[109] The action plan, a document entitled "*Countering Money Laundering*", offers a set of measures to be taken. The content of this action plan derives directly from the Forty Recom-

---

[104] Ibid., Recommendation 13.
[105] Ibid., Recommendation 15.
[106] Ibid., Recommendation 22.
[107] Ibid., Recommendation 25.
[108] Ibid., Recommendation 31.
[109] Political Declaration and Action Plan against Money Laundering, adopted at the Twentieth Special Session of the United Nations General Assembly devoted to "countering the world drug problem together", New York, 10 June, 1988, Political Declaration 15.

mendations, covering the legislative level, the financial level and the enforcement level.

However, the Forty Recommendations are simply recommendations after all. Following normal international practice, they have no binding force. Although some Recommendations are reflected in the provisions of existing multilateral conventions and binding on parties or already embodied in domestic anti-money laundering laws, the others are not fixed in legislations. In this case, the function of the Recommendations depends on endorsement and practical implementation by member countries.

2.5.2.3 The Eight Special Recommendations on Terrorist Financing

After the terrorist attack on the United States on 11 September 2001, the fight against terrorism has reached its climax throughout the world. The FATF also made a quick response to the shocking events. On 29—30 October 2001, the FATF members called an extraordinary session in Washington DC to consider the necessary steps for preventing and combating terrorist financing activity. At the very important meeting, the FATF decided to extend its mandate to include terrorist financing. The FATF set up a new international standard for combating terrorist financing—the Eight Special Recommendations on Terrorist Financing. These Recommendations have been developed in addition to the existing Forty Recommendations, which are already accepted proverbially. The set of new Recommendations commit FATF members to undertake the following action:[110]

- Take immediate steps to ratify and implement the relevant United Nations instruments.[111]

- Criminalize the financing of terrorism, terrorist acts and terrorist organization.

- Freeze, seize and confiscate terrorist assets.

- Report suspicious transaction linked to terrorism.

- Provide the widest possible range of assistance to other countries' law enforcement and regulatory authorities for terrorist financial investigations.

---

[110] See *Financial Action Task Force on Money laundering Annual Report 2001—2002*, I. See also, *Guidance Notes for the Special Recommendations on Terrorist Financing and the Self-assessment Questionnaire*.

[111] Untied Nations instruments include the 1999 United Nations International Convention for the Suppression of the Financing of Terrorism and five UN Security Council Resolutions: S/RES/1267(1999), S/RES/1269 (1999), S/RES/1333(2000), S/RES/1373(2001) and S/RES/1390(2001).

• Impose anti-money laundering requirements on money remittance systems, including informal value transfer system;

• Strengthen customer identification measures in international and domestic wire transfers; and

• Ensure that entities, in particular non-profit organizations, cannot be misused to finance terrorist.

It is significant to note that the FATF will not be contented with merely drawing up recommendations, rather it will urge members to truly implement the Recommendations. In order to secure the swift and effective implementation of the Special Recommendations, the FATF developed a self-assessment questionnaire to help evaluate the level of implementation of the new standards. In January 2002, FATF members completed the first phase of a self-assessment exercise against the Special Recommendations and submitted responses to the questionnaire on terrorist financing. In addition, the FATF is conscious of the fact that the fight against terrorist financing requires the concert effort of all countries, both FATF and non-FATF members. For this reason, on 1 February 2002, the FATF held a special forum on terrorist financing at the conclusion of its plenary meeting in Hong Kong, China. Sixty-five jurisdictions and nine international organizations participated in the forum. All jurisdictions present agreed on joining the FATF's efforts to combat terrorist financing. The participating non-FATF members also agreed to take part in a self-assessment exercise and to turn the completed self-assessment questionnaire to the FATF Secretariat before 1 May 2002. Furthermore, the FATF President wrote to all UN Ambassadors to invite their governments to participate in the self-assessment exercise. By June 2002, 58 non-FATF members had returned a completed questionnaire to the FATF Secretariat.[112]

2.5.2.4　The 2003 Revised 40 Recommendations

As mentioned above, the 1996 Forty Recommendations have been the international anti-money laundering standard since they are set out. However, money laundering methods and techniques changed in response to the developing countermeasures. In recent years, the FATF has noted "*increasingly sophisticated combinations of*

---

[112]　See *Financial Action Task Force on Money laundering Annual Report 2001—2002*, http://www.fatf-gafi.org/dataoecd/13/1/34328160.pdf, 20 June 2006.

techniques, such as the increased use of legal persons to disguise the true ownership and control of illegal proceeds, and an increased use of professionals to provide advice and assistance in laundering criminal funds."[113] And also FATF gained much experience through the FATF's Non-Cooperative Countries and Territories (NCCT) process. All these led to the FATF deciding to review and revise the Forty Recommendations.

The process of review and revision of the 40 Recommendation began in May 2002, when the FATF issued a public consultation document, which examined the issues, proposed options for dealing with them, and invited all countries, international organizations, the financial sector and other interested parties to express their views, and finished in June 2003, when the revised Forty Recommendations were formally agreed in Berlin.

The revised Forty Recommendations now apply not only to money laundering but also to terrorist financing. They now provide a comprehensive and consistent framework of measures for anti-money laundering and combating terrorist financing. They cover all aspects of a national system, including the criminal justice elements; the preventive measures to be taken by financial institutions and certain other businesses and professions; the institutional framework and transparency of legal persons; and international co-operation.

The most important changes are as follows:

- Specifying a list of crimes that must underpin the money laundering offence;[114]

---

[113] *Financial Action Task Force on Money laundering Annual Report 2002—2003*, http://www.fatf-gafi.org/dataoecd/13/0/34328221.pdf, 20 June 2006.

[114] See *The 2003 Revised 40 Recommendations*, Recommendation 1. Countries must make all serious offences predicate offences to the crime of money laundering. At a minimum, each country should include as predicate offences a range of offences within each of the 20 designated categories of offences. If the country determines the predicate offences by reference to a threshold linked to the term of imprisonment for the underlying offences, then certain alternative minimum thresholds are set out. Foreign predicate offences should be as wide as the domestic predicates.

- The expansion of the customer due diligence process for financial institutions;[115]

- Enhanced measures for higher risk customers and transactions, including correspondent banking and politically exposed persons;[116]

- The extension of anti-money laundering measures to designated non-financial businesses and professions;[117]

- The inclusion of key institutional measures;[118]

- The improvement of transparency requirements through adequate and timely information on the beneficial ownership of legal persons such as companies, or arrangements such as trusts;[119]

---

[115] See *The 2003 Revised 40 Recommendations*, Recommendation 5. The new Recommendation and its Interpretative Note sets out the fundamental measures that financial institutions must take to identify and verify the identity of customers and beneficial owners, and to conduct ongoing due diligence. These requirements set firmer and more detailed standards, but also provide the necessary degree of flexibility, and are in line with current industry practice. In addition to the fundamental obligations, the Recommendation also deals with other issues such as the timing of verification, the measures to be taken with respect to existing customers and for legal persons or arrangements, and when simplified CDD measures may be appropriate.

[116] See *The 2003 Revised 40 Recommendations*, Recommendations 6 and 7. The FATF identified these two areas as requiring additional due diligence measures, due to the risks of money laundering or terrorist financing. The extra steps will help to ensure that financial institutions have the necessary information and the systems required to deal with the enhanced risks.

[117] See *The 2003 Revised 40 Recommendations*, Recommendations 12 and 16. For a number of years the FATF has observed a displacement effect, whereby money launderers seek to use businesses or professions outside the financial sector, due to the preventive measures being put in place in the financial sector. After examining the available data, it was agreed that the following businesses and professions should be covered by the Forty Recommendations: Casinos; Real estate agents; Dealers in precious metals and Dealers in precious stones; Lawyers, notaries, other independent legal professionals and accountants; and Trust and Company Service Providers.

[118] See *The 2003 Revised 40 Recommendations*, Recommendations 26—32. These Recommendations require countries to establish a financial intelligence unit (FIU), which will receive suspicions transaction report (STR); to designate law enforcement agencies for anti-money laundering investigations; and for financial supervisors to have a role in anti-money laundering. These authorities should have appropriate duties and powers, the necessary resources, and effective mechanisms to cooperate and coordinate. To ensure that systems are effective and that this can be reviewed, comprehensive anti-money laundering statistics must be kept e. g. the number of STR received.

[119] See *The 2003 Revised 40 Recommendations*, Recommendations 33 and 34. The FATF has consistently found that the lack of transparency concerning the ownership and control of legal persons (e. g. companies) and legal arrangements (e. g. trusts) is a problem for money laundering investigations. The measures required under commercial or other laws regarding the obtaining or access to such information vary widely from country to country. These Recommendations therefore set out the key objective of ensuring that adequate, accurate and timely information on the beneficial ownership and control of legal persons and arrangements is obtainable or accessible. In particular, countries must be able to show that companies issuing bearer shares cannot be misused for money laundering.

- Reliance on third parties and introduced business;[120]
- The prohibition of shell banks.[121][122]

2.5.3 Monitoring the Implementation of the 40 Recommendations

The Task Force is not simply content with drawing up recommendations to set up a standard for combating money laundering. Its endeavor also focuses on monitoring implementation of the forty Recommendations. In order to urge its membership to implement the Forty Recommendations, the Task Force develops many mechanisms for promoting effective actions by member states. In its second year of operation (1990/1991), the FATF commenced a process of self-assessment of its membership. In the third year of operation (1991/1992), the FATF commences a process of mutual evaluation of its members. It was recognized that "*a regular assessment of progress realized in enforcing money laundering measures would stimulated countries to give to these issues a high priority, and would contribute to a better mutual understanding and hence to an improvement of the national systems to combat money laundering.*"[123] In recent years, other mechanisms of monitoring the implementation of the Forty Recommendations are also launched. In 1996, the FATF adopted a formalized policy for sanctioning members that failed to comply with the 40 Recommendations. In order to foster the establishment of world-wide anti-money laundering network, in 2000, the FATF issued a report describing a process to identify jurisdictions that were not cooperation in taking measures against money laundering and encourage them to implement international standards adopted by the FATF. It is worth noting that the jurisdictions reviewed are both within and outside the FATF memberships.

---

[120] See *The 2003 Revised 40 Recommendations*, Recommendation 9. Some countries allow their financial institutions to rely on persons other than employees and agents to perform some of the required customer due diligence (CDD) measures on customers. The FATF recognizes that this is a common commercial practice, and permits countries to allow their institutions to rely on third parties provided that the conditions laid out in the Recommendation are met. The ultimate responsibility remains with the financial institutions relying on the third party.

[121] A shell bank is a bank incorporated in a jurisdiction in which it has no physical presence and which is unaffiliated with a regulated financial group.

[122] See *The 2003 Revised 40 Recommendations*, Recommendation 18. Countries should not allow the establishment of shell banks nor allow their financial institutions to have correspondent relations with such banks.

[123] *Financial Action Task Force on Money Laundering Report of 6 February 1990*, Conclusion.

2.5.3.1 Self-assessment Exercise

In the self-assessment exercise, every member country provides information on the status of its implementation of the Forty Recommendations by responding to a standard questionnaire each year. This information is then compiled and analyzed. Through this information it can be approximately concluded that to which extent the Forty Recommendations have been implemented by every member state.

2.5.3.2 Mutual Evaluation Process

The second element for monitoring the implementation of the Forty Recommendations is the mutual evaluation process. The mutual evaluation process started from its third year of operation (1991/1992), which is used to ensure that the 40 Recommendations were being put into practice.[124] Each member country is examined in turn by a team of three or four selected experts from the legal, financial and law enforcement fields from other member governments. The mutual evaluation process makes member states open them to independent scrutiny, and are evaluated and subject to criticism. The mutual evaluation process has led to improvements in the standard of anti-money laundering measures in all FATF members because these evaluated countries receive an independent and objective analysis of its anti-money laundering system.

2.5.3.3 Policy on Non-compliance Members

In 1996, more than five years after FATF was established, it was found that most members had reached a satisfactory standard of compliance with the Forty Recommendations. However, few members clearly damaged these recommendations. The FATF decided it had a responsibility to make every effort to ensure that necessary actions were taken. Consequently, FATF defined a policy for dealing with these few members that were not in compliance with the Forty Recommendations. The measures consists of 5 graduated steps: requiring the members to provide regular reports on their progress in implementing the Recommendations within a fixed timeframe; sending a letter from the FATF President to the relevant ministers in the member jurisdiction drawing their attention to non-compliance with the FATF Recommendations; arranging a high-level mission to the member jurisdiction in question to reinforce this

---

[124] See *Financial Action Task Force on Money Laundering Report (1990—1991)*, Paris, 13 May 1991.

message; in the context of application of Recommendation 21[125] by its members, issuing a formal FATF statement to the effect that a member jurisdiction is insufficiently in compliance with the FATF Recommendations; and suspending the jurisdiction's membership of the FATF until the Recommendations have been implemented.[126]

Under this policy, Turkey was the first example, although it was not expelled in the end. It was from the conclusion of the 1995—1996 self-assessment exercise that FATF noticed the fact, that Turkey was the only FATF member which had not passed any anti-money laundering legislation and whose compliance with the Forty Recommendations was seriously deficient. Therefore the President of the FATF wrote a letter to the relevant ministers. Subsequently, a FATF high-level mission met with several members of the Turkish Government in April 1996 in order to encourage Turkey to expedite the enactment of its anti-money laundering Bill. In October 1996, the FATF issued a press release cautioning financial institutions to scrutinize transactions with persons or business domiciled in Turkey. The public shame created by the statement and Turkish political objectives to become a member of the European Community led Turkey to enact a law making money laundering a criminal offence, and to implement other mandatory FATF standards.[127]

Another example and also the last one up to now is Austria, which was investigated by FATF in 1999 with regard to its anonymous passbooks. On 3 February 2000, the FATF threatened the member state with the ultimate sanction—suspension from the group unless it fulfilled two conditions: making a clear statement that all necessary steps to eliminate the system of anonymous passbook accounts would be taken by June 2002; the introduction and support of a bill into Parliament to prohibit the opening of anonymous passbook accounts and to eliminate existing anonymous accounts. The Austrian government responded by stating that it would conform completely to the FATF demands in June 2000 and the Parliament adopted an amendment to the Bank-

---

[125] Recommendation 21 requires financial institutions to pay special attention to business relations and transactions with persons, including companies and financial institutions in countries that do not or insufficiently apply these Recommendations.

[126] See Financial Action Task Force on Money Laundering, *Review of FATF Anti-Money laundering Systems and Mutual Evaluation Procedures 1992—1999*, IV (A).

[127] See Financial Action Task Force on Money Laundering Annual Report 1995—1996, see also Kern Alexander, The International Anti-Money-Laundering Regime: The Role of the Financial Action Task Force, *Journal of Money Laundering Control*, V-4. N.3, p.241.

ing Act on 7 June 2000. Thus Austria will not be suspended from the FATF.[128] These examples clearly demonstrated how the FATF policy on non-compliance members could lead to a more effective anti-money laundering system.

2.5.3.4 Designating Non-cooperative Jurisdictions

As mentioned above, FATF regularly reviews its members to check their compliance with Forty Recommendations through self-assessment exercises and mutual evaluations and taking sanctions against non-compliance members. These measures did improve the members' standards of implementation of the Forty Recommendations and make the anti-money laundering systems more effective. However, with its members strengthening their systems to combat money laundering, the criminals have sought to exploit weaknesses in other jurisdictions to continue their laundering activities. In order to reduce the vulnerability of the international financial system, and increase the worldwide effectiveness of anti-money laundering measures, it is also important to secure non-member countries to adopt adequate anti-money laundering measures. Therefore, from 1999, the FATF began the process to identify jurisdictions with serious deficiencies in their anti-money laundering regimes. The process involves 25 criteria to which are employed to identify detrimental rules and practices that impede international cooperation in the fight against money laundering. The criteria, which are consistent with Forty Recommendations, are divided into four aspects:[129]

　　a. Loopholes in financial regulations that allow no, or inadequate, supervision of financial institutions, weak licensing or customer identification requirement, excessive financial secrecy provisions, or lack of suspicious transactions reporting systems;

　　b. Weak commercial regulations, including the identification of beneficial ownership and the registration procedures of business entities;

　　c. Obstacles to international cooperation, regarding both administrative and judicial work;

　　d. Inadequate resources for preventing, detecting and repressing money-laundering activities.

　　As part of the review process, the FATF began to review the anti-money launde-

---

[128] See *Financial Action Task Force on Money Laundering Annual Report 1999—2000*, II (C).
[129] See Financial Action Task Force on Money Laundering, *Report on Non-Cooperative Countries and Territories*, 14 February 2000.

ring regimes of a number of jurisdictions, both within and outside the FATF memberships, with above-mentioned criteria. In June 2000, the FATF published the names of non-cooperative jurisdictions. They are: Bahamas, Cayman Islands, Cook Islands, Dominica, Israel, Lebanon, Liechtenstein, Marshall Islands, Nauru, Niue, Panama, Philippines, Russia, St. Kitts and Nevis, St. Vincent and the Grenadines. The FATF is continued to review the situation in the fifteen countries named as non-cooperative, as well as in other countries that had not yet been subject to the NCCT Survey. As the NCCT list is an open one, it is expected that some names will be deleted while some others could be added. In September 2001, the FATF identified two new jurisdictions—Grenada and Ukraine—as non-cooperative in the fight against money laundering. On the other hand, based on the progress they made during the year, Hungary, Israel, Lebanon and St. Kitts and Nevis were removed from the list of NCCTs. Thus, the list of NCCT now comprises the following jurisdictions: Cook Islands, Dominica, Egypt, Grenada, Guatemala, Indonesia, Marshall Islands, Myanmar, Nauru, Nigeria, Niue, Philippines, Russia, St. Vincent and Grenadines, and Ukraine.[130]

The FATF threatens to impose sanctions against these jurisdictions unless these jurisdictions comply with international minimum standards set forth by the FATF. It is in evidence that the aim of the exercise is to bring all jurisdictions to apply the international standards in the fight against money laundering. Of course, *"the best result to be achieved by the NCCT exercise would be to arrive at the conclusion that there are no countries to be listed"*[131].

2.5.4　Evaluation

The FATF, as an international body specializing in the fight against money laundering, plays a particular and also crucial role in this area. Despite its having a rather limited membership and informal legal status, it establishes an international standard for effective money laundering prevention system. And its Recommendations have

---

[130] See Financial Action Task Force on Money Laundering, *Review to Identify Non-Cooperative Countries or Territories: Increasing The World-Wide Effectiveness of Anti-Money Laundering Measures*, 21 June 2002, V.

[131] Gil Galvao, Countering Money Laundering: The FATF, The European Union and The Portuguese Experiences, Past and Current Developments, *United Nations Asia and Far East Institute*, 15 January 2001, p.268.

international recognition and application. From its more than ten years' efforts, it can be concluded that the following contributions of the FATF are in evidence.

First, the FATF not only puts forward Recommendations but also urges members to implement its Recommendations in practice, by the way of self-assessment exercise and mutual evaluation process. The influence from the FATF is obvious. For example, at the time of formulation of the 1990 Report, money laundering was a specific criminal offence in only several FATF jurisdictions. However, by 1997, drug money laundering was an offence in all members, and in 1999, the final FATF member countries made the laundering of the proceeds of serious predicate crimes an offence.[132] Another example, mandatory suspicious transactions reporting procedures, virtually non-existent before the FATF came into being, however they are in place in all but one of the FATF member jurisdictions in 2001.[133] Second, the influence of the FATF is getting more far-reaching. More and more countries now are subject to the FATF. In its first year of operation, there are only fifteen countries. By June 2003, it amounts to 31 members and two regional organizations. In addition, the FATF exert much effort to spread anti-money laundering information to non-members and thus have a profound impact over non-members on their mechanisms of controlling money-laundering activities. Its regular efforts consist of development of FATF-style regional bodies in the various parts of the world, cooperation with other international organizations and designating non-cooperative countries or territories. Third, as money-laundering techniques evolve, the FATF anti-money laundering measures also evolve. Specifically, from original 1990 Forty Recommendations to the 1996 revised Recommendations and in the end to the 2003 devised Recommendations, every stage goes further to establish stricter obligations for membership, such as from drug-related money laundering to the extended predicate offences; from financial institutions to the broadened coverage of non-financial businesses; from voluntary obligation to the mandatory reporting of suspicious transactions and the like. This progress resulted from its paying close attentions to the new trends of money laundering activity and the accompanying new challenges. Every year the FATF will produce a typology report to review

---

[132] See *Review of FATF Anti-Money Laundering System and Mutual Evaluation Procedure 1992—1999*, 16 February 2001.

[133] See Kern Alexander, The International Anti-Money-Laundering Regime: The Role of the Financial Action Task Force, *Journal of Money Laundering Control*, Vol. 4 No. 3, p. 242.

money laundering techniques and countermeasures in order to ensure that the Forty Recommendations remain up to date and effective. In addition to this constant effort, the FATF is also sensitive to the changes of circumstance, for example, after the event of terrorist attack on the United States, the FATF made a swift response to the terrorism and put forward the Eight Special Recommendations on Terrorist Financing, which now is resounded throughout the world. Last, although "*it is not a permanent international organization nor a body managing a legally-binding convention*"[134], the monitoring force of the FATF Recommendations is getting from strength to strength. This can be concluded from the recent exercises of the FATF. That is imposing sanctions on non-compliance members and designating non-cooperative jurisdictions. Turkey, Austria as the previous examples of non-compliance members, and Hungary, Israel, Lebanon and St. Kitts and Nevis, as previous examples of non-cooperative jurisdictions, all do better in controlling money laundering activities under the surveillance of the FATF. They are striking proofs that both the sanctions on non-compliance members and the measures of designating non-cooperative jurisdictions bring positive and beneficial results.

2.6 Interpol

2.6.1 Introduction to Interpol

The International Criminal Police Organization (ICPO/Interpol), the successor to the International Criminal Police Commission which was established in 1923, is the largest international police organization in the world. With its headquarters in Lyon, France, it has 181 member countries spread over five continents.[135]

The principle aims of Interpol, as expressed in the Article 2 of its constitution, are to "*ensure and promote the widest possible mutual assistance between all criminal police authorities with the limits of the law existing in the different countries and in the*

---

[134] William C. Gilmore, *Dirty money, The Evolution of money laundering counter-measures*, Council of Europe Press, p. 97.

[135] See *The Introduction to Interpol*, http://www.interpol.int/Public/Icpo/introduction.asp, 25 July 2003.

spirit of the Universal Declaration of Human Rights", and to "*establish and develop all institutions likely to contribute effectively to the prevention and suppression of ordinary law crimes*"[136]. It should be stressed that Interpol is an international organization aiming at facilitating cross-border police cooperation on a global scale and it has no operational policing mandate. "*One of its two major functions is to facilitate communication between its members through the provision of a modern, safe and secure communications network. ... The Second major function performed by Interpol is to act as a source of information on criminals and on developing trends and patterns of criminality.*"[137]

Interpol provides essential tools for international police cooperation: a global communication and messaging systems; a system of international notices requesting action and/or information from members; a range of databases based on information exchanged between members and/or provided by them direct to headquarters; forensic services related to fingerprints, DNA, and disaster victim identification; criminal analysis relating to trends as well as specific cases.[138] With its most advanced intelligence system, the widest communication network and the largest databases, the information interchange between the headquarters and its 184 members is timely, accurate, and complete. Interpol indeed acts as the intelligence hub of coordinating members to combat transnational crimes throughout the world.

2.6.2 Efforts on Combating Money Laundering

Interpol, as an international organization to fight against ordinary law crimes, its priority activities concern three broad categories of criminality at present: first, terrorism and crimes against people and property, such as crimes against children, trafficking in human beings, illegal immigration; second, economic, financial and high-tech crime, such as banking fraud, money laundering, counterfeit banknotes, counterfeit payment cards, cybercrime, corruption; third, criminal organizations and

---

[136] *ICPO-Interpol Constitution*, Article 2, http://www.interpol.int/Public/Icpo/LegalMaterials/constitution/constitutionGenReg/constitution.asp, 28 July 2003.

[137] William C. Gilmore, *Dirty Money, the evolution of money laundering counter-measures*, Council of Europe Press, p. 83.

[138] See *Funds Derived from Criminal Activities*, http://www.interpol.int/public/ICPO/InterpolOverview.pdf, 30 July 2003.

drugs, such as organized crime, cocaine, heroin, cannabis.[139] Among these activities, combating money laundering is one of its focal points. In recent years Interpol has made great efforts to prevent and suppress money-laundering crime.

2.6.2.1 The Definition of Money Laundering Given by the Interpol

A concise working definition was adopted by Interpol General Secretariat Assembly in 1995, which defines money laundering as: *"Any act or attempted act to conceal or disguise the identity of illegally obtained proceeds so that they appear to have originated from legitimate sources."*[140]

Under this definition, money laundering has the following elements: First, money laundering depends upon the existence of an underlying crime that has generated the illicit proceeds. It is apparent that the Interpol doesn't confine the scope of predicate offences, whether they are drug-related crimes or not. Second, the behavior patterns of money laundering include "conceal" and "disguise". From these words of "conceal" and "disguise", the third element of money laundering under this definition can be concluded, the mens rea of money launderer is scienter, namely the actor has already known that the property which he is dealing with came from a crime. Fourth, this definition doesn't exclude the case that the money launderer may be the owner of the proceeds.

Compared with the definition of money laundering given by the United Nations Conventions (1988 Vienna Convention and the 2000 Palermo Convention), the Strasbourg Convention, the EC Directive, this definition given by the Interpol is very simple and concise. For this reason, it should be stressed that the description of money laundering given by the Interpol couldn't be considered as a strict legal definition, but only a concise working definition.

2.6.2.2 The Resolutions Adopted by the General Assembly

It was in the mid-1980s that the Interpol started to pay close attention to the money laundering activities. The ICPO (International Criminal Police Organization)-Interpol General Assembly, meeting in Belgrade from 6th to 13th October 1986 at its

---

[139] Ibid.
[140] *Money Laundering-Interpol's Definition*, http://www.interpol.int/Public/Icpo/introduction.asp, 25 July 2003.

55 session, decided that the General Secretariat should create a working group to improve cooperation between the banking and financial institutions and associations and law enforcement agencies.[141] Then at the meeting at the Interpol General Secretariat in March 1987, the Memorandum of Cooperation was concluded and at the end of the Memorandum, member states were encouraged to adopt laws that make the laundering of monies obtained from criminal enterprise a criminal offence.[142]

The Interpol has assumed a leading role among international organizations in combating the laundering of funds derived from criminal activities. This is not only because the Interpol took the early effort to focus on the problem of money laundering but also because its later General Assembly Resolutions on money laundering.

Acknowledging the value of the existing international mechanisms such as the United Nations Convention against illicit traffic in narcotic drugs and psychotropic substances, the 1992 OAS (the Organization of America States) Model regulations concerning laundering offenses, the forty recommendation of the FATF, the Convention on laundering, search, seizure and confiscation of the proceeds from crime (Council of Europe, 1990) and the European Council Directive on prevention of the use of the financial system for the purpose of money laundering (Council of European Communities, 1991), the ICPO-Interpol General Assembly, meeting in New Delhi from 15th to 21st October 1997 at its 66th Session adopted these comprehensive resolutions AGN/66/RES/15, AGN/66/RES/17, and AGN/66/RES/18. These resolutions called on the member countries to adopt national laws that specifically make the laundering of illegal proceeds a criminal act and to develop effective enforcement strategies at national as well as international levels.[143]

AGN/66/RES/15[144] Money laundering: Legislations

This Resolution calls upon member countries which have not yet done so to ratify the 1988 United Nations Convention against illicit traffic in narcotic drugs and psy-

---

[141] See *Resolution No AGN/55/RES/18*, http://www.interpol.int/Public/ICPO/GeneralAssembly/AGN55/Resolutions/AGN55RES18.asp, 25 July 2003.

[142] See *Resolution No AGN/56/RES/11*, http://www.interpol.int/Public/ICPO/GeneralAssembly/AGN56/Resolutions/AGN56RES11.asp, 25 July 2003.

[143] See *Funds Derived from Criminal Activities*, http://www.interpol.int/Public/FinancialCrime/Money-Laundering/default.asp.

[144] See *Resolution No AGN/66/RES/15*, http://www.interpol.int/Public/ICPO/GeneralAssembly/AGN66/Resolutions/AGN66RES15.asp.

chotropic substances, and to urge their governments to implement the Convention in order to give their law enforcement institutions the powers it provides for. Besides, this Resolution recommends that member countries consider adopting national laws which would:

"(1) Provide for the criminal prosecution of individuals and legal entities that knowingly participate in the laundering of assets derived from criminal activities;

(2) Allow for the confiscation of such assets, and give law enforcement officials the power to identify, trace, and freeze assets derived from illegal activities in order to prevent those assets from being placed beyond the reach of appropriate authorities;

(3) Make provision for the repatriation of assets derived from illegal activities;

(4) Allow for the possibility of sharing out confiscated illicit assets among law-enforcement services, including the ICPO-Interpol to be used in the fight against drug trafficking and the prevention of drug abuse;

(5) Require banks and other financial institutions to report unusual or suspect currency or other transactions to appropriate officials who would have authority to conduct further investigations to determine if the transactions reported involved funds derived from illegal activities;

(6) Require financial institutions to maintain, for at least five years after the conclusion of the transaction, records on both domestic and international transactions so that money laundering cases can be properly investigated;

(7) Facilitate international co-operation by enabling member countries to respond to each others' requests for such records;

(8) Forbid the acceptance of anonymous accounts by banks and financial institutions;

(9) Allow for the expeditious extradition of individuals charged with money laundering offences."

It is apparent that this Resolution focuses on the legislation of member states concerning the prevention and suppression of money laundering. It requires members states to take necessary steps to criminalize money laundering; to deal with the assets derived from criminal activities appropriately, such as confiscating, repatriating and sharing the proceeds; to impose necessary responsibilities on financial institutions, such as suspicious transactions reporting and record keeping; and to strengthen international cooperation. This Resolution fully absorbs the policies and measures of anti-money laundering, adopted by the 1988 UN Convention, the 1990 Strasbourg Convention, the EC Directive, the FATF Recommendations and the others. It is commendable that these legislative requirements comprise the most important strategies of anti-money laundering crime with quite clear and concise wording.

AGN/66/RES/17[145] **Money laundering: Investigations and international police cooperation**

In view of the difficulties encountered by law enforcement authorities in their efforts to identify and prosecute money laundering crime, and the need to confiscate the proceeds of crime, the ICPO-Interpol General Assembly adopted this Resolution, which, Recommends that member countries extend cooperation in investigations to other members, and that the General Secretariat compiles and distributes information submitted by the member states on good investigative practices;

Recommends that member countries consider adopting effective laws that give law enforcement officials the powers they need to combat money laundering both domestically and internationally, by taking the measures listed below:

"(1) *Simplify procedures for the production of relevant financial records, overcome obstacles hindering or delaying the sharing of financial and criminal information by appropriate agencies, and improve the effectiveness of disclosure systems by increasing contacts with financial institutions in order to facilitate the gathering of intelligence;*

(2) Grant law enforcement officials the authority they need to investigate such cases, waive bank secrecy rules when there are reasonable grounds for suspecting that certain transactions are connected with criminal activities, authorize law enforcement departments to use techniques such as covert (undercover) investigations, technical surveillance and controlled deliveries when dealing with cases relating to assets known or suspected to be the proceeds of crime, and provide adequate

---

[145] See *Resolution No AGN/66/RES/17*, http://www. interpol. int/Public/ICPO/GeneralAssembly/ AGN66/Resolutions/AGN66RES17. asp, 25 July 2003.

resources for law enforcement departments, in order to increase the likelihood of a successful outcome for investigations;

(3) In the context of criminal procedure, allow courts to consider circumstantial or indirect evidence of the illegal origin of assets, provide protection or ensure anonymity for witnesses who give evidence in money laundering cases, and subject to the fundamental principles of each country's domestic law, allow the appropriate authorities to consider granting immunity from prosecution, or reducing penalties, or providing protection, for accomplices who testify to illegal activities;

(4) Subject to the fundamental principles of each country's domestic law, reverse the burden of proof (use the concept of reverse onus) in respect of the confiscation of alleged proceeds of crime."

If the former Resolution concerns the legislative requirement of member states, this Resolution focuses on the issue of law enforcement. It is widely acknowledged that the aim of legislation is to carry out the law. Though much legislation has already been adopted by many countries, a great deal of difficulty comes forth in the efforts to identify and prosecute money-laundering crime, or to confiscate the proceeds of crime. For this reason, this Resolution puts forward several constructive suggestions to alleviate the difficulties encountered by law enforcement authorities. Lifting bank secrecy, reversing burden of proof, simplifying relevant procedures, considering circumstantial or indirect evidence, using techniques such as covert (undercover) investigations, technical surveillance and controlled deliveries, all will be of great significance in the process of investigation, prosecution and conviction of money laundering crime, as well as will contribute to the confiscation of the proceeds derived from crimes.

AGN/66/RES/18[146] **Money laundering: Statistics**

Recognizing that any assessment of the progress achieved in combating the laundering of funds derived from crime must be based on statistical data, and the relevant statistics are not currently available, The ICPO-Interpol General Assembly recommends that member countries collect and circulate such data, particularly through In-

---

[146] See *Resolution No AGN/66/RES/18*, http://www.interpol.int/Public/ICPO/GeneralAssembly/AGN66/Resolutions/AGN66RES18.asp, 25 July 2003.

terpol channels;

Also recommends that such data include, at least:

"(1) The number of reports on suspicious transactions received from financial institutions and the number of such reports referred for further investigation (giving the outcome of the case where known);

(2) The number of convictions for money laundering and related charges;

(3) The number of cases where assets were seized and/or confiscated and the value of the assets forfeited."

Statistics about money laundering is highly essential in the process of assessing the progress achieved in combating money laundering crime. And one of the major functions of Interpol is to act as a source of information on criminals and on developing trends and patterns of criminality. This Resolution calls on members to collect and circulate relevant data so that can provide the possibilities for information exchange and information share and can support law enforcement or judicial authorities to cope with money laundering effectively and efficiently.

2.6.3 Evaluation

Interpol, as the largest international police organization in the world, is an effective tool in the fight against transnational money laundering crime. Firstly, the continuous efforts of Interpol facilitate the establishment and improvement of anti-money laundering mechanism of member states. The policies and action adopted by the Interpol, especially these anti-money laundering resolutions, surely can exert great influence on member states. As provided under the Constitution of the Interpol, "*member shall do all within their power, in so far as is compatible with their own obligation, to carry out the decisions of the General Assembly.*"[147] Since 181 members have taken part in the Interpol, the achievement obtained by the Interpol certainly looms large. Secondly, the Interpol promotes the elaboration of international anti-money laundering mechanism. The Interpol works closely with other international organizations with the

---

[147] *Constitution of the Interpol*, Article 9, ICPO-Interpol Constitution and General Regulations, http://www.interpol.int/public/ICPO/Legalmaterials/constitution/constitutionGenReg/constitution.asp#gp, 20 June 2006.

purpose of fight against money laundering, such as Financial Action Task Force (FATF) and Caribbean Financial Action Task Force (CFATF), Asia Pacific Group on Money Laundering (APG), Council of Europe, and so on. Most importantly, this liaison and cooperation are aimed at supporting each international organization's efforts in combating transnational money laundering crime and other serious crimes.[148] Thirdly, the Interpol contributes to the effective operation of anti-money laundering mechanism. As money-laundering crimes have no direct victims and are often masked as legal activities, it is difficult to be detected. Effective control on money laundering extremely depends on the relevant information. Interpol, as a source of information on criminals and on developing trends and patterns of criminality, it can serve as a clearinghouse of money laundering information for the benefit of all national and international anti-money laundering agencies. Thus, the Interpol can have unparalleled functions during the process of investigating and detecting money laundering offences.

2.7 Conclusions

Money laundering is an international problem and therefore international action is needed if it is to be combated effectively. In the last two decades, the Basel Committee Statement, the 1988 Vienna UN Convention, the 2000 Palermo UN Convention, the Financial Action Task Force, and the Interpol, all expressed their common awareness of the growing gravity of money laundering and showed their resolve and capability to deal with this problem in every possible way.

The Basel Committee issued its Statement Principles on the prevention of criminal use of the banking system for the purpose of money laundering. Customer identification, compliance with law and cooperation with law enforcement authorities, which covered by the statement, are regarded as the central components of anti-money laundering program. Though it is not a legal document, its pioneering role in the fight against money laundering is unassailable.

The two conventions of the United Nations are undoubtedly of great importance in the history of the fight against money laundering. The 1988 Vienna UN Convention

---

[148] See *Funds Derived from Crimind Activities*, http://www.interpol.int/Public/FinancialCrime/Money-Laundering/default.asp, 28 July 2003.

criminalized drug-related money laundering offence for the first time, set up an integrated confiscation system and established international standards for mutual legal assistance. It is considered as the foundation of the international legal regime in the fight against money laundering. The 2000 Palermo UN Convention strengthened the international cooperation mechanism and legal measures provided in the 1988 Vienna UN Convention and extended well beyond the sphere of drug-related money laundering. It adopted criminal, financial and administrative measures to control transnational organized crime in general and money laundering in particular, and succeeded in transferring the single international criminal cooperation system into the multiple and integrative cooperation mechanism.

The FATF, as an international body specializing in the fight against money laundering, plays a particular role in this area. It established an international standard for effective money laundering prevention system. And its Recommendations have international recognition and application. Most importantly, the FATF not only put forward Recommendations but also urged members to implement its Recommendations in practice by the way of self-assessment exercise and mutual evaluation process.

The Interpol, as the largest international police organization in the world, has the most advanced intelligence system, the widest communication network and the largest databases. It serves as a clearinghouse of money laundering information for the benefit of all national and international anti-money laundering agencies. Thus, the Interpol has unparalleled functions during the process of investigating and detecting money laundering offence.

Chapter 3

Western European Responses to Money Laundering

3.1 Introduction

In this chapter, two levels of efforts in the fight against money laundering will be discussed. One level is within the Council of Europe. The Council of Europe, as an intergovernmental organization, was established in 1949, its *"principal aims are to promote European unity, foster social and economic progress and protect human rights"*[149]. At first, the Council's membership was limited to the countries of Western Europe. With the collapse of the former Soviet Union, the Council expanded its sphere to the newly emerging nations of Central and Eastern Europe.[150] Now the Council of Europe has about 50 members.

The Council of Europe has played a significant role in the field of combating money laundering in the European region. This is not only because of its later Convention on laundering, search, seizure and confiscation of the proceeds from crime (hereafter referred to as the 1990 Strasbourg Convention), which plays a leading role in the fight against money laundering within the European region, but also because it

---

[149] William C. Gilmore, *Dirty Money, The Evolution of Money Laundering Counter-measures*, Council of Europe Press, p.133.

[150] Several of these emerging democracies have obtained full membership in the Council. These include Bulgaria, the Czech Republic, Estonia, Hungary, Lithuania, Poland, Romania, Slovakia and Slovenia. A number of additional applications for admission are under consideration. See Gilmore, ibid., p.134.

is the Council of Europe that took the initiative in focusing on the problem of money laundering in 1980, that is the Council of Europe Recommendation entitled "*Measures Against the Transfer and Safekeeping of Funds of Criminal Origin*". In this chapter, within the level of the Council of Europe, the focus will be put on the 1980 Council of Europe Recommendation and the 1990 Strasbourg Convention.

The other level is within the European Union (EU). The European Union, set up after the Second World War, is a family of democratic European countries, committed to working together for peace and prosperity. The EU now has 25 member states. The EU is underpinned by three pillars. The first pillar is composed of European Community, the European Coal and Steel Community (ECSC), and the European Atomic Energy Community (Eu-ratom), which assumes the good part of traditional EU responsibilities. The second pillar is about common foreign and security policy. The third pillar, introduced by the Treaty on European Union which was signed in Maastricht on 7 February 1992, and entered into force on 1 November 1993, is about the policies on cooperation in justice and home affairs (CJHA).

In the last decade, money-laundering has been given strategic priority at EU level. Under the first pillar, the 1991 anti-money laundering directive and the 2001 Amendment to this Directive, play significant role in the prevention and control of money laundering.

Under the third pillar, Main measures adopted to combat money laundering include:

—The Second Protocol to the Convention on the Protection of European Communities' Financial Interests (1997). Under this Protocol, member states are required to take necessary measures to establish money laundering as a criminal offence. In addition, liability of legal persons, sanctions for legal persons and confiscation measures are stipulated in this protocol;

—The Joint action of 3 December 1998 on money laundering, the identification, tracing, freezing, seizing and confiscation of instrumentalities and the

Chapter 3   Western European Responses to Money Laundering

proceeds from crime;[151]

—The decision of October 2000 concerning arrangements for cooperation between financial intelligence units (FIUs) of the Member States;

—The framework decision on money laundering, dealing with the identification, tracing, freezing and confiscation of criminal assets and the proceeds of crime, adopted on 26 June 2001. Since this framework decision covers part contents of the above-mentioned the Joint action of 3 December 1998, several articles of the Joint action are repealed;

—The protocol to the Convention of 29 May 2000 on Mutual Assistance in Criminal Matters between the Member States, at a subsequent joint EU Council of Finance and Justice and Home Affairs Ministers held in October 2001, Member States signed The protocol represents an important improvement of the cooperation between Member States in fighting economic and financial crime.

Besides, under the third pillar, the European Police Office (Europol) and the European Union's Judicial Cooperation Unit (Eruojust) also greatly contribute to the fight against money laundering.

In this chapter, within the level of European Union, the Council Directive 91/308/EEC of June 1991 on the prevention of the use of the financial system for the purpose of money laundering and its amendment, Directive 2001/97/EC of the European Parliament and of the Council of 4 December 2001 will be examined in detail. In addition, equal justice will be done to other efforts made by Europol and Eurojust.

3.2   The Council of Europe Recommendation

3.2.1   Background

In the 1970s, the large number of acts of criminal violence such as hold-ups and kidnappings are becoming more frequent in many European countries. The European

---

[151]   Prior to 1 May 1999, the day when the Treaty of Amsterdam entered into force, the Council of the European Union was able to adopt joint actions. Since 1 May 1999, the instruments within the third pillar are common positions, framework decisions and decisions, conventions, resolutions, recommendations, declarations, conclusion etc.

Committee on Crime Problems (CDPC) at its 26 Plenary Session in 1977 set up a Select Committee of Experts on Violence in Present-Day Society and gave it the task of studying the general and specific problems raised by crime of violence. The first phase of the study given by the Select Committee is *"to examine the serious problems raised in many countries by the illicit transfer of funds of criminal origin frequently used for the perpetration of further crime"*[152].

The Committee drew up a questionnaire on banking questions, which was distributed to member states. From the information collected on banking questions, it shows that banking practices represent a weak spot in the system that criminals are able to take advantage of in order to launder money acquired from violent crimes.[153] In view of the close ties between money laundering activities and banking practices, it is accepted that the stricter the requirements regarding identity checks, the greater the chances of discovering the money obtained through criminal activities. Thus, the coordination between the activities of banks and of the authorities competent in the prevention and control of criminal deeds is essential. To that effect, it seems that particular obligations should be imposed on banks. These considerations lead to a formal recommendation entitled *"Measures Against the Transfer and Safekeeping of Funds of Criminal Origin"*, adopted by the Committee of Ministers of the Council of Europe on 27 June 1980.

3.2.2 Measures to Be Taken by Banking System

"Customer identification", as a fundamental part of anti-money laundering system, is provided in the Basel Committee Statement, the FATF Recommendations, the EC Directive and other anti-money laundering documents. It should be noted that this rule originates from the 1980 Council of European Recommendation. Based on the conviction that *"the banking system can play a highly effective preventive role, while the cooperation of the banks also assists in the repression of such criminal acts by the ju-*

---

[152] Measures Against the Transfer and Safekeeping of Funds of Criminal Origin: Recommendation No. (80) 10 Adopted by the Committee of Ministers of the Council of Europe on 27 June 1980 and Explanatory Memorandum, International Efforts to Combat Money Laundering, *Cambridge international documents series*, Volume 4, p.171.

[153] Ibid., p.173.

dicial authorities and the police"[154], the Council of Europe of Recommendation puts stress on the "customer identification" rule. The Recommendation states that all private and public banks or other agencies performing similar activities should, leastwise, undertake identity checks on customers whenever "*an account or a securities deposit is opened; safe-deposits are rented; cash transactions involving sums of a certain magnitude are effected, bearing in mind the possibility of transactions in several parts; inter-bank transfers involving sums of a certain magnitude are made, bearing in mind the possibility of transactions in several parts*"[155]. "Customer" here means both the owner of the funds and the persons who represents him in his relations with the bank. "*These checks must be made on the basis of an official document or, where the relationship with the customer has been established through correspondence or through a third party, by equivalent means.*"[156]

The rental of safe-deposits is the easiest and most immediate means of safeguarding almost any proceeds of crime. According to the Council of Europe of Recommendation, only under the two situations, can the banks rent the safe-deposits to persons or firms: one is the situation where the bank has already had dealings with the persons or firms over a certain period, the other is the person whom the bank can regard as trustworthy on the strength of references.[157] The committee of experts had also envisaged what banks were bound to do: draw up a list of customers to whom safe-deposits were rented and to forward the list to the appropriate authorities; forward the list to a judicial authority upon request; keep an inventory of objects and funds placed in the safe. This idea, however, did not meet with the unanimous approval of the committee.[158]

The Council of Europe Recommendation also provides for banks to hold stocks of banknotes whose serial numbers are made known to the authorities if the banknotes have been used in connection with criminal offences.[159] Since the only individual characteristic of any single banknote is its serial number, the recording of the serial

---

[154] Ibid., p. 169.
[155] Ibid., Recommendation a (i), p. 170.
[156] Ibid.
[157] Ibid., Recommendation a (ii), p. 170.
[158] Ibid., Explanatory memorandum, p. 175.
[159] Ibid., Recommendation s (iii), p. 170.

numbers of banknote should be useful for relevant authorities.

In view of the fact that the effectiveness of most Recommendations depends on the judgment of the employees, the discrimination of the employees is of great of importance. Therefore, the Recommendation stipulates that "*suitable training for cashiers, particularly in checking identity papers and detecting criminal behavior*"[160]. It is notable that this Recommendation concerning staff training was subsequently adopted by FATF Recommendation, EC Directive and Basle Committee statement of principles.

3.2.3 Cooperation between Banks and Appropriate Authorities

The Recommendation addresses the issue about cooperation, which is also an essential means in the fight against money laundering. "*Banknotes which entered into circulation as a result of a criminal act and whose serial numbers are recorded, must be traced in order to prevent them from being laundered. To that effect, close cooperation is recommended between, on one side, the police and judicial or other appropriate authorities, and on the other side, banks.*"[161] This Recommendation requires that cooperation should be both at national and international level. The essence of this Recommendation also has a profound impact on many later international documents, such as the Council of Europe Convention, FATF Recommendation and Basle Committee statement of principles.

3.2.4 Evaluation

The Council of Europe Recommendation is very concise, in contrast with the Recommendations of the Financial Action of Task Force. Probably it was ahead of its times, the Council of Europe Recommendation was neither widely accepted nor implemented in practice.[162] Even so, the significance of the Council of Europe Recommendation should not be underestimated. After all, it for the first time recognized the fact that banking system not only can play a preventive role in the fight against money

---

[160] Ibid., Recommendation s (ⅳ), p.170.
[161] Ibid., p.173.
[162] See William C. Gilmore, *Dirty Money, The Evolution of Money Laundering Counter-measures*, Council of Europe Press, 1995, p.136.

laundering but also can assist the judicial authorities and the police to repress such activities. And its recommended measures, such as staff training and cooperation between financial institutions and competent authorities, now are widely accepted and considered as central components of comprehensive anti-money laundering measures both at national level and international level. In particular, the Recommendation focuses on "know your customer" rule, which resurfaces in subsequent national regulations and international instruments, is regarded as one of the three most important obligations of the financial system and other vulnerable professions and activities.

3.3 The Council of Europe Convention on Laundering, Search, Seizure and Confiscation of the Proceeds from Crime

3.3.1 Background

Before the 1990 Convention on Laundering, Search, Seizure and Confiscation of the Proceeds from Crime (hereinafter referred to as the 1990 Strasbourg Convention), the Council of Europe had already set up a high priority to legal sphere activities for many years. 160 international treaties and conventions had been created by the Council of Europe and of these 20 are related to the penal field.[163] Among these efforts, the European Convention on Extradition of 1957 and the European Convention on Mutual Assistance on Criminal Matters of 1959 were considered as the pillars of European cooperative efforts to combat crimes. However, these instruments were insufficient in combating money laundering. Therefore one of the purposes of the 1990 Strasbourg Convention is to complement already existing instruments to strengthen international cooperation concerning investigative assistance, search, seizure and confiscation of the proceeds from criminality.

In addition, it should be acknowledged that the 1988 Vienna UN Convention effectively pushed the creation of 1990 Strasbourg Convention. One important issue under the 1988 Vienna Convention is to identify, trace, seize, freeze and forfeit pro-

---

[163] Ibid., p. 134.

ceeds derived from and instrumentalities used in drug trafficking. However, implementing this Convention still depends on bilateral and multilateral treaties, agreements or arrangements to enhance the effectiveness of international cooperation.[164] The Strasbourg Convention, as a multilateral treaty to specify the obligations under the Vienna Convention, emerged as the occasion arose. The 1990 Strasbourg Convention was opened for signature in Strasbourg in November 1990 and entered into force in September 1993.

The 1990 Convention has four chapters: the first explains the use of terms; the second sets forth measures to be taken at a national level; the third defines the obligations and parameters of international cooperation; and the fourth contains final provisions. This Convention adopts and retains the achievements that have been fixed in the 1988 Vienna UN Convention on the one hand; on the other hand, it improved and complemented already existing articles under the 1988 Vienna UN Convention.

3.3.2 Money Laundering Crime

In the 1990 Strasbourg Convention, laundering offence is formulated under Article 6(1). It states: *"Each party shall adopt such legislative and other measures as may be necessary to establish as offences under its domestic law, when committed intentionally:*

a. the conversion or transfer of property, knowing that such property is proceeds, for the purpose of concealing or disguising the illicit origin of the property or of assisting any person who is involved in the commission of the predicate offence to evade the legal consequence of his action;

b. the concealment or disguise of the true nature, source, location, disposition, movement, rights with respect to, or ownership of, property, knowing that such property is proceeds;

and, subject to its constitutional principles and the basic concepts of its legal system:

c. The acquisition, possession or use of property, knowing, at the time of re-

---

[164] See *United Nations Convention Against Illicit Traffic in Narcotic Drugs and Psychotropic Substances*, Article 5 (4) g, 6 (11), 7 (20), 10 (3) and 17 (9).

ceipt, that such property was proceeds;

  d. *participation in, association or conspiracy to commit, attempts to commit and aiding, abetting, facilitating and counseling the commission of any of the offences established in accordance with this article.*"

It is obvious that laundering offences of Article 6(1) is largely based on the 1988 Vienna UN Convention. The categories of laundering offences under the two conventions[165] are largely identical. However, several significant breakthroughs have been made about money laundering in Strasbourg Convention, in contrast to Vienna Convention.

Firstly, laundering offence, as a special term, is put forward in an international convention for the first time. And also it is an independent crime, no longer as one of the offences of drug trafficking, which are formulated in the 1988 Vienna UN Convention. This reflects the fact that the growing gravity of money laundering crime attracts more attentions of international community.

Secondly, and most importantly, the obligation to criminalize money laundering is not restricted to drug trafficking. Instead it extends to any predicate offence. It is also the first time to expand the definition of money laundering in a binding international agreement, although it has been proposed by FATF in the fifth of the 40 Recommendations contained in its February 1990 Report, and also the same idea can be found in Article 305 (bis) of the Penal Code of Switzerland, which came into force on 1 August 1990 (a month before the Convention was adopted by the Committee of Ministers of the Council of Europe).[166]

Thirdly, the 1990 Strasbourg Convention permits, but does not require, the criminalisation of negligent laundering, which is formulated under paragraph 3 of Article 6. It reads, "*Each party may adopt such measures as it considers necessary to establish also as offences under its domestic law all or some of the acts referred to in paragraph 1 of this article, in any or all of the following cases where the offender:*

---

[165] 1990 Council of Europe Convention on Laundering, Search, Seizure, and Confiscation of the proceeds from Crime, Article 6(1); United Nations Convention Against Illicit Traffic in Narcotic Drugs and Psychotropic Substances, Article 3(b)(i), (b)(ii), (c)(i), and (c)(iv).

[166] See William C. Gilmore, *Dirty Money, The evolution of money laundering counter-measures*, Council of Europe Press, 1995, p.140.

      a. ought to have assumed that the property was proceeds; ... "

    Advantages of the extension of mens rea of laundering are obvious: negligence can be proved more easily than willfulness in judicial practical work. But we must not lose sight of the fact that criminalisation anywhere at any time is to sufficiently protect the society, meanwhile it also shrinks the freedom of people absolutely. Such concerns must have been felt by the 1990 Strasbourg Convention. In this regard, therefore, the Convention provides not absolute obligation but flexible suggestion.

    Last, A significant difference can also be found on the way of jurisdiction between the Council of Europe Convention and the Vienna UN Convention. Under the Vienna Convention, traditional ways of jurisdiction are stimulated, namely territorial jurisdiction, personal jurisdiction[167]. Although it does not exclude the exercises of any criminal jurisdiction established by a Party in accordance with its domestic law[168], it does not require its parties to adopt legislative provisions in such circumstances that the predicate offence was committed extraterritorially either. According to the 1990 Strasbourg Convention, the article reads: *"For the purpose of implementing or applying paragraph 1 of this article:*

    a. it shall not matter whether the predicate offence was subject to the criminal jurisdiction of the Party;"[169]

    The experts wanted to make it clear that the 1990 Strasbourg Convention was intended to cover extraterritorial offences.[170] In view of the transnational character of money laundering, and the situation, that predicate offence and money laundering crime are frequently scattered in different countries, the provisions on jurisdiction under the 1990 Convention is of great significance in the fight against transnational money laundering.

---

    [167] See *United Nations Convention Against Illicit Traffic in Narcotic Drugs and Psychotropic Substances*, Article 4(1), (2).

    [168] Ibid., Article 4(3).

    [169] *1990 Council of Europe Convention on Laundering, Search, Seizure and Confiscation of the Proceeds from Crime*, Article 6(2)(a).

    [170] See Explanatory Report on the Convention on Laundering, Search, Seizure and Confiscation of the Proceeds from crime, *Cambridge International Document Series*, Volume 4, 1992, p. 207.

3.3.3 Investigative and Provisional Measures and Confiscation both at the National and International Level

The main purpose of the 1990 Strasbourg Convention is to facilitate international cooperation as regards investigative assistance, search, seizure and confiscation of the proceeds from all types of criminality.[171] In order to be able to cooperate at the international level, states should adopt efficient measures in their national laws at first to deprive criminals of the fruits of their illicit activities.

At the national level, the committee noted that the national law of the member states differ widely and sometimes does not contain the necessary powers for law enforcement agencies. This situation may in fact impede the successful fight against serious criminality, which is tending to become better-organized, more international and increasingly dangerous to society.[172] For this reason, The 1990 Strasbourg Convention requires states to adopt legislative and other appropriate measures to investigate offences, to implement provisional measures and to confiscate the instrumentalities and profits of illegal activities at national level.

In order to provide a flexible and effective mechanism of international cooperation to the widest extent possible to deprive criminals of the instruments and fruits of their illegal activities, the Convention seeks to provide a complete set of rules, covering all the stages of the procedure from the first investigation to the imposition and enforcement of confiscation sentences.[173] Investigative assistance, provisional measures, confiscation, refusal and postponement of cooperation, notification and protection of third parties' rights, procedural and other general rules consist in Chapter 3. "*In certain respects this scheme seeks merely to reflect established and accepted forms of best practice. In other areas, however, the text seeks to improve upon and extend the cooperative mechanism embodied in pre-existing international agreements.*"[174]

In regard to the seizure and eventual forfeiture of assets, the Strasbourg Conven-

---

[171] See Explanatory Report on the Convention on Laundering, Search, Seizure and Confiscation of the Proceeds from crime, *Cambridge International Document Series*, Volume 4, 1992, p.193.
[172] Ibid., p.196.
[173] Ibid., p.195.
[174] William C. Gilmore, *Dirty Money, The evolution of money laundering counter-measures*, Council of Europe Press, 1995, p.145.

tion is perhaps the most forceful instrument yet contemplated.[175] First, the Strasbourg Convention focuses mainly on investigative measures, provisional measures and confiscation both at national and international level. No other international agreements have basically focused on so narrow a problem concerning depriving criminals of instrumentalities and illicit proceeds. Second, although the 1988 Vienna UN Convention represents several forms of inter-cooperation in penal matters, due to 100-plus nations that participated in the elaboration in the Convention, this instrument sometimes is limited by its global scope for compromise. While the finite nations comprise the Council of Europe are more cohesive and have more similarities. On account of this condition, the 1990 Strasbourg Convention provides more feasible provisions in respect of both substantive and procedural rules.

3.3.4 Legal Remedy and the Rights of Bona Fide Third Parties

The 1990 Strasbourg Convention, as a powerful weapon in the fight against money laundering, focusing on international cooperation and deprival of proceeds from criminal activities, no doubt is highly intrusive. Experts must have been aware of the fact that when we put stress on combating crimes, it is important as well to protect human rights and civil liberties. Accordingly, the 1990 Strasbourg Convention requires each party to adopt legislative and other measures to ensure that interested parties affected shall have effective legal remedies in order to preserve their rights.[176]

Moreover, this obligation has been officially described as follows: "*The legal provisions required by this article should guarantee effective legal remedies for interested third parties. This implies that there should be a system where such parties, if known, are duly informed by the authorities of the possibilities to challenge decisions or measures taken, that such challenges may be made even if a confiscation order has already become enforceable, if the party had no earlier opportunity to do so, that such remedies should allow for a hearing in court, that the interested party has the right to be assisted or represented by a lawyer and to present witnesses and other evidence, and that the*

---

[175] See Ernesto U. Savona, *Responding to Money Laundering, International Perspectives*, Harwood Academic Publishers, 1997, p. 128.

[176] See *1990 Council of Europe Convention on Laundering, Search, Seizure and Confiscation of the Proceeds from Crime*, Article 5.

party has a right to have the court decision reviewed."[177]

The measures stated above should be taken at the national level. Besides, the 1990 Convention requires parties to take measures to protect the rights of bona fide third parties at the international level. According to the Convention, the parties should render each other the widest measures of mutual assistance in the serving of judicial documents to persons affected by provisional measures and confiscation. When serving judicial documents to persons abroad affected by provisional measures or confiscation orders issued in the sending Party, this Party shall indicate what legal remedies are available under its law to such person.[178] When dealing with a request for cooperation, the requested party shall recognize any judicial decision taken in the requesting party regarding rights claimed by third parties. However, recognition may be refused if third parties did not have adequate opportunity to assert their rights.[179]

As shown above, not only at the national level but also at the international level, necessary measures should be taken to protect the rights of bona fide third parties under 1990 Strasbourg Convention. This reflects the fact that the 1990 Convention strives to seek an appropriate balance between combating money laundering and protecting the rights of affected individuals. Fighting crimes aims at maintaining the order of society and creating a stable living environment and ultimately, ensuring individuals' rights and freedom. But things will develop in the opposite direction when they become extreme. In other words, if we exceed a fitting degree to fight against crime, it will do damage to people's rights and liberties. This clear dialectic must have been felt by the drafters of the 1990 Strasbourg Convention.

3.3.5 Evaluation

The 1990 Strasbourg Convention no doubt is an effective international agreement in regard to establishing an important legal system on combating transnational money-laundering crime. The Convention lays stress upon two issues: requiring states to

---

[177] Explanatory Report on the Convention on Laundering, Search, Seizure and Confiscation of the Proceeds from crime, *Cambridge International Document Series*, Volume 4, 1992, pp. 206—207.
[178] See *1990 Council of Europe Convention on Laundering, Search, Seizure and Confiscation of the Proceeds from Crime*, Article 21(3).
[179] Ibid., Article 22(1), (2)(a).

criminalize the offence of money laundering and providing states the means to confiscate proceeds from crime both at national level and international level. In the first place, the Convention requires states to enlarge the scope of predicate offences, thus overcoming the 1988 Vienna UN Convention's biggest infirmity, which is restricted to drug-related offences. In the second place, the Convention provides a complete set of rules, covering all the stages of the procedure from investigation to confiscation and international cooperation mechanisms as well, thus expecting to effectively destroy the economic base of all types of criminality, especially serious crimes that generate large profits.

On the whole, the 1990 Strasbourg Convention has the following characteristics:

First, the Convention fully absorbs existing achievements of combating money laundering and inter-state penal cooperation, such as the former conventions of Council of Europe and the 1988 Vienna UN Convention. At the same time, as discussed above, the Convention addresses many questions and issues about which these former conventions are either silent or insufficient.

Second, the Convention sets up a legal mechanism of combating crime both at national level and international level. In view of transnational characteristic of serious crimes, the Convention strives to seek an effective international penal cooperation mechanism. While differences in national legislation may impede the successful and effective cooperation, the Convention requires states to innovate in national legislation to enable them to cooperate more effectively. "*The Convention makes significant achievements in recognizing the need to harmonize domestic legislation with international norms.*"[180]

Third, the Convention provides effective and flexible means of combating money laundering, such as the scope of predicate offences. On the one hand, the Convention expresses its expectation to states that the scope of application of the Convention should be made as wide as possible. On the other hand, the Convention also allows states to have a reservation right, as it is premature to consider it as a compulsive obligation. The sensible thought of "*more haste, less speed*" was fully embodied in this Convention.

---

[180] Ernesto U. Savona, *Responding to Money Laundering*, *International Perspectives*, Harwood Academic Publishers, 1997, p. 109.

Last, the Convention pays close attention to human rights while it puts stress on combating serious crimes. It is not advisable to carry things into extremes. For this reason, the Convention strives to seek an appropriate balance between retaliation and protection. This reflects the fact that the Convention is subject to the requirements of the European Convention on Human Rights, which was signed on 4 November 1950 and entered into force in September 1953.

Since the 1990 Strasbourg Convention is an excellent example of the integrated approach to inter-state penal cooperation, it is not only binding to all contracting parties, but also have an influence over other countries. Moreover, the Convention makes the 1988 Vienna UN Convention more effective. The Convention, however, due to its limited ambition, is not an all-inclusive agreement but only a criminal law agreement. It is impossible for this Convention to resolve all problems of controlling transnational money laundering crime, since a penal approach is not the only way to combat money laundering.

3.4 Council Directive of 10 June 1991 on Prevention of the Use of the Financial System for the Purpose of Money Laundering

3.4.1 Background

With the creation of the Single Market, the freedom of capital movements and freedom of financial services offer great opportunities for legitimate enterprise as well as criminal activities, such as money laundering. The European Communities considered it necessary to take preventive measures to impede money launderers from taking advantage of this environment.

Since credit and financial institutions are frequently used to carry out these kinds of activities by money launderers on the one hand, on the other hand, the financial system itself can play a highly effective preventive role in the struggle against money laundering, the European Communities intend to *"ensure the soundness and stability of the European financial system"*[181].

In June 1991, the Council of the European Communities adopted a directive on the *"Prevention of the Use of the Financial System for the Purpose of Money Laundering"*. The 1991 Directive was the first legislative measure to be adopted by EC in this area. As one of the major international instruments in the fight against money laundering, it did play an important role in preventing abuse of the financial system and detecting laundering offence.

3.4.2 Prohibiting Money Laundering by Member States

Money laundering has an evident influence on the rise of organized crime in general and drug trafficking in particular, and combating money laundering is one of the most effective means of opposing drug trafficking and other serious crimes. Moreover, the soundness and stability of credit and financial institutions could be jeopardized, since these institutions are vulnerable to be used to launder proceeds from criminal activities.[182] For these main reasons, the 1991 Directive requires all member states to ensure that money laundering is prohibited.[183]

Although the definition of laundering contained in Article 1 is derived from that used in the 1988 Vienna Convention and the 1990 Strasbourg Convention, an obvious difference between the two Conventions and the Directive is easily identified. That is, both the 1988 Vienna Convention and the 1990 Strasbourg Convention require states to criminalize the phenomenon of money laundering, while the 1991 Directive merely requires member states to prohibit this phenomenon.

In fact, the proposal for a Council Directive also required that *"member states shall ensure that money laundering of proceeds from any serious crime is treated as a criminal offence according to their national legislation."*[184] Just as it was interpreted in the explanatory memorandum: *"Criminalizing money laundering by member states*

---

[181] The 1990 Commission Proposal and Explanatory Memorandum, *Cambridge International Document Series*, Volume 4, 1992, pp. 243—244.

[182] *Council Directive of 10 June 1991 on Prevention of the Use of the Financial System for the Purpose of Money laundering*, Preamble.

[183] Ibid., Article 2.

[184] Proposal for a Council Directive on Prevention of Use of the Financial System for the Purpose of Money Laundering. Article 2. *Cambridge International Document Series*, Volume 4, 1992, p. 248.

is not only a necessary repressive means of combating money laundering, but also a previous prerequisite for cooperation between financial institution and judicial or law enforcement authorities."[185] Such an agreement, however, was not reached at that time. The core of this issue is the violent controversy about whether an EC measure of this kind has the competence to require the imposition of a criminal penalty.[186] One viewpoint is that the Community could assert the competence to compel member states to criminalize certain forms of conduct, provided that this was necessary to achieve the Community objective in question. Another one is that the Community has no jurisdiction in the field of criminal law.[187]

At last a compromising outcome was reached as a result of the concession of both sides. The Directive does not follow the Commission's draft in this respect and merely requires the member states "*to ensure that money laundering as defined in this Directive is prohibited*". In order to complement the provision of only prohibition of money laundering, Article 15 of the Directive provides that "*the member states may adopt or retain in force stricter provision in the field covered by this Directive to prevent money laundering.*"[188] As a matter of fact, the member states promised to take all necessary steps by 31 December 1992 at the latest to enact criminal legislation enabling them to comply with their obligations under the Directive.[189]

Although the Directive provides that money laundering shall be prohibited, according to the Second Commission Report to the European Parliament and the Council on the implementation of the Money Laundering Directive, all of the member states in fact made money laundering a criminal offence.

---

[185] The 1990 Commission Proposal and Explanatory Memorandum, *Cambridge International Document Series*, Volume 4, 1992, p. 245.

[186] See William C. Gilmore, *Dirty Money, The evolution of money laundering counter-measures*, Council of Europe Press, p. 164.

[187] See Peter J Cullen, The European Community Directive, Money Laundering, *Hume paper on public policy*, Vol. 1 No. 2, 1993, p. 37.

[188] *Council Directive of 10 June 1991 on Prevention of the Use of the Financial System for the Purpose of Money Laundering*, preamble, Article 15.

[189] See Statement by the Representatives of the Governments of the Member States of the European Communities Meeting within the Council Concerning the Council Directive of 10 June 1991, *Cambridge International Document Series*, Volume 4, 1992, p. 268.

3.4.3 General Coverage of the Whole Financial System

The Directive applies to not only banks, but also all kinds of credit and financial institutions, including the insurance industry. *"Credit institution means a credit institution, as defined in the first indent of Article 1 of the Directive 77/780/EEC*[190] *, at last amended by Directive 89/646/EEC*[191] *and includes branches within the meaning of the third indent of that Article and located in the Community, of credit institutions having their head offices outside the Community."*[192] *"Financial institution means an undertaking other than a credit institution whose principle activity is to carry out one or more of the operations included in number 2 to 12 and number 14 of the list annexed to Directive 89/646/EEC*[193] *, or an insurance company duly authorized in accordance*

---

[190] Directive 77/780/EEC provides: "Credit institution means an undertaking whose business is to receive deposits or other repayable funds from the public and to grant credits for its own account." See OJ No. L 322, 17.12.1977, p.30.

[191] This Directive adopts without change the definition in Directive 77/780. However, the directive contains a number of substantive provisions relating to credit institutions generally. See OJ No. L 386, 30.12.1989, p.1.

[192] *Council Directive of 10 June 1991 on Prevention of the Use of the Financial System for the Purpose of Money laundering*, Article 1.

[193] Directive 89/646/EEC provides:
ANNEX
LIST OF ACTIVITIES SUBJECT TO MUTUAL RECOGNITION
(1) Acceptance of deposits and other repayable funds;
(2) Lending (Including inter alia: consumer credit; mortgage credit; factoring, with or without recourse; financing of commercial transactions, including forfeiting);
(3) Financing leasing;
(4) Money transmission services;
(5) Issuing and administering means of payment (e.g. credit cards, travelers "cheques and bankers" drafts);
(6) Guarantees and commitments;
(7) Trading for own account or for account of customers in: a. money market instruments (cheques, bills, CDs, etc.); b. foreign exchange; c. financial futures and options; d. exchange and interest rate instruments; e. transferable securities;
(8) Participation in share issues and the provision of services related to such issues;
(9) Advice to undertakings on capital structure, industrial strategy and related questions and advice and services relating to mergers and the purchase of undertakings;
(10) Money broking;
(11) Portfolio management and advice;
(12) Safekeeping and administration of securities;
(13) Credit reference services;
(14) Safe custody services.

with Directive *79/267/EEC*[194] *at last amended by Directive 90/619/EEC*[195] , *insofar as it carries out activities covered by that Directive*; *this definition includes branches located in the community of financial institutions whose head offices are outside the Community.* "[196] The general coverage of the whole financial system reflects the feeling that "*a partial coverage of the financial system could provoke a shift in money laundering from one to another kind of financial institutions.* "[197]

Due to the difficulty of establishing the exact scope and the fact that they do not usually have any supervisory authorities, "Non-formal financial institutions" are not directly covered by the Directive.[198] However, money laundering can be carried out not only through credit and financial institutions but also through other types of professions and categories of undertakings. In the light of this concern, the Directive requires member states to ensure the provisions of this Directive is extended in whole or in part, to include those professions and categories of undertakings whose activities

---

[194] Directive 79/267/EEC provides:
Article 6
(1) Each member states shall make the taking up of the activities referred to in this Directive in its territory subject to an official authorization.
(2) Such authorization shall be sought from the competent authority of the member state in question by:
(a) any undertaking which establishes its head office in the territory of such state;
(b) any undertaking whose head office is situated in another member state and which opens an agency or branch in the territory of the member states in question;
(c) any undertaking, which, having received the authorization required under (a) or (b) above, extends its business in the territory of such state to other classes;
(d) any undertaking which, having obtained, in accordance with Article 7(1), an authorization for a part of the national territory, extends its activity beyond such part.
(3) Member states shall not make authorization subject to the lodging of a deposit or the provision of security.
Article 7
(1) An authorization shall be valid for the entire national territory unless, and in so far as national laws permit, the applicant seeks permission to carry out his business only in a part of the national territory.
(2) Authorization shall be given for a particular class of insurance. The classification by class appears in the Annex. Authorization shall cover the entire class unless the applicant wishes to cover only part of the risks pertaining to such class.
The supervisory authorities may restrict an authorization requested for one of the classes to the operations set out in the scheme of operations referred to in Articles 9 and 11.
(3) Each member state may grant an authorization for two or more of the classes, where its national laws permit such classes to be carried on simultaneously.
See OJ No. L63, 13.3.1979, p.1.
[195] This directive contains no provision affecting the provisions on authorization in Directive 79/267.
[196] *Council Directive of 10 June 1991 on Prevention of the Use of the Financial System for the Purpose of Money laundering*, Article 1.
[197] The 1990 Commission Proposal and Explanatory Memorandum, *Cambridge International Document Series*, Volume 4, 1992, p.244.
[198] Ibid.

are particularly likely to be used for money laundering purpose.[199] Nevertheless, this ambiguous wording is far from enough. This deficiency of the Directive led to the creation of the 2001 Amendment to this Directive, which will be discussed below.

3.4.4 The Scope of the Predicate Offences

Since money laundering occurs not only in relation to the proceeds of drug-related offences but also in relation to the proceeds of other criminal activities, the Commission originally proposed that the Directive's prohibition of money laundering should apply in respect of the proceeds of "serious crime". "*Serious crime means a crime specified in Article 3, paragraph 1(a) and (c), of the Vienna Convention, terrorism and other serious criminal offence (including in particular organized crime), whether or not connected with drugs, as defined by the Member States.*"[200]

However there was a wide divergence among the European Community countries on the interpretation of "serious crimes". A consensus could not even be reached to include terrorism.[201] The pragmatic approach to resolving this problem is to leave member states with the discretion to decide the scope of the predicate offence. Therefore, under this Directive, "criminal activity" replaces serious drug trafficking offences, which is defined in the 1988 Vienna Convention. "*Criminal activity means a crime specified in Article 3(1)(a) of the Vienna Convention and any other criminal activity designated as such for the purposes of this Directive by each member states*".[202]

Although money laundering always relates to drug trafficking, it would not be appropriate to exclude laundering of other serious crimes. Whereas it is also difficult for the 1991 Directive to decide how far it should seek to encompass criminal activities, which were unconnected with drug trafficking. This is also one of the main faults of the 1991 Directive, which was amended by the 2001 amendment to this Directive.

---

[199] See *Council Directive of 10 June 1991 on Prevention of the Use of the Financial System for the Purpose of Money laundering*, preamble, Article 12.

[200] Proposal for a Council Directive on Prevention of the Use of the Financial System for the Purpose of Money Laundering. Article 1. *Cambridge International Document Series*, Volume 4, 1992, p. 248.

[201] See Peter J Cullen, The European Community Directive, Money Laundering, *Hume Paper on Public Policy*, Vol. 1 No. 2, 1993, p. 39.

[202] *Council Directive of 10 June 1991 on Prevention of the Use of the Financial System for the Purpose of Money laundering*, Article 1.

3.4.5 Concrete Obligations for Credit and Financial Institutions

The preamble of the Directive explains that the penal approach to combating laundering should be used along with other strategies of prevention. It is the Directive's belief that the financial system can protect itself against money laundering to a significant degree. For this reason, the Directive imposes a number of specific obligations on credit and financial institutions.

Firstly, it requires the identification of customers and beneficial owners when they entering into business relations *"particularly when opening an account or savings account, or when offering safe custody facilities"*[203]. The identification requirement shall also apply to any other transaction involving a sum amounting to ECU 15000 or more, *"whether the transaction is carried out in a single operation or in several operations which seem to be linked."*[204] Furthermore, *"Credit and financial institutions shall carry out such identification even where the amount of the transaction is lower than the thresholds laid down, wherever there is suspicion of money laundering."*[205] Identification of customers or beneficial owners is considered as an essential measure on prevention of use of the financial system for money laundering.

Secondly, the Directive requires member states to keep certain records for a period of at least five years to be used as evidence in any investigation into money laundering. The certain records include, *"in the case of identification, a copy or the references of the evidence required"* and *"in the case of transaction, the supporting evidence and records, consisting of the original documents or copies admissible in court proceedings under the applicable national legislation."*[206] The obligation of keeping records not only is closely allied to the requirements concerning identification, but also is useful in any investigation into money laundering.

Thirdly, obligations are imposed to ensure cooperation between relevant institutions and the authorities responsible for combating money-laundering activities. Just as mentioned in the preamble of the Directive, *"preventing the financial system from*

---

[203] Ibid., Article 3(1).
[204] Ibid., Article 3(2).
[205] Ibid., Article 3(6).
[206] Ibid., Article 4.

being used for money laundering is a task which cannot be carried out by the authorities responsible for combating this phenomenon without the cooperation of credit and financial institutions and their supervisory authorities."

According to the Article 6 of the Directive, the cooperation encompasses two different obligations for credit and financial institutions and their directors and employees: one is about informing the judicial or law enforcement competent authorities, on their own initiative, of any fact which might be an indication of money laundering; the other one is about furnishing those authorities, at their request, with all necessary information, in accordance with the procedures established by the applicable legislation. The former, namely the mandatory system of suspicious transactions reporting is considered as the most effective measure to accomplish such cooperation.[207] The latter, namely furnishing the relevant authorities with all necessary information, must not be brought to the attention of the customer concerned or to any other third parties in order to safeguard the integrity of any subsequent investigation.[208]

Finally, it should be noted that the Directive requires the establishment by credit and financial institutions of procedures of internal control and training programs in this field. Adequate procedures of internal control and communication can forestall and prevent operations related to money laundering. Appropriate training programs can help the employees in credit and financial institutions to recognize operations which may be related to money laundering as well as to instruct them as to how to proceed in such cases.[209] These internal control procedures and training programs are complementary provisions, without which the other measures contained in this Directive could become ineffective.[210]

3.4.6 Evaluation

The 1991 European Community Directive was a landmark in the international efforts against money laundering. The Directive absorbed and reinforced international a-

---

[207] See Proposal for a Council Directive on Prevention of the Use of the Financial System for the Purpose of Money Laundering. *Cambridge International Document Series*, Volume 4, 1992, p. 247.
[208] See *Council Directive of 10 June 1991 on Prevention of the Use of the Financial System for the Purpose of Money laundering*, Article 8.
[209] Ibid., Article 11.
[210] Ibid., Preamble.

chievements in this field. These former achievements include the 1980 Recommendations of the Council of Europe, the 1988 Basle Committee statement of principles, the 1988 Vienna Convention, the 1990 Strasbourg Convention and the 1990 Recommendations of the Financial Task Action Force. Compared with these instruments, the European Community did play a unique role in the fight against money laundering.

By way of contrast, the 1980 Recommendations of the Council of Europe recognized that the coordination between banks and the competent authorities was of great importance. To that effect, particular obligations were imposed on banks. However, this initiative failed at the time to find a receptive audience and the recommendations were not generally implemented.[211]

Although the 1988 Basle Committee statement of principles has been more influential in establishing preventive strategies on control money laundering activities, it merely laid particular stress on banks not being used to hide or launder funds acquired through criminal activities. While the Directive requires member states that those relevant provisions apply to not only banks, but also all kinds of credit and financial institutions, including the insurance industry. In addition, the 1988 Basle Committee statement of principles is only a statement and it has no direct legal effect in the domestic law of any country.

Similarly, the 1990 Recommendations of FATF also have no legal constraining force. In this regard, the European Directive, in contrast to the 1988 Basle Committee statement of principles and the Recommendations of FATF, no doubt has greater influence on member states in the area that resort to preventive approach to control money-laundering activities.

Both the 1988 Vienna Convention and the 1990 Strasbourg Convention resorted to criminal repressive approach toward money laundering and emphasized particularly criminal law and cooperation in criminal matters, while the Directive focused on preventive strategies and laid stress on financial regulations and cooperation in administrative fields.

Thus, just as summarized by other scholars, while the Vienna Convention and Strasbourg Convention "*were directed to articulating a repressive approach towards this*

---

[211] See International Efforts to Combat Money Laundering, *Cambridge International Document Series*, Volume 4, 1992, xvi.

issue, the Directive is primarily addressed to credit and financial institutions and imposes obligations on them which are designed to ensure that laundering is detected before the stage of criminal investigation is reached"[212].

Nevertheless, the Directive only "prohibited" the offence of money laundering as it was not within its competence to "criminalize" activity, although all the member states in fact made money laundering a criminal offence in their domestic criminal law in the following years. Besides, the Directive did not create a system of "complete uniformity" at national level but leave a measure of discretion to the member states as to the exact way to achieve the object described in the Directive. Therefore several provisions, such as the scope of predicate offences, the coverage of non-financial institutions, are ambiguous. Thus it was not strange that regulations and practice as well differed widely from country to country on these points.

3.5 Directive 2001/97/EC of the European Parliament and of the Council, Amending Council Directive 91/308/EEC on Prevention of the Use of the Financial System for the Purpose of Money Laundering

3.5.1 Background

As mentioned above, the 1991 Directive was a landmark in the fight against money laundering and was frequently cited as one of the major international instruments, alongside the 1988 Vienna UN Convention, the 1990 Strasbourg Convention and the Forty Recommendations of the Financial Action Task Force on Money Laundering. However, in view of changes both at national level and at international level, it is no longer considered as an effective and adequate legislative instrument in this field.

At national level, many member states have already gone beyond the minimum standards established by the 1991 Directive, since Article 15 under the Directive stip-

---

[212] William C. Gilmore, *Dirty Money, The evolution of money laundering counter-measures*, Council of Europe Press, 1995, p.162.

Chapter 3 Western European Responses to Money Laundering

ulate that "*The Member States may adopt or retain in force stricter provisions in the field covered by this directive to prevent money laundering.*" By way of illustration, all Member States criminalize money laundering rather than only prohibit this phenomenon, which obviously go beyond the duty required by the Directive. In addition, the Directive does not require but merely encourages the prohibition of non-drug related money laundering, while most Member States have already extended the scope of predicate offences to other crimes in their legislation.

At international level, some new efforts have already been made to respond to the development of money laundering activities. The FATF revised the original forty Recommendations and resulted in the conclusion of 1996 Recommendations. For example, the FATF requires that, "*each country should extend the offence of drug money laundering to one based on serious offences.*"[213] The FATF has noted a shift of laundering activities from the traditional financial sector to non-financial professions or enterprises.[214] Furthermore, some time after the 1999 proposal to amend Council Directive 91/308/EC while one year before the formal amendment of the Directive in 2001, the United Nations Convention against Transnational Organized Crime came into being in December 2000, which requires contracting parties to apply to the widest range of predicate offences[215] and to extend the coverage to other bodies apart from banks and non-bank financial institutions.[216] In general, these efforts put forward higher requirements to combat money laundering since the schemes of money laundering activities evolve a lot.

In the same way, at European level, much response has already been made to strive to improve the measures against money laundering. The Action Plan on organized crime adopted by the Amsterdam European Council referred to these envisions that extended the obligation of suspicious transaction reporting to persons and professions outside the financial sector and to the proceeds of all offences connected with serious crime (rather than just drug trafficking)[217]. And also the Action Plan men-

---

[213] *Financial Action Task Force on Money Laundering 1996*, Recommendation 4.
[214] Ibid., Recommendation 9.
[215] See *United Nations Convention against Transnational Organized Crime*, Article 6 (2).
[216] Ibid., Article 7 (1).
[217] See *Action Plan to Combat Organized Crime (Adopted by the Council on 28 April 1997)*, Recommendation 26 (e).

tioned that criminalisation of laundering of the proceeds of crime should be made as general as possible.[218] Similarly, the European Parliament also noted that the 1991 Directive failed to respond adequately to the increased money laundering activity and called for additional measures to enhance the European Union's anti-money laundering effort. The Parliament "*called on the Commission to present a proposal for a further directive to fill in the gaps it perceived in the European Union's anti-money laundering defenses*"[219]. And it called for the money laundering offence to apply to the laundering of the proceeds of all organized crime and wanted the Directive to cover directly all the occupations and types of undertaking involved or likely to be involved in money laundering.[220]

Since the Directive was adopted in 1991 both the money laundering threat and the response to the threat have evolved. It is the view of the Commission, supported by the European Parliament and the Member States, that the response of the European Union must also move forward.[221] In fact, the Commission was quite serious in considering the necessity to modify the directive in the 1997 Second Commission Report on the implementation of the 1991 Directive. The second Report concluded that, "*the 1991 money laundering Directive risks appearing somewhat out-of-date in certain respects and this naturally poses the question of whether it should be updated.*"[222] At the same time the report stressed the need for extension outside the financial sector of the obligation to report suspicion of money laundering and also it concerned about the issue to cover other predicate offences.

Based on the above-mentioned aspects, the European Commission, who has the right of initiative under community law, put forward a proposal to update and extend the 1991 Directive to counter money laundering on 14 July 1999. The EU's Council of Ministers reached political agreement on the proposal in September 2000, and for-

---

[218] Ibid., Recommendation 26 (b).
[219] *Second Commission Report to the European Parliament and the Council on the Implementation of the Money Laundering Directive*, Introduction.
[220] Ibid.
[221] See *Proposal for a European parliament and Council Directive Amending Council Directive 91/308/EEC of the 10 June 1991 on Prevention of the Use of the Financial System for the Purpose of Money Laundering*, Explanatory memorandum.
[222] *Second Commission Report to the European Parliament and the Council on the Implementation of the Money Laundering Directive*, Conclusions.

mally adopted its Common Position on 30 November 2000. However, the Parliament voted a series of amendments to the Common Position at its 5 April 2001 plenary session. These amendments were not accepted by the Council, so that a conciliation procedure had to be convened on 18 September 2001 to seek a compromise. A compromise was agreed by the Committee of Member States' Permanent Representative on 10 October and by a parliamentary delegation on 17 October.[223] Thus, through concerted efforts in several years from the beginning of the 1999 proposal, Directive 2001/97/EC of the European Parliament and of the Council, amending Council Directive 91/308/EEC on prevention of the use of the financial system for the purpose of money laundering, was set down on 4 December 2001.

3.5.2 The Extension of Coverage of Financial System and Certain Non-financial System

One of the main changes of the 1991 Directive is the extensive coverage of financial system and certain non-financial system. The 1991 Directive applies to credit institutions and to financial institutions in the widest sense. However, the activities of currency exchange offices ("bureaux de change") and money transmitters (money remittance offices) are vulnerable to money laundering. These activities should already fall within the scope of the Directive. In order to dispel any doubt in this matter the Directive clearly confirms that these activities are covered.[224] The Investment Services Directive (ISD) having been adopted in 1993, some time after the adoption of the Money Laundering Directive, in order to ensure the fullest possible coverage of the financial sector and to remove any doubt, the Directive also confirms that the activities of investment firms as defined in Council Directive 93/22/EEC of 10 May 1993 on investment services in the securities field are covered.[225]

The most striking contrast between the Amendment and the 1991 Directive is the

---

[223] http://europa.eu.int/comm/internal_market/en/finances/banks/01-1580.htm.

[224] See *Directive 2001/97/EC of the European Parliament and of the Council of 4 December 2001 Amending Council Directive 91/308/EEC on Prevention of the Use of the Financial System for the Purpose of Money Laundering*. Preamble.

[225] See *Proposal for a European parliament and Council Directive Amending Council Directive 91/308/EEC of the 10 June 1991 on Prevention of the Use of the Financial System for the Purpose of Money Laundering*, Explanatory memorandum.

extension of the obligations imposed therein to several non-financial businesses and professions. As anti-money laundering measures executed by the banking sector have become stronger, money launderers have sought alternative ways of disguising the criminal origin of their funds. Just as the annual Typologies Reports of FATF have already stated: *"As regards money laundering techniques, the most noticeable trend is the continuing increase in the use by money launderers of non-bank financial institutions and non-financial businesses relative to banking institutions. This is believed to reflect the increased level of compliance by banks with anti-money laundering measures ... Money launderers continue to receive the assistance of professional facilitators, who assist in a range of ways to mask the origin and ownership of tainted funds."*[226] Besides, the 1998 Report of the UN Office for Drug Control and Crime Prevention on financial havens, banking secrecy and money laundering refers to the frequent misuse of lawyers and accounts to help criminal funds. And also there have been numerous cases where the real estate sector is used for money laundering purposes.[227]

The 1991 Directive applies basically to credit institutions and to financial institutions. Although Article 12 of the Directive provides that *"member states shall ensure that the provision of this Directive are extended in whole or in part to professions and to categories of undertakings, other than the credit and financial institutions referred to in Article 1, which engages in activities which are particularly likely to be used for money-laundering purpose"*, its wording is too broad and ambiguous for Member States to apply to this article. Based on this belief that a number of professions and activities can also play an active role in combating money laundering crime, the Amendment of the Directive determines to extend relevant obligations to some legal or natural persons acting in the exercise of their professional activities, which have been shown to be vulnerable to money laundering. Thus, Article 2 (a) under the amendment to the Directive now reads: member States shall ensure that the obligations laid down in this Directive are imposed on the following institution:

- credit institutions as defined in point A of Article 1;

---

[226] Financial Action Task Force on Money Laundering, *1996—1997 Report on Money Laundering Typologies*.

[227] See *Proposal for a European parliament and Council Directive Amending Council Directive 91/308/EEC of the 10 June 1991 on Prevention of the Use of the Financial System for the Purpose of Money Laundering*, Explanatory memorandum.

- financial institutions as defined in point B of Article 1;
- auditors, external accountants and advisors;
- real estate agents;
- notaries and other independent legal professionals;
- dealers in high-value goods, such as precious stones or metals, or works of art, auctioneers, whenever payment is made in cash, and in an amount of EUR 15000 or more;
- casinos.[228]

In consideration of the fact that notaries and other independent legal professions have the privilege of professional confidentiality on the one side, on the other side, sometimes these professionals perform tasks similar to those of banks, the Amendment to the Directive provides that the obligations of the notaries and other independent legal professionals laid down in the Directive merely apply to two different situations: (1) when they assist in the planning or execution of certain transactions for their client; (2) when they act on behalf of and for their client in any financial or real estate transaction. The former refers to specific financial or company law activities where the money laundering risk is the greatest. Specifically, the following activities are covered: buying and selling of real property or business entities; managing of client money, securities or other assets; opening or management of bank, savings or securities accounts; organization of contributions necessary for the creation, operation or management of companies; creation, operation or management of trusts, companies or similar structures.[229]

3.5.3 The Widening of Scope of Predicate Offences

The second major change of the 1991 Directive is the definition of criminal activity, namely the scope of the predicate offence. Under the 1991 Directive, "criminal activity" means "*a crime specified in Article 3 (1)(a) of the Vienna Convention and any other criminal activity designated as such for the purposes of this Directive by each*

---

[228] See *Directive 2001/97/EC of the European Parliament and of the Council of 4 December 2001 Amending Council Directive 91/308/EEC on Prevention of the Use of the Financial System for the Purpose of Money Laundering*, Article 2a-(3)-(7).

[229] Ibid., Article 2a-5.

Member States"[230]. It can be concluded that the 1991 Directive merely requires Member States to prohibit drug-related money laundering, and leave the member states with the discretion to extend to the proceeds of other forms of criminal activity. This was a narrow scope, which was already left behind by the revision of the FATF Forty Recommendation, namely Recommendation 4, which refers to serious crimes.

Although it is a long debate in respect of the scope of the predicate offences within the European Union, in fact, several agreements have already been reached to include a wide range of predicate offences. By way of illustration, the Second Protocol to the Convention on the Protection of the European Communities' Financial Interests (1997)[231] provided that, money laundering means the conduct defined in the 1991 Directive, related to the proceeds of fraud, at least in serious cases, and of active and passive corruption.[232] The extension of the concept of money laundering signifies the European Union's readiness to accept a wider provision in this area of law. Another example, on 3 December 1998 the council adopted a Joint Action on the basis of Article K.3 of the Treaty on European Union, on money laundering, the identification, tracing, freezing, seizing and confiscation of instrumentalities and the proceeds from crime[233]. In this Joint Action Member States agreed that no reservations should be made or upheld in respect of Article 6 of the Strasbourg Convention in so far as serious offences are concerned. Serious offences "*should in any event include offences which are punishable by deprivation of liberty or a detention order of a maximum of more than one year, or as regards those States which have a minimum threshold for offences in their legal system, offences punishable by deprivation of liberty or a detention order of a minimum of more than six months.*"[234] The result of the Joint Action reflects that the Member States have agreed to criminalize the laundering of the proceeds of all serious offences.

Now, under the Amendment to the Directive, "criminal activity" means any

---

[230] Ibid., Article 1.

[231] See *Official Journal of the European Commission No. C221*, 19.07. 1997, p. 11.

[232] See *Second Protocol to the Convention on the Prevention of the European Communities' Financial Interests (1997)*, Article 1 (e).

[233] See *OJL 333*, 9.12.1998, p. 1.

[234] *Joint Action of 3 December 1998 adopted by the Council on the basis of Article K. 3 of the Treaty on European Union, on Money Laundering, the Identification, Tracing, Freezing, Seizing and Confiscation of Instrumentalities and proceeds from crime*, Article 1 (b).

Chapter 3 Western European Responses to Money Laundering

kind of criminal involved in the commission of a serious crime. Serious crimes are, at least:

- *"any of the offences defined in Article 3(1)(a) of the Vienna Convention;*
- *the activities of a criminal organizations as defined in Article 1 of Joint Action 98/773/JHA*[235];
- *fraud, at least serious, as defined in Article 1(1) and Article 2 of the Convention on the protection of the European Communities' financial interests*[236];

---

[235]　See *OJL 351*, 29.12.1998, p.1.
Joint Action 98/773/JHA provides:
Article 1
Within the meaning of this joint action, a criminal organization shall mean a structured association, established over a period of time, of more than two persons, acting in concert with a view to committing offences which are punishable by deprivation of liberty or a detention order of a maximum of at least four years or a more serious penalty, whether such offences are an end in themselves or a means of obtaining material benefits and, where appropriate, of improperly influencing the operation of public authorities.
The offences referred to in the first subparagraph include those mentioned in Article 2 of the Europol Convention and in the Annex thereto and carrying a sentence at least equivalent to that provided for in the first subparagraph.

[236]　See *OJ C 316*, 27.11.1995, p.48.
Convention on the Protection of the European Communities' Financial Interests (1995) provides:
Article 1—General provisions
(1) For the purpose of this Convention, fraud affecting the European Communities' financial interests shall consist of:
(a) in respect of expenditure, any intentional act or omission relating to:
—the use or presentation of false, incorrect or incomplete statements of documents, which has as its effect the misappropriation or wrongful retention of funds from the general budget of the European Communities or budgets managed by, or on behalf of, the European Communities;
—non-disclosure of information in violation of a specific obligation, with the same effect;
—the misapplication of such funds for purposes other than those for which they were originally granted;
(b) in respect of revenue, any intentional act or omission relating to:
—the use or presentation of false, incorrect or incomplete statements of documents, which has as its effect the illegal diminution of the resources of the general budget of the European Communities or budgets managed by, or on behalf of, the European Communities;
—non-disclosure of information in violation of a specific obligation, with the same effect;
—misapplication of a legally obtained benefit, with the same effect.
Article 2—Penalties
(1) Each Member State shall take the necessary measures to ensure that the conduct referred to in Article 1, and participating in, instigating, or attempting the conduct referred to in Article 1(1), are punishable by effective, proportionate and dissuasive criminal penalties, including, at least in cases of serious fraud, penalties involving deprivation of liberty which can give rise to extradition, it being understood that serious fraud shall be considered to be fraud involving a minimum amount to be set in each Member States. This minimum amount may not be set at a sum exceeding ECU 50,000.
(2) However in cases of minor fraud involving a total amount of less than ECU 4000 and not involving particularly serious circumstances under its laws, a Member State may provide for penalties of a different type from those laid down in paragraph 1.
(3) The Council of the European Union, acting unanimously, may alter the amount referred to in paragraph 2.

- *corruption*;
- *an offence which may generates substantial proceeds and which is punishable by a severe sentence of imprisonment in accordance with the penal law of the member states.* "[237]

In order to oblige the member states to carry out relevant obligations, the amended Directive imposes a time limit for implementation; "*Member States shall before 15 December 2004 amend the definition provided for in this indent in order to bring this definition into line with the definition of serious crime of Joint Action98/699/JHA*[238]. *The Council invites the Commission to present before 15 December 2004 a proposal for a Directive amending in that respect this Directive.*"[239] In addition, the Amendment again expresses the desire that the scope of predicate offences provided in Article 1 (e) is the minimum requirement, "*Member States may designate any other offence as a criminal activity for the purpose of this Directive.*"[240] This article reflects the idea that the scope of predicate offences should be as wide as possible.

3.5.4 The Obligation of Suspicious Transactions Reporting

Under 1991 EC Directive, three main duties concerning customer identification, record keeping and reporting of suspicious transactions are imposed on financial institutions. Now under the amendment to the Directive, these obligations should be ex-

---

[237] Directive 2001/97/EC of the European Parliament and of the Council of 4 December 2001, amending Council Directive 91/308/EEC on prevention of the use of the financial system for the purpose of money laundering, Article 1(1) e.

[238] See *OJL 333*, 9.12.1998, p.1.
Joint Action98/699/JHA provides:

Article 1

(1) In order to enhance effective action against organized crime, Member States shall ensure that no reservations are made or upheld in respect of the following Articles of the 1990 Council of Europe Convention on Laundering, Search, Seizure and Confiscation of the Proceeds from Crime:

(a) ...

(b) Article 6: in so far as serious offences are concerned. Such offences should in any event include offences which are punishable by deprivation of liberty or a detention order of a maximum of more than one year, or, as regards those States which have a minimum threshold for offences in their legal system, offences punishable by deprivation of liberty or a detention order of a minimum of more than six months.

[239] Directive 2001/97/EC of the European Parliament and of the Council of 4 December 2001, amending Council Directive 91/308/EEC on prevention of the use of the financial system for the purpose of money laundering, Article 1(1) e.

[240] Ibid.

tended to a limited number of activities and professions that are vulnerable to money laundering, just as mentioned above. However, in respect of the obligation of reporting of suspicious transactions, there are some special provisions, which are in relations to the notaries and other independent legal professionals.

Although the notaries and other independent legal professionals have the privilege of professional confidentiality, in the above-mentioned situations, they are still made subject to obligation of the reporting of suspicious transactions according to the Amendment to the Directive. *"The rationale for this situation is the idea that the privilege of professional confidentiality was granted to the lawyer/customer relationship to safeguard the fundamental right of defense. The intervention in financial transactions, namely in the transactions referred to in the new directive, cannot be construed as a typical act of the lawyer's profession, and therefore does not deserve that kind of protection. On the other hand, from the axiological point of view, the value of the fight against serious criminality precedes, in these cases, other values.*"[241]

Of course, when these people are performing their traditional role of legal adviser or representative, it is necessary for them to be able to preserve the confidentiality of their clients. After all it is also important to pays close attention to human rights while putting stress on combating crimes, since the rights are clearly laid down in the European Convention for the Protection of Human Rights and Fundamental Freedoms (ECHR) and the Treaty of the European Union. For this reason, according to the Amendment to the Directive, notaries, independent legal professionals, auditors, external accountants and tax advisors would be exempted from the obligation to report any information obtained either before, during or after judicial proceedings, or in the course of ascertaining the legal position for a client.[242] However, at the same time it is also not appropriate to leave these professionals alone to face with a suspicion of serious criminal activity. To solve this problem, the Directive stipulates that, *"In the case of the notaries and independent legal professionals referred to Article 2a (5),*

---

[241] Gil Galvao, Countering Money Laundering: The FATF, The European Union and The Portuguese Experience, Past and Current Developments, *Work Product of 117th International Seminar "Current Situation and Countermeasures against Money Laundering"*.

[242] See *Directive 2001/97/EC of the European Parliament and of the Council of 4 December 2001, amending Council Directive 91/308/EEC on prevention of the use of the financial system for the purpose of money laundering*, Article 6(3).

member states may designate an appropriate self-regulatory body of the profession concerned as the authority to be informed of the facts referred to in paragraph 1 (a)[243] and in such case shall lay down the appropriate forms of cooperation between that body and the authorities responsible for combating money laundering. "[244] That is to say, in view of their particular status, the member states are given the option of allowing these independent professionals to communicate their suspicions of money laundering not to the normal anti-money laundering authorities but to their bar associations or other self-regulatory bodies. In this case, the rules governing the treatment of such reports and their possible onward transmission to the authorities responsible for combating money laundering and the appropriate forms of cooperation between the bar associations or professional bodies and these authorities should be determined by the member states.[245]

3.5.5 The Obligation of Customer Identification

Article 3 of the 1991 Directive requires that financial institutions should identify their clients, keep appropriate records and take reasonable measures to seek to identify beneficial owners. According to FATF 1996—1997 annual report, identification regimes in FATF members are deemed satisfactory.[246] However, with the emergence of internet banking, direct banking and other types of non-face to face transactions, it becomes more difficult to perform the duty of customer identification. In the action plan to combat organized crime, Recommendation 26 (f) also addresses the issue of money laundering on the internet and via electronic money products, and requires, in electronic payment and message system, that the messages sent give details of the originator and the beneficiary.

In consideration of this fact, the Amendment to the Directive addresses this issue

---

[243] The obligation about informing authorities responsible for combating money laundering of any fact, which might be an indication of money laundering.
[244] See *Directive 2001/97/EC of the European Parliament and of the Council of 4 December 2001, amending Council Directive 91/308/EEC on prevention of the use of the financial system for the purpose of money laundering*, Article 6(3).
[245] Ibid., preamble.
[246] See *Second Commission Report to the European Parliament and the Council on the implementation of the Money Laundering Directive*.

under Article 3 (11), which reads: "*member states shall in any case, ensure that the institutions and persons subject to this Directive take specific and adequate measures necessary to compensate for the greater risk of money laundering which arises when establishing business relations or entering into a transaction with a customer who has not physically present for identification purposes (non-face to face operations).*" Furthermore, several measures are illustrated under this article, "*by requiring additional documentary evidence, or supplementary measures to verify or certify the documents supplied, or confirmatory certification by an institution subject to this Directive, or by requiring that the first payment opened in the customer's name with a credit institution subject to this Directive.*" Moreover, in order to oblige the member states to implement this obligation, the Amendment to the Directive imposes a time limit for implementation. It provides that within three years of the entry into force of this Directive, the Commission shall carry out a particular examination relating to the implementation of the identification of clients in non-face to face transaction and possible implementations for electronic commerce.[247]

3.5.6 Evaluation

Nowadays it is generally accepted that prevention is no less important than repression in the fight against money laundering. The 1991 Directive, however, as a preventive instrument, was considered to be insufficient, given the changes of recent money-laundering schemes. Therefore the European Union has decided to amend the 1991 Directive for a long time. The process leading to the proposal of a draft directive amending the original 1991 Directive began as early as 1996.[248] The proposal for a European Parliament and Council Directive came into being on 14 July 1999. While the formal amended Directive emerged on 4 December 2001. This short review only wants to make it known that the European Union has spent much time, exerted great effort and expanded plenty of resources to amend the 1991 Directive.

---

[247] See *Directive 2001/97/EC of the European Parliament and of the Council of 4 December 2001, amending Council Directive 91/308/EEC on prevention of the use of the financial system for the purpose of money laundering*, Article 2.

[248] See Constantin Stefanou and Helen Xanthaki, The New EU Draft Money Laundering Directive: A Case of Inter-Institutional Synergy, *Journal of Money Laundering Control*, Vol. 3 No. 4, 2000, p. 325.

The Amendment to the Directive addresses the most sensitive issues in the fight against money laundering. That is the scope of predicate offences, the coverage of non-financial professions and activities, the contradiction between the privilege of professional secrecy and the obligation on combating money laundering, and the new challenge created by high-technology and the like. All of the issues are not undertaken lightly since right balances should be sought between fighting crime and developing economy, protecting human rights and punishing criminals, and also respective contributions and harmonization of laws. The Amendment is fully in consideration of these thorny problems and once again sets a new world standard in the fight against money laundering. This great achievement resulted from its great ambition, which can be concluded from the Explanatory Memorandum of the Draft Directive, "*as the 1991 Directive moved ahead of the original FATF 40 Recommendations in requiring obligatory suspicious transaction reporting, the European Union should continue to impose a high standard on its Member States, giving effect to or even going beyond the 1996 update of the FATF 40 Recommendations. In particular the EU can show the way in seeking to involve certain professions more actively in the fight against money laundering alongside the financial sector.*"

Owing to the great efforts of the European Union for several years, the great ambition of its proposal and the innovative fresh contents in the articles, it will not be over-praised to say that the Amendment to the Directive continues to be a leading international instrument in the fight against money laundering and this instrument will be sure to have profound impacts on the domestic laws of the member states of the European Union as well as the other countries throughout the world.

3.6 Europol

3.6.1 Introduction

The European Police Office (hereafter referred to as "Europol"), Interpol's European equivalent, is the European Union law enforcement organization that handles criminal intelligence. Its aim is to improve the effectiveness and cooperation between the competent authorities of the member states in "*preventing and combating terrorism, unlawful drug trafficking and other serious forms of international crime*"[249].

The establishment of Europol was agreed in the Maastricht Treaty on European Union of 7 February 1992. Based in the Netherlands in the Hague, Europol started limited operations on 3 January 1994 in the form of the Europol Drugs Unit (EDU), fighting against drugs. With other important areas of criminality added to its scope of powers and functions, it was necessary to replace the Europol Drugs Unit with a new body, which could not only fight against drugs offences but also other serious transnational crimes. On 18 July 1995 the Europol Convention was concluded and it came into force on 1 October 1998. Europol commenced full activities as of 1 July 1999.[250]

Europol will have competence only if the crime is an organized one involving at least two or more member states. Europol can only take part in investigations into crimes, which fall within its mandate. Europol was initially engaging in preventing and combating unlawful drug trafficking, trafficking in nuclear and radioactive substances, illegal immigrants smuggling, trade in human beings, motor vehicle crime and money laundering.[251] Its competence was subsequently extended to cover terrorism, Euro counterfeiting, racism, cyber-and environmental crime, extortion, kidnapping, corruption and other forms of crime listed in the Annex to the Europol Convention.[252] Europol has no executive powers and it can't carry out cross-border operations and has no supranational power. Europol has the following principle tasks:[253]

- "*To facilitate the exchange of information between the member states*;
- *To obtain, collate and analyze information and intelligence*;
- *To notify the competent authorities of the member states without delay via the national units of information concerning them and of any connections identified between criminal offences*;

---

[249] Convention based on Article K. 3 of the Treaty on European Union, on the establishment of European Police Office (Europol Convention), Article 2 (1).

[250] See *2003 Europe Information Service European Report*, 28 June 2003.

[251] See Convention based on Article K. 3 of the Treaty on European Union, on the establishment of European Police Office (Europol Convention), Article 2 (2), (3).

[252] See *2002 Europe Information Service European Report*, 27 February 2002.

[253] See Convention based on Article K. 3 of the Treaty on European Union, on the establishment of European Police Office (Europol Convention), Article 3 (1).

- *To aid investigation in the member states by forwarding all relevant information to the national units.*
- *To maintain a computerized system of collected information."*

In order to perform the above-mentioned tasks, the Europol Convention states that Europol shall establish and maintain a computerised system to allow the input, access to and analysis of data. The Europol Computer System has three principal components: an information system, an analysis system and an index system.[254]

3.6.2 Europol's Role in the Fight against Money Laundering

In recent years, money laundering has indeed increased at the international level. It poses a global threat to the integrity, reliability and stability of financial and economic systems and even to government structures. In order to enhance the results at law enforcement and judicial level, it is required that the international cooperation shall be improved. In this context, Europol offers an excellent structure to support and co-ordinate international investigations and to provide expertise, knowledge and training in this field.

3.6.2.1 Contributions to the Member States

Although Europol has no executive power, with real-time information, sophisticated intelligence analysis, expertise and training, Europol can contribute to relevant national authorities to fight against money laundering. Europol is a central office that obtains information, analyzes information and if necessary then presents it to an appropriate government authority in support of its national anti-money laundering effort.

It is reported in the 1999 annual report that in the area of money laundering, Europol contributed to the operational investigations by facilitating the exchange of information via the Europol Liaison Network in 145 cases, approximately 7% of the total number in 1999, and by giving analytical support to 4 operational money laundering investigations and to the financial aspects of several other investigations.[255] More importantly, the number of information exchange is growing. Statistics produced by

---

[254] Ibid., Article 6.
[255] http://www.europol.eu.int/index.asp? page = publ_ar1999#FINANCIAL%20CRIME, 30 July 2003.

Europol for 2002 show that the member states are making more use of it. There was increase of 50% in the number of information exchanges between Europol's liaison offices in the member states, from 45,222 to 69,822.[256]

In 2001, Europol opened an Analytic Work File (AWF) for suspicious transactions. The AWF, based on the article 30—1 B of the Treaty on the European Union, has the main objective to gather suspicious transactions handled by police or justice authorities of the member states. It aims to identify potential links between suspicious transactions, and to provide specialized law enforcement agencies of the member states with a long-term analytic support.[257]

3.6.2.2 Cooperation at the International Level

According to Article 42 of the Europol Convention, Europol may establish and maintain relationship with third states and third bodies, so far as is relevant or required for the performance of the Europol's tasks.

Information exchange between Europol and non-EU countries and bodies is based on a three-level grading system. Level one consists of informal exchanges on general strategy and operating methods. Level two focuses on training methods for officers and instilling best practices. Level three involves transmitting information on individuals and is the most sensitive type of cooperation. In level one and two, the Council will authorize Europol negotiate multilaterally. However, with level three Europol negotiate on a country-by-country basis and submit each agreement for Council approval.[258]

To date the agency has reached agreements with Poland, Estonia, Slovenia, Hungary, the USA, Norway, Iceland, Interpol, the European Central Bank and the EU drugs agency EMCDDA. Talks are underway for cooperation deals with the European Commission, the World Customs Organization and the United Nations Drug Control and Crime Prevention Office. Meanwhile, twenty-five liaison officers from non-EU states and bodies are being dispatched to the agency in 2002.[259]

---

[256] See Justice and home affaires: Europol shifts to operational side, *Europe Information Service*, *European Report*, 14 May 2003.

[257] http://www.europol.eu.int/index.asp?page=publ_moneylaundering, 30 July 2003.

[258] See EU/US: agreement on transfer of personal data with Europol imminent, *Copyright 2002 Europe Information Service*, *European Report*, 16 November 2002.

[259] See *2002 Europe Information Service European Report*, 29 May 2002.

3.6.3 Evaluation

The Europol is a support service for the law enforcement agencies of the EU member states. Europol's emphasis is on practical support to police and other investigators in the European Union, through the exchange of information and intelligence, and by providing a range of services, especially analysis and coordination. In recent years, its powers have been boosted, enabling it to take part in joint investigation teams set up by the member states, and to ask the member states to initiate an investigation.[260] Its remit has gradually been extended to cover drug trafficking, human trafficking, child pornography, money laundering, Euro counterfeiting, cyber crime, environmental crime, terrorism and racism. Besides, it has also asked for access to the Schengen Information System (SIS), the database of stolen objects, missing and wanted persons used by national police forces.[261]

Although Europol carries no weapons and is not allowed conduct wire-tapping, house searches or arrests, it is an important center contributing to information exchange, crime analysis and providing coordination at EU level. With the enlargement of the European Union, it can be predicted that more data will be exchanged between Europol and the extended scope of member states. Thus Europol will play more important role in the fight against money laundering.

3.7 Eurojust

3.7.1 Background

Establishing an area of freedom, security and justice is one of the objectives of European Union. To that end, judicial cooperation in criminal matters must be placed in a high priority. With the challenge of cross-border crime in an area of free movement, the traditional means of mutual judicial assistance, with lengthy and onerous

---

[260] See *2003 Europe Information Service European Report*, 14 May 2003.

[261] In this regard, the Spanish EU Presidency has shown enthusiasm for this, While Belgium recently voiced its doubts. See European Report 2672, section IV, *Europe Information Service European Report*, 29 May 2002.

Chapter 3 Western European Responses to Money Laundering

procedures, are no longer sufficient. Although the European Union has adopted some initial steps to fight against cross-border crime, such as setting up Europol, OLAF (the EU's anti-fraud organisation) and the European Judicial Network, it seems that a certain central structure providing cooperation and coordination of national prosecuting authorities is indispensable.

To achieve this central coordination, the European Council of Tampere Summit in October 1999, agreed that, by the end of 2001, a unit (Eurojust) should be set up composed of national prosecutors, magistrates, or police officers of equivalent competence, detached from each member state according to its legal system.[262]

On 14 December 2000, the Council of the European Union established the Provisional Judicial Cooperation Unit. It was also referred to as the Pro-Eurojust as it was treated as a transnational body until replaced by Eurojust. Work by the Pro-Eurojust began on 1 March 2001, when it was temporarily based in Brussels. It is clear, however, that "Pro-Eurojust" is not able to fulfill the high expectations people have for Eurojust itself, as its legal foundation, structure and resources are provisional. On 15 December 2001, the Council Declaration of Laeken suggested that Eurojust would be located in the Hague. The decisions to locate Eurojust in the Hague will enable it to cooperate and work closely with Europol which is also based in the Hague. And lastly by the Council Decision of 28 February 2002[263] Eurojust was formally established.

3.7.2 Objectives and Competences

Eurojust is a new European Union body. With a high level team of prosecutors, magistrates, or police officers of equivalent competence, working as a team in the same place, in the same building, it aims at enhancing the effectiveness of the competent authorities within member states when they are dealing with the investigation and prosecution of serious cross-border crime, particularly when it is organized. According to the Council Decision, the objectives of Eurojust are as follows:[264]

- *"To stimulate and improve the coordination between competent authorities in*

---

[262] See *Tampere European Council, 15 and 16 October 1999, Presidency conclusion*, Point 46.
[263] See OJEC, 6 March 2002.
[264] See *Council Decision of 28 Feb. 2002 Setting up Eurojust with a view to reinforcing the fight against serious crime*, 2002/187/JHA.

the member states, of investigations and prosecutions in the member states, taking into account any request emanating from a competent authority of a Member State and any information provided by any body competent by virtue of provisions adopted within the framework of the Treaties;

- To improve co-operation between the competent authorities of the member states, in particular by facilitating the execution of international mutual legal assistance and the implementation of extradition requests; and,

- To otherwise support the competent authorities of the member states in order to render their investigations and prosecutions more effective."

Article 4 of the Council Decision indicates that the offences which are within the competence of Eurojust are the crimes listed in Article 2 of the Europol Convention and computer crime, fraud and corruption affecting the European Community's financial interests, the laundering of the proceeds of crime, environmental crime, participation in a criminal organization, other offences committed in conjunction with the enumerated offences. Eurojust may also assist in the investigation and prosecution of other offences at the request of a member state's competent authority.

3.7.3 Evaluation

It seems that, to a large extent, European Judicial Network[265] and Eurojust are playing the similar roles in judicial cooperation and coordination between member states, such as providing information on national law, building up a documentary basis, arranging contacts among investigating national bodies, transferring information on the stage of proceedings or on judgments, exchanging experience and legal advice and so on. However, the advantages of Eurojust are obvious, compared with the European Judicial Network. The European Judicial Network is a decentralized Network. Its work is carried out by contact points, which can be contacted and asked for advice. While Eurojust is a central unit. Eurojust is a high level team of senior law-

---

[265] The European Council adopted in 1997 an Action Plan to combat organized crime, which was prepared by a High Level Group of experts from the Member States. Several of the recommendations of this Action Plan aim at improving the standards of co-operation between judicial authorities in criminal matters. On the basis of this Action Plan, and amongst other measures, the Council adopted on 29 June 1998 a Joint Action on the creation of a European Judicial Network. This Network was officially inaugurated on 25 September 1998.

yers, magistrates, prosecutors, judges and other legal experts seconded from every EU country, working as a team in the same place, in the same building. It is apparent that it will be easier to communicate within a team working in a joint office than among decentralized contact points in the member states, even in the light of improved technical means of communication.

In addition, Eurojust will cooperate closely and effectively with Europol, Eurojust will provide legal advice on certain judicial questions to Europol and will act on information received from Europol. However, Eurojust will remain a judicial unit, not being directly involved in administrative, political or legislative work of the Parliament, the Council and the Commission.[266]

3.8 Conclusions

From this selective overview it is obvious that in the last two decades, the countries of Western Europe have made great contributions to the world-wide efforts to counter money laundering. This is not only because it was the western European countries took the first effort to focus on the problem of money laundering as early as twenties years ago, but also the money laundering legislations in western European countries provided a modern and comprehensive basis in the field of combating money laundering.

In respect of improving domestic criminal law, western European countries were required to establish money laundering as a criminal offence long ago. In addition, confiscation measures were repeatedly emphasized in order to eliminate the main incentive for money laundering offence. As to enhancing international cooperation, great efforts both under the Council of Europe level, such as the 1990 Strasbourg Convention and the European level, such as Europol and Eurojust have been made significantly. Besides, in regard to securing the preventive role of financial institutions and other vulnerable institutions, the EC Directive provided a well-defined format for the anti-money laundering provisions and no doubt played a leading role in this field.

---

[266] See *Communication from the Commission on the Establishment of Eurojust, Brussels, 22. 11. 2000 COM(2000) 746 final.*

What is commendable is the western European countries pay equal attention to making advantage of suppressive and preventive approaches to cope with money laundering problem. For example, the 1990 Strasbourg Convention resorted to criminal repressive approach toward money laundering and emphasized particularly criminal law and cooperation in criminal matters, while the Directive focused on preventive strategies and laid stress on financial regulations and cooperation in administrative fields. More importantly, the western European countries succeeded in seeking an appropriate balance between combating crimes and protecting human right, which is significantly worth recommending.

Chapter 4

Chinese Criminal Law Concerning Money Laundering

4.1 Introduction

　　This chapter first describes the evolution of the Chinese Criminal Law. It points out the historical background and development of the provisions of money laundering. It then addresses the constituent elements of money laundering in detail, such as the scope of the predicate offence, mens rea of money laundering, subject and behavior patterns of money laundering, legal interest that money laundering infringed. Also this chapter presents the relationship between money laundering and relevant offences, one being concealing, transferring, purchasing and disposing of plunder, formulated under Article 312; the other being the crime of harboring, transferring or covering up narcotic drugs or gains from relevant crimes, under Article 349. Finally this chapter introduces the legal consequences of money laundering according to the Chinese Criminal Law.

4.2 Evolution of the Criminal Law

4.2.1 Lack of Money Laundering Offence in Criminal Law during More Than 40 Years since the Founding of PRC (1949—1990)

China is a country with the legal tradition of laying more stress on criminal law and paying less attention to civil law. But during the first 30 years after the founding of the People's Republic of China (PRC), China did not make a criminal code although a criminal law was critically needed to keep social order and safeguard public security. The drafting work of Criminal Code was constantly held back due to several grand historical events, such as the national Anti-Rightist Movement[267] and the ten years' "*Cultural Revolution*"[268]. During those 30 years, social order and public security were maintained with several separated criminal regulations. Of those regulations, the most important were Regulation for Suppression of Counter-Revolutionists, Regulation for Suppression of Corruption, Provisional Regulation on Crimes of Interfering with National Currency, etc. Those criminal regulations were tinged with distinctive ideological and political color. They were regarded as tools the newly born revolutionary dictatorship used for the struggle against the class enemies. Under the condition when the criminal law was incomplete, for a long period of time, the punishments for crimes were practiced according to commands and indications of the leaders. The commands of officials and instructions of the leaders could determine the fate of the life, freedom, wealth and honor of the people. The replacement of the criminal law with internal policies, official replies and instructions had caused serious consequences.[269]

---

[267] During the process of "the Anti-Rightist Movement" from June 1957 to the summer of 1958, several hundred thousand "Bourgeois Rightists" were assessed and criticized. All legislative and judicial were regarded as "rightist tendency" and legal system was damaged seriously.

[268] The "Cultural Revolution" was a civil strife, which existed from May 1966 to October 1976. During the "Culture Revolution", legal nihilism prevailed and the position of law was replaced by policies or the political will of the leaders. The socialist legal system was seriously destroyed.

[269] See Xin Chunying, *Chinese Legal System and Current Legal Reform*, Law Press 1999, pp.614—618.

After the "*Cultural Revolution*", in 1978, the First Session of the Fifth National People's Congress (NPC) decided to revise and formulate laws, especially those which were urgently needed. In late February 1979, the Commission of Legislative Affairs of the NPC Standing Committee established and started criminal lawmaking on the basis of existing legislative and judicial experience. In the end the Criminal Code draft was submitted to the Second Session of the Fifth NPC in June 1979 and was adopted in July First. The 1979 Criminal Code took effect on 1 January 1980.

However, because the 1979 Criminal Code was formulated in the period of traditional planned economy, when our government had a strong control over finance and economy, and at that time we did not adopt open-door policy, it was impossible for international criminal gang to have the opportunity to enter into China to commit economic crimes. Neither was there suitable external environment for large-scale organized crime, such as drug trafficking, smuggling and mafia. Economic crimes or property crimes under planed economy system mainly include speculation, forging or scalping coupons of goods under planned supply, counterfeiting trademarks, theft, fraud, robbery and corruption and others. And criminals often made use of simple and traditional ways, such as concealing or selling plunder to deal with illegally acquired money and booties. Therefore, crimes of concealing or disposing of plunder was formulated under Article 172 in 1979 Criminal Code, which reads, "*Whoever knowingly conceals or helps to sell illegally acquired goods shall be sentenced to fixed-term imprisonment of not more than three years, criminal detention or public surveillance and shall also, or shall only, be fined.*"

The overview of the historical background of the 1979 Chinese Criminal Code indicates the reason why there were no provisions of money laundering crime for more than 40 years since the founding of the PRC.

4.2.2 Money Laundering Offence in "*Decision on Suppressing Drug Dealing*"

Since 1980s, with the transition of economic system, from planed economy to market economy, China came into a period of vigorous development. Under the circumstance of market economy system, new situation emerged which did not exist when the 1979 Criminal Code was formulated, and the situation of crimes also changed soon. Thus the defects of 1979 Criminal Code were getting more obvious. To deal with this problem, legislative organs had to issue constantly separate criminal regulations as supplements to the 1979 Criminal Code in accordance with the development of market economy and the practical need of fighting against various kinds of crimes. From June 1981 to October 1995, the Standing Committee of the NPC adopted 23 special criminal ordinances successively. Under the 1990 "*Decision on Suppressing Drug Dealing*", laundering illicit money acquired from drug-related crimes was definitely provided as a crime.

There were double reasons at that time to criminalize the act of laundering money illegally acquired from drug-related crimes. On the one hand, drug-related crimes were getting increasingly serious, and the criminals who gained large amounts of profit from these crimes tried every means to conceal and disguise the nature of the illicit money and to evade criminal sanctions. It was evident that laundering illicit money could do great harm to the society, however, the traditional crimes of concealing or disposing of plunder could not meet the needs of retaliation against money laundering, which had the nature of ever-growing gravity. On the other hand, the UN Convention against Illicit Traffic in Narcotic Drugs and Psychotropic Substances was adopted in Vienna in December 1988, which was ratified by Chinese government on 4 September 1989. This Convention required the member countries to stipulate a crime of covering up or concealing the proceeds from drug trafficking in domestic criminal law. In order to carry out the obligation required by the UN Convention, on 28 December 1990, the Standing Committee of the NPC enacted a regulation named *Decision on Suppressing Drug Dealing*, of which Article 4 clearly defined that the act covering up and concealing the source or nature of the proceeds from drug trafficking will be sentenced to fixed-term imprisonment of not more than 7 years, criminal detention or public surveillance and also can be fined. This was the first time that Chinese criminal law formulated the money laundering activity, although at that time there wasn't the special term of money laundering.

4.2.3 Money Laundering Offence in the 1997 Criminal Code

Owing to the historical limitations and insufficient experience of legislators, the phrase that "*it is better to be general rather than be specific*" was the guideline for

1979 Criminal Code. Therefore the Criminal Code was too simple compared with the social needs. Within the 192 articles, many of them are ambiguous. Furthermore, during the 17 years' of implementation of the Criminal Law, great changes have taken place. Generally speaking, China has transformed from a country of petrifying thought and ideology, with the planned economy system as the base and with the former Soviet Union as the model, into a vigorous country with a booming market economy. New social reality results in fresh crimes. But the 1979 Criminal Code represented its obvious lag, especially in the field of economic crimes. Besides, with the economic reform and opening up, the gap between the rich and the poor was enlarged and the social conflict was aggravated. Some crimes developed more rapidly and seriously. And Punishment needed intensifying for it was not strict enough to repress these crimes. In addition, with the integration of the world economy, many countries are facing some common crimes, such as drug dealing, smuggling, money laundering, etc. China must face all those problems while taking part in the process of economic globalization. Although the 23 special criminal ordinances once served the purpose of supplementing the 1979 Criminal Code, these ordinances were separated from the Criminal code and thus damaged the systematic integrality and disrupted the contents of the Criminal Code. For all above-mentioned reasons, it was inevitable to modify the 1979 Criminal Code.

In the process of amendment, it was decided that the crime of money laundering should be provided on the basis of the *"Decision on Suppressing Drug Dealing"*. This decision is closely related to the great changes of Chinese economic situation. First, with the transition of economic system, form planed economy to market economy, the exclusively state-owned economy turned to be the mixed economy, which includes collective economy, private economy, foreign capital economy, etc. Due to the multi-benefits, the desire to get illegal benefits through illegal means has been strengthened. Second, since the policy of economic reform and opening up, the amount of foreign capital increases rapidly. Within 18 years from 1979 to 1997, the number of foreign capital projects approved by Chinese government was up to 280,000 and the total amount was up to 177 billions.[270] Due to the lack of regulations for checking the

---

[270] See Feng Zhaokui: We Welcome Foreign Capital—The Relation Between Introducing Foreign Capital and developing National Industry, *World Knowledge*, Vol. 13, 1997.

source and nature of the foreign capital, some capital must have been invested just for the purpose of laundering. Third, the fields allowed for foreign investment expands continuously, from original processing industry, tourism to IT industry, insurance and finance. As of 1997, there had been 540 foreign financial institutions created in China. The total assets of foreign capital banks were up to 30 billions.[271] Along with the opening of the Chinese financial market to the world financial market, it is easier for the international criminal organizations to cross the boundary for money laundering.

It is reported that the money laundering is a true problem now with the development of the financial business in China. In some areas, especially in south-east part of China, relatively often are the activities of money laundering, which committed by members of the drug-deal organization, smuggling organization or Mafia-like organizations.[272] On the other hand, foreign criminal organizations bring money, gained from illegal activities such as smuggling, drug-deal or swindle, into China in the name of investment, running service businesses such as bar, ballroom, restaurant, night-club or pleasure ground, in order to launder money.[273] So, it becomes necessary to punish and prevent money laundering in China. In the end, the money laundering crime was normalized in Article 191 in the 1997 Chinese Criminal Code.

Under Article 191, the crime of money laundering is: "*Whoever, while clearly knowing that the funds are proceeds illegally obtained from drug-related crimes or from crimes committed by mafia-like organizations or smugglers and gains derived therefrom, commits any of the following acts in order to cover up or conceal the source or nature of the funds shall, in addition to being confiscated of the said proceeds and gains, be sentenced to fixed-term imprisonment of not more than 5 years or criminal detention and shall also, or shall only, be fined not less than 5 percent but not more than 20 percent of the amount of money laundered; if the circumstance are serious, he shall be sentenced to fixed-term imprisonment of not less than 5 years but not more than 10 years and shall also be fined not less than 5 percent but not more than 20 percent of the amount of money laundered:*

---

[271] See Gao Degui: The Achievement and future of the Financial Reform in China, *People's Daily*, 11 December 1997.

[272] See Guo Weicheng: Observing Trend from the Lujiazui, *People's Daily*, 2 December 1997; Bai Peng-fei: The Way of Getting Money by the Criminal Organizations, *The Economy and Law*, the 9th issue, p. 24.

[273] See China Sternly Crack down on the New Kind of Crimes, *Reference of Reading*, the 14th issue, p. 14.

—providing fund accounts;

—helping exchange property into cash or any financially negotiable instruments;

—helping transfer capital through transferring accounts or any other form of settlement;

—helping remit funds to any other country;

—covering up or concealing by any other means the nature or source of illegally obtained proceeds and gains derived therefrom. Where an organization commits any of the crimes mentioned in the preceding paragraph, it shall be fined, and the persons who are directly in charge and the other persons who are directly responsible for the crime shall be sentenced to fixed-term imprisonment of not more than 5 years or criminal detention."

4.2.4 Money Laundering Offence in the Third Amendment to the 1997 Criminal Code

After the terrorist attack on Washington and New York in America on 11 September 2001, the world made a quick response to the shocking terrorism. Every country has recognized that it is an urgent task to fight terrorism to ensure the worldwide security and stability. China will not be an exception. In order to punish terrorism crime, to safeguard security of the state and to protect people's life and property, as well as to maintain social order, the third sets of amendments to the Chinese Criminal Law were adopted at the 25 Meeting of the Standing Committee of the Ninth NPC on 29 December 2001 to meet the need of fighting terrorism.

Under Article 7 of these Amendments, the crime of money laundering was revised. First, the predicate offences of money laundering expand to four kinds of crimes: smuggling, drug-related crimes, organized underworld crime and terrorism. Second, the maximum term limit of statutory sentence for organizations committing money laundering was raised. The amendment to the article reads: *"If the circumstances are serious, the persons who are directly in charge and the other persons who are directly responsible for the crime shall be sentenced to fixed-term imprisonment of not less that 5 years but not more than 10 years."* According to this article, natural person and the responsible person in an organization will have an equal statutory sentence.

It is worth noting that China used to issue separated criminal regulations to supplement the 1979 Criminal Code before 1997, while these years China prefer to modify Criminal Code by the means of amendment. No doubt the latter is more desirable because the amendment directly referred to the Criminal Code. Thus, the close relation between Criminal Code and Amendment is strengthened and the integrality and unity of the Criminal Code is also maintained.

4.3　The Elements of Money Laundering Crime by Criminal Law

4.3.1　The Scope of the Predicate Offences[274]

Under the 1997 Chinese Criminal Code and the 2001 Amendments to the Criminal Code, the scope of the predicate offence is confined to four kinds of crimes: drug-related crimes, organized underworld crime, smuggling and terrorism. Although the scope has been broadened compared with the "*Decision on Suppressing Drug Dealing*" enacted in 1990, it is still considered too narrow.

The predicate offences captured by the definition of money laundering under the 1997 Chinese Criminal Code and its amendments highlighted the focal point of the issue and stressed the emphasis on suppression, but the extent was too limited and not compatible with the spirit embodied in international conventions or other soft laws. Of course there are many other serious crimes, such as crimes of trafficking in people, kidnapping, crimes concerning securities, crimes of financial fraud etc, generating large amounts of wealth which the criminals have an urgent need to launder.

In addition, more attention should be paid to the issue that legalizes the proceeds of crimes of corruption or accepting bribes, by means of money laundering. The Chinese government has taken many measures to fight against corruption, such as requiring bank accounts to be under authentic names and stipulating as a crime the holding of a huge amount of property with unidentified sources. All of these necessary meas-

---

[274]　In 1990 Council of Europe Convention on Laundering, Search, Seizure, and Confiscation of the Proceeds from Crime, "predicate offence" means any criminal offence as a result of which proceeds were generated that may become the subject of money laundering.

ures make it difficult to conceal or squander dirty money. Therefore corrupt public officials have to work hard to launder dirty money. In recent years many corruption cases have been exposed in China. It is a pity that among those cases, criminals have not been punished under the ambit of anti-money laundering, because laundering money from corruption and embezzlement is not a money laundering offence in China. This is a shortcoming of legislation in criminal law.

Observing the evolution of worldwide criminal legislation, national strategies for criminalizing money laundering differ in some ways. The predicate offences that generate proceeds vary from one country to another. But the scale has a tendency to grow and expand, which is in agreement with the Financial Action Task Force Recommendation 5 that the criminalisation of money laundering should be based on all serious offences. The approach that has been taken with regard to the predicate offences for the crime of money laundering can be divided into three broad categories:[275]

—All predicate crimes, or those that may be tried in a higher court, e. g. Australia, Finland, Italy, UK.

—Crimes with a specified minimum period of imprisonment, e. g. Austria (greater than three years). New Zealand (greater than five years), Switzerland (greater than one year).

—A list of predicate offences, e. g. Canada (45 crimes), Greece (20 crimes), USA (130 + crimes).

As money laundering is an international crime, the fight against money laundering should be a common effort by the international community and the laws governing money laundering crime in various countries should be as similar as possible. For this reason, concerning the Chinese Criminal Code, it should be concluded that the scope of underlying crimes of money laundering should be adjusted and improved to be compatible with the direction of worldwide legislation.

4.3.2 The mens rea of Money Laundering

According to Chinese Criminal Code, the mens rea of money laundering is scien-

---

[275] See Financial Action Task Force on Money Laundering, *Review of FATF Anti-Money Laundering Systems and Mutual Evaluation Procedures 1992—1999*.

ter. Specifically speaking, it must be proved against the defendant that he knew the funds were derived from drug crimes, organized underworld crimes, terrorism or smuggling. "*He who claims is to provide evidence*" is a legal principle. In criminal cases, the burden of proof rests on the public prosecutor, who should demonstrate that the defendants must have been aware that the wealth was generated from one of the four special kinds of crimes, and that they preceded the activities of money laundering.

The key point of this issue is to grasp firmly the meaning of "*scienter*". The literal interpretation of the word is "*precise knowledge*". However, this is difficult for the public prosecutor to demonstrate in practice. Moreover almost all defendants would deny this in order to play down their responsibility or to dismiss the charge. For this reason, another interpretation of "*scienter*" is "*obligatory knowledge*", and the public prosecutor is in a position to prove that the defendant *should* know that the proceeds were derived from these four kinds of crime.[276]

The Supreme People's Court and the Supreme Procuratorate have issued several judicial interpretations about the meaning of "*scienter*", such as "*the interpretation on dealing with theft and the application of the law*" on 11th December 1992. It reads: "*To settle whether the defendant holds scienter in the crimes of concealing or disposing of plunder, cannot depend on the oral statement of the accused but the objective circumstance must be analyzed on the basis of the case. It is enough to demonstrate that the defendant already knew or should have known that the proceeds were derived from criminal activities.*" In addition, the Supreme People's Court, the Supreme People's Procuratorate, the Ministry of Public Security, and the Administration for Industry and Commerce issued a combined interpretation about "*the regulation of investigating the case of stealing and robbing power-driven vehicles*" on 8th May, 1998. It says again: "*scienter refers to precise knowledge or obligatory knowledge. Any of the following acts should be viewed as that the accused should know the proceeds are derived from criminal activities, except that there are proofs which demonstrate he was kept in the dark . . . .*"

The two interpretations are useful in providing a norm for understanding the meaning of scienter. But the words "*obligatory knowledge*" means that the accused

---

[276] See Zhao Zuojun, Research on Money Laundering, *Law Science*, Volume 5, 1997.

really did not know the wealth was crime-derived at that time because of his negligence. "*Obligatory knowledge*" is different from "*presumptive knowledge.*" "*Presumptive knowledge*" means the judicial organs proved the accused already held *scienter* through indirect proof, although the accused denied it. As the crimes mentioned in the two interpretations are not negligent crimes but willful crimes, it would seem more logical if "*presumptive knowledge*" were substituted for "*obligatory knowledge*" in the interpretations. In fact, presumptive knowledge is also different from scienter. So the interpretations are expanded explanations. Of course, judicial interpretation is not legislation, but only interpretation. The loopholes of legislation can only be filled through legislation, or the authority and solemnity of the law will be damaged.

To solve the problem about the mens rea of money laundering, the only thing to be done is to improve legislation. First, as mentioned above, the predicate offences should be expanded from four kinds of crime to other serious crimes. In reality, the general public has neither the obligation nor the capacity to know precisely where other people find their property and financial gain. Second, the mens rea of money laundering should be expanded from scienter to presumptive knowledge and obligatory knowledge. Scienter indicates that the prosecutor has direct evidence to prove that the defendant has knowledge that the proceeds are from certain crimes. Presumptive knowledge means that the prosecutor demonstrates the defendant has knowledge of something through indirect proof. Obligatory knowledge means the defendant should realize the proceeds are from specified crimes, based on his age, knowledge, profession, life experience, the quantity, variety and price of the goods and the time and place of the deal. But in fact he did not know the proceeds were obtained through committing specified crimes at that time, because of his negligence.

4.3.3 Subject of Money Laundering Crime

According to the Chinese Criminal Code, the subjects of crime of money laundering include both natural persons and organizations. Article 191(1) is about the crime by natural persons, while Article 191(2) is about organizational crimes. Under this subheading, there is another issue worth discussing, that is whether it is possible to decide that the owner of the dirty money is a money launderer. In other words, can the drug dealer be sentenced for money laundering on account of laundering his own proceeds?

According to the traditional criminal law theory, the essence of money laundering crime is the disposal of plunder. It is not a crime for somebody to deal with the plunder which originated from his own offence. This is called an inculpable after-act.[277] For example, the criminal stole something, and then disposed of the plunder himself. In regard to this problem, both in theory and in practice the criminal will not be considered as having committed two crimes, theft and disposing of plunder, but only one crime, theft.

On these grounds, some scholars believe that the subject of money laundering should not be the executor or accomplice of the predicate crime.[278] Article 191 of the 1997 Chinese Criminal Code illustrates five kinds of conducts. From these terms of "*providing*" and "*helping*", it can be concluded that it is not possible to sentence the owner of the criminal money as a money launderer. Money laundering is looked on as fencing, which means a sort of favor. It is obvious that legislative intent was influenced by the theory of inculpable after-act.

However, money laundering is quite different from booty-related crimes. Booty-related crimes depend on the existence of traditional crimes against property, such as larceny, robbery or extortion. These crimes have obvious victims. But money laundering is frequently associated with drug dealing, smuggling and other crimes. It is a so-called "*consensual*" crime, where there are no direct injured parties. "*Money laundering is the process of converting or cleansing property knowing that such property is derived from serious crime for the purpose of disguising its origin.*"[279] Money laundering is a relatively independent process, which is separated from predicate offences. Besides, there is no substantial difference between the person committing the predicate crime of laundering money and the fencer doing so. This is derived from mens rea, the consequence of the perpetrator's method. That there should be different consequences for different persons seems to violate the basic principle of "everyone is equal before law".

---

[277] See Gao Mingxuan, Wang Zuofu, *The Dictionary of Chinese Criminal Law*, Xue Lin Press 1989, p. 18.

[278] See Zhao Zuojin, The Research on Money Laundering, *Law Science*, Vol. 5, 1997.

[279] Tom Sherman, International Efforts to combat Money Laundering: The Role of the Financial Action Task Force, Money Laundering, *Hume Papers on Public policy*, Vol. 1 No. 2, 1993, p. 13.

For these reasons, money laundering should not be an example of doing a favor, but should be an independent, autonomous crime. In other words, if the drug dealer laundered his money, it should be possible to prosecute and sentence the drug dealer for not only dealing drugs, but also for money laundering.

4.3.4 Behavioral Patterns of Money Laundering Crime

Under the Chinese Criminal Code, there are five types of money laundering behavior:

—*providing fund accounts*;

—*helping exchange property into cash or any financially negotiable instruments*;

—*helping transfer capital through transferring accounts or any other form of settlement*;

—*helping remit funds to any other country*;

—*covering up or concealing by any other means the nature or source of illegally obtained proceeds and gains derived therefrom.*

Among these the first four money laundering activities are concrete, while the last one is an open item, which summarizes other behaviors by using the expression "*any other means*". With the advancement of modern technology and economic prosperity, money laundering comes in various guises. Traditional methods are the use of secret havens, shell companies and underworld bank systems, with the recent advent of electronic money laundering and online money laundering. It is necessary to use vague legal expressions to disguise the limitations of legislation and to meet the needs of various social circumstances.

Another problem needs to be addressed—behavioral patterns. Can nonfeasance be a behavioral pattern of money laundering? Nonfeasance means the actor has a special legal obligation and also has the capacity to perform it, but he doesn't. Nonfeasance presupposes a legal obligation. Financial regulations, such as reporting suspicious transactions, client identification and record keeping are imposed on financial institutions and employees in many countries. For example, banks have to identify the client when the business is over FF50,000 in France. In England, suspicious *transactions have to be reported even when the business is only* 1 pound.[280] According to these provisions, financial institutions and employees must carry out these obligations, or they will be charged with criminal responsibility. So in these countries, nonfeasance can be a behavioral pattern of money laundering. As for China, though there are some legal obligations on suspicious transactions reporting, client identification and record keeping for financial institutions, no criminal responsibility attaches for failing to carry out these obligations. Therefore in China the behavioral pattern of money laundering is not a failure to act.

4.3.5 The Legal Interests that Money Laundering Crime Infringes

In terms of various legal interests, the special provisions of the 1997 Criminal Code consist of ten chapters and each chapter deals with one kind of crime. These ten chapters are put in order on the basis of extent of injury on the whole. The ten chapters are as follows:

- Crimes of Endangering National Security;
- Crimes Endangering Public Security;
- Crimes of Disrupting the Order of the Socialist Market Economy (there are 8 Sections in this chapter);
- Crimes of Infringing upon Citizens' Right of the person and democratic rights;
- Crimes of Property Violation;
- Crimes of Obstructing the Administration of Public Order (there are 9 Sections in this chapter);
- Crimes of Impairing the Interests of National Defense;
- Crimes of Embezzlement and Bribery;
- Crimes of Dereliction of Duty;
- Crimes of Servicemen's Transgression of Duties.

The offence of money laundering is placed in Section 4 "Crimes of Disrupting the Order of Financial Administration", and Chapter 3 "Crimes of Disrupting the Order

---

[280] See Zhao Bingzhi, *The Strategy on Confused Problems in Crimes of Undermining the Order of the Socialist Market Economy*, Ji Lin People's Press 2000, p.439.

of the Socialist Market Economy". This arrangement indicates that the crime of money laundering is considered as encroaching upon the order of financial administration, because criminals often make use of financial institutions to commit money-laundering which undermines the integrity of financial institutions and thus undermines public confidence in the financial system.

From the international legislation of money laundering, the nature of money laundering varies from country to country. Some consider that money laundering is a type of property crime; some regard money laundering as a crime that impairs judicial administration. And in some countries, money laundering is arranged behind specific predicate offences, which means that laundering illicit proceeds acquired from other crimes is not a crime.[281] The provision of the crime of money laundering is given at Section 4 Chapter 3 in the Specific Provisions in the Chinese Criminal Code because criminals often launder money from illegal activities through financial institutions and money-laundering crime has a direct negative impact on the order of financial administration. In fact, money laundering not only disrupts the order of financial administration, but also impairs judicial administration and infringes on ownership as well.

Moreover, with the evolution of money laundering schemes, financial institutions are not the sole industry which is exploited by money launderers. Money laundering activities penetrate many other business industries that can produce a large amount of currency. Criminals can conceal the illegal origin of currency by way of purchasing cars, precious metals, valuable jewelry and antiques. Criminals also can disguise the nature of illegal proceeds by means of operating restaurants, hotels, shops and casinos through which they integrate dirty money with legal earnings. Furthermore, money launderers now use the expertise of lawyers, notaries, accountants and other professionals to aid them to minimize suspicion surrounding their criminal activities. In view of this fact, money laundering should be regarded as a crime of sabotaging judicial order as a whole and should be placed in Section 2 "*Crimes of Impairing Judicial Administration*" Chapter 6 "*Crimes of Obstructing the Administration of Public Order*".

---

[281] See Zhao Zuojun, The Research on Money Laundering, *Law Science*, Vol. 5, 1997.

4.4 The Relationship between Money Laundering and Relevant Offences

Since the 1980s many countries have legislated against money laundering, as a result of the ever-growing gravity of drug trafficking. Before this, many countries had legislated against crimes relating to theft etc. It must be acknowledged that there are some similarities between money laundering and traditional crimes. At present, the legislative forms of money laundering vary from country to country or from region to region. Some stipulate money laundering in the criminal code, such as China, France and Italy; some formulate specific money laundering control ordinances, such as America and Taiwan; others, like Japan, still consider money laundering as a form of crime related to theft. Under the first two legislative forms, it is possible that money laundering and theft-related crime coexist. This is the Chinese situation.

Under the 1997 Chinese Criminal Code, money laundering crimes are very similar to two other crimes. One is concealing, transferring, purchasing and disposing of plunder, which is placed under Article 312. It states that: "*Whoever knowingly conceals, transfers, purchases or helps to sell illegally acquired goods shall be sentenced to fixed-term imprisonment of not more than three years, criminal detention or public surveillance and shall also, or shall only be fined.*" The other is the crime of harboring, transferring or covering up narcotic drugs or gains from relevant crimes, under Article 349. It states that: "*Whoever harbors, transfers or covers up, for such offenders engaged in smuggling, trafficking in, transporting or manufacturing of narcotic drugs, narcotic drugs or their pecuniary and other gains from such criminal activities shall be sentenced to fixed-term imprisonment of not more than three years, criminal detention or public surveillance; if the circumstances are serious, he shall be sentenced to fixed-term imprisonment of not less than three years but not more than ten years.*"

From the above two Articles, it is obvious that the definitions of these two crimes overlap somewhat. If someone goes against the two Articles, it would seem logical that he would be sentenced under Article 349 because a "special" Article (applicable to particular situations) derogates a "general" Article (applicable to ordinary situations) and a "heavy" Article (which carries a more severe punishment) derogates a "light" Article (one which carries a lighter punishment).

But what is the difference between money laundering and these two crimes, especially between money laundering and the crime of harboring, transferring or covering up narcotic drugs or gains from relevant crimes? The key difference lies in the criminal intent and objective fact. It is important to bear in mind that money laundering is a process, often a highly complex one, rather than a single act. One complete process of money laundering includes three stages:[282]

—*Placement stage*: *where cash derived directly from criminal activity is first placed either in a financial institution or used to purchase assets.*

—*Layering stage*: *the stage at which there is the first attempt at concealment or disguise of the source of the ownership of the funds.*

—*Integration stage*: *the stage at which the money is integrated into the legitimate economic and financial system and is assimilated with all other assets in the system.*

In short, money laundering is a very complicated process. Money laundering is an act of accounting or a fiscal act designed to bypass the law and "*legalize*" money from illegal activities, which totally alters the nature and source of the property, so that criminals can freely spend and circulate this money in their other economic activities. But the crimes articulated in Article 312 and Article 349 are neither intended to result in legitimacy nor to go through such complex stages as money laundering. They are not crimes of money laundering but of money channeling. Of course, they could be a first step in a money laundering procedure (the pre-wash).[283]

4.5 The Punishment for Money Laundering Crime

The legal consequences of money laundering according to the Chinese Criminal Code and its amendments are as follows:

the person who commits this crime, "*in addition to being confiscated of the said*

---

[282] See William C. Gilmore, *Dirty Money*, *The Evolution of Money Laundering Counter-measures*, Council of Europe Press 1995, p. 37.

[283] See Petrus C. Van Duyne, Money Laundering: Estimate in Fog, *The Journal of Asset Protection and Financial Crime*, Vol. 2 No. 1, 1994.

proceeds and gains, shall be sentenced to fixed-term imprisonment of not more than five years or criminal detention and shall also, or shall only, be fined not less than 5 per cent but not more than 20 per cent of the amount of money laundered; if the circumstances are serious, he shall be sentenced to fixed-term imprisonment of not less than five years but not more than 10 years and shall also be fined not less than five per cent but not more than 20 per cent of the amount of money laundered."

"Where an organization commits any of the crimes mentioned in the preceding paragraph, it shall be fined, and the persons who are directly in charge and the other persons who are directly responsible for the crime shall be sentenced to fixed-term imprisonment of not more than five years or criminal detention; if the circumstances are serious, they shall be sentenced to fixed-term imprisonment of not less than five years but not more than 10 years."

It can be concluded on the basis of above-mentioned provisions that money launderers will bear the legal consequences detailed below.

4.5.1 Loss of Freedom

Either criminal detention or fixed-term imprisonment will be applied to a money laundering offence. There are two kinds of criterion for sentencing. The basic statutory sentence is fixed-term imprisonment of not more than five years or criminal detention, while the aggravated statutory sentence is fixed-term imprisonment of not less than five years but not more than 10 years, no matter who commits the crime, be it an individual or an organization. But neither legislative interpretation nor judicial interpretation has definitive explanations for "*serious circumstances*". Theoretically, the following can be regarded as "*serious circumstances*": laundering money in especially huge amounts; making laundering a profession; organizing a money laundering group; being involved in organized international money laundering.

4.5.2 Financial Penalty

In addition to loss of liberty, money launderers will also, or will only, be fined not less than 5 per cent but not more than 20 per cent of the amount of money laundered. In other words, a floating financial penalty will be applicable to money laundering crime. This penalty has many advantages. It is conducive not only to the principle of fitting the punishment to the crime but also to the consideration of the criminal's economic situation, as well as to the stability and continuity of criminal law.

4.5.3　Confiscation of Illegal Gains

Except for the preceding legal consequences, confiscation of the proceeds from predicate offences has also been mentioned under Article 191. It should be pointed out that confiscation of illegal gains here is different from confiscation of property. The former is a criminal coercive measure, while the latter, as one of the four supplementary punishments[284], refers to the confiscation of part or all of the property personally owned by a criminal.

Under Article 64 of the Chinese Criminal Code, *"All money and property illegally obtained by a criminal shall be recovered, or compensation shall be ordered; the lawful property of the victim shall be returned without delay; and contrabands and possessions of the criminal that are used in the commission of the crime shall be confiscated. All the confiscated money and property and fines shall be turned over to the State treasury, and no one may misappropriate or privately dispose of them."*

Under Article 64, two different articles shall be subject to this criminal confiscation measure. One is the money and property illegally obtained by a criminal, which shall be pursued compulsorily by judicial authority and shall be turned over to the State treasury. The others are contrabands or possessions used in the commission of the crime. Contrabands refer to articles that are forbidden to be held by citizens, such as drugs, pornography and counterfeit money. Possessions used in the commission of the crime often refer to criminal tools, such as the vehicles for carrying drugs, or deposits for purchasing counterfeit money. According to Article 64, the laundered money should be confiscated since it derives from drug-related crimes, smuggling, organized underworld crime or from terrorism.

From the viewpoint of legislative coverage, there are several aspects of the confiscation of illegal gains under Article 191 which need to be explored. First, the leg-

---

[284]　Under the 1997 Chinese Criminal Code, there are four types of supplementary punishment: fine, deprivation of political rights, confiscation of property and deportation.

islation is duplicated. It has already been provided that all money and property illegally obtained by a criminal shall be recovered under the General Provisions (Article 64). The General Provisions deal with the basic questions concerning the Criminal Law and its implementation, while the Special Provisions cover various types of crimes and punishments as well as the necessary conditions that constitute various kinds of crimes. The General Provisions guide the Special Provisions. It is not necessary for Article 191 to repeat the same contents. Second, the location of confiscation is not correct. Confiscation of illegal gains is found in Article 191, s. 1 (for an individual). With this provision, it is as if there was no need to confiscate illegal gains from organizations involved in money laundering crime. It should be formulated so that the confiscation of illegal gains is not only applicable to individuals but also to organizations.

In addition, compared with the international requirements concerning confiscation measures, the provisions of confiscation measures under the Chinese Criminal Code are simple and abstract. In order to deprive criminals of their economic benefit and to weaken criminals' economic strength effectively and efficiently, it is necessary to provide value confiscation and substitute confiscation system, thus preventing criminals from escaping being confiscated in the case of proceeds of crime that have been converted into other property or proceeds of crime that have been intermingled with property acquired from legitimate sources. Besides, the mechanism of confiscated assets sharing should be in place to raise the enthusiasm of related authorities or institutions.

Confiscation measures are considered as an important tool with which to combat money laundering and its predicate crimes. The confiscation of illegal gains will not only deprive criminals of their economic benefit from crimes, thus discouraging them from pursuing illegal profits, but will also to weaken criminals' economic strength and improve efficiency in the fight against money laundering and related crimes. For this reason, confiscation measures are provided in the most significant international documents concerning the fight against money laundering. Chinese legislation on confiscation should conform to the obligations that have been proposed by the international community.

4.6 Conclusions

Although it is a short history since China turned into a country under the rule of law, from the above overview it is clear that the Chinese Criminal Law has made considerable progress on the issue of money laundering in a period of more than ten years. The measures on confiscation of illegal gains do exist in the Chinese Criminal Law. Corporate criminal liability also has been established. Additionally, some visible improvement has been made on the money laundering provisions. For instance, the scope of predicate offences has been expanded to four kinds of crimes from only drug-related crime. And the penalty of money laundering for organizations is increased in the third set of amendments to the 1997 Chinese Criminal Code.

Despite the fact that these provisions largely comply with the international requirements, there are a number of significant shortcomings. Predicate offences do not cover all serious crimes. Negligent laundering is not provided by the Criminal Code. As to the confiscation system, value confiscation and substitute confiscation systems have not been set up. And the mechanism of confiscated assets sharing has not been put in place in China. For these reasons, it can be concluded that there is an absolute need for continuing action to improve the Chinese Criminal Law concerning money laundering in order to match the international standards.

Chapter 5

The Chinese Financial Institution Campaign against Money Laundering

5.1 Introduction

In January 2003, the People's Bank of China (PBC) promulgated three rules, namely Rules for Anti-money Laundering by Financial Institutions, Administrative Rules for the Reporting of Large-Value and Suspicious RMB (Ren Min Bi) Payment Transactions, Administrative Rules for the Reporting by Financial Institutions of Large-Value and Suspicious Foreign Exchange Transactions. All of them came into force as of 1 March 2003. The three rules provide the criteria for Chinese financial institutions to take responsibility in the fight against money laundering. This chapter deals with the background and major contents of the three rules, along with comments on the status quo of anti-money laundering legislation in China from the perspective of international standards of anti-money laundering experience.

5.2 Background

Since the 1980s, with the ever-growing seriousness of money laundering activities, the international community has paid proper attention to the money laundering problem. Anti-money laundering laws have been shaping up and are constantly updated. New institutions that specialize in the fight against money laundering are developing. After the terrorist attack on Washington and New York on 11 September 2001, the fight against money laundering has gone even further, since terrorism is closely tied to money laundering. There is no doubt that the effective check on money laundering has, to a certain extent, had an impact on the incidence of those predicate offences and at the same time helped in maintaining social order and creating a peaceful and stable environment.

Drawing on experience from other countries, China has learned that the financial institutions are the most prone to be abused by money laundering criminals. These institutions have become the focus of anti-money laundering efforts in various parts of the world and laws have been passed to define the obligations and functions of financial institutions in order to effectively prevent them from being abused. As the central bank, the PBC is charged with regulating and supervising financial institutions and their operation and safeguarding the legitimate and sound performance of the financial industry. Over the years, the PBC has been working to improve the corporate governance of financial institutions and has issued a series of rules and regulations, which have, to some extent, prevented their abuse. For example, the PBC issued the Notice on Management over Large-Value Cash Payment on 15 August 1997, establishing a reporting system for large-value cash transactions and an appointment mechanism for withdrawal of large-value cash. Additionally, the banking sector has adopted the practice of using real names for individual deposit accounts and account management. Though these rules and practice have to some extent contained money-laundering activities, financial institutions have yet to create competent anti-money laundering departments, or establish standards for identifying suspicious transactions. Also, there is not yet any mechanism for data collection and analysis. Anti-money laundering rules are needed to provide a solution to these issues. As a consequence, the Rules for Anti-Money Laundering by Financial Institutions, the Administrative Rules for the Reporting of Large-Value and Suspicious RMB Payment Transactions, and the Administrative Rules for the Reporting by Financial Institutions of Large-Value and Suspicious Foreign Exchange Transactions, came into being in January 2003.

5.3　Major Contents

5.3.1　The Coverage of Financial Institutions

Since financial institutions are frequently abused by money launderers, the anti-money laundering legislation in various countries always focus on those institutions as mainly responsible in the fight against money laundering. China is no exception. The three rules issued in January 2003 are primarily to get financial institutions involved. In Article 2 of the Rules for Anti-Money Laundering by Financial Institutions, financial institutions are defined as institutions legally established and engaged in financial business within the territory of the People's Republic of China, which include:

(a) *banks, such as policy banks*[285], *wholly state owned commercial banks, joint stock banks, commercial city banks and commercial rural banks;*

(b) *credit cooperatives, such as urban credit cooperatives and their unions and rural credit cooperatives and their unions;*

(c) *postal savings institutions;*

(d) *non-bank financial institutions, including enterprise finance companies,*

---

[285]　Prior to the year 1978, there was only one bank, namely the People's Bank of China. This bank led, supervised and took care of all the banks in China and the financial business world, at the same time dealing for itself with industrial and commercial credit loans and savings business. Thus it served the double purposes as the central bank and a commercial bank. Since 1979, in order to divorce what the central bank does from what commercial banks do, the China Agricultural Bank, the Bank of China, the China Industrial and Commercial Bank, the China Construction Bank and the like have been brought back into operation one after another, thus establishing such dealings as the domestic savings and savings of foreign currency, obtaining of loans, settlements and individual savings. Being a state organ charged with the responsibility of supervising all financial business, the People's Bank of China doesn't handle credit loans with individuals and businesses for its unique position as the bank under the Party's Central Committee to be established. But the above specialized banks are responsible for both policy-based and industrial financial dealings. For the separation of policy-based financial dealings from industrial financial business, the Chinese government decided to have policy banks set up to solve the problem—the specialized banks having double function, cutting off the immediate link between the policy loans and the basic currency and to ensure that the bank under the Party's Central Committee is entitled to adjust and control the basic currency. In 1994 the National Development Bank and the Import and Export Bank of China, therefore, came into being. The policy banks are to be responsible for their own risks, operating within the purview of their own profits, while avoiding competing with commercially financial banks. Under these working principles, to meet the needs of the national industries' policies being their major tasks, the policy banks largely fund the national infrastructure, the basic industries and the pillar industries. What the policy banks do comes under the supervision of the bank under the Party's Central Committee.

trust and investment companies and financial leasing companies;

(e) foreign capital financial institutions, such as wholly foreign-funded banks, Sino-foreign joint equity banks, branches of foreign banks, wholly foreign-funded finance companies and Sino-foreign joint equity finance companies and other kinds of foreign-funded non-bank financial institutions.

It is clear that in China at present, banking and non-banking financial institutions should bear the responsibilities for preventing money-laundering activities. It has to be recognized that there is a big gap between Chinese legislation and international requirements on this issue. This gap is due to the short history of the anti-money laundering campaign in China. The revised Forty Recommendations of the Financial Action Task Force (FATF) require the financial activities of non-financial businesses or professions to be subject to the recommendations. In the amendment to the 1991 Directive, which came into being on 4 December 2001, not only financial institutions but also non-financial persons or entities, such as auditors, external accountants and advisors, real estate agents, notaries and other independent legal professionals, dealers in high-value goods and casinos operators, all should assume anti-money laundering obligations. While Western countries already have a history of dozens of years fighting against money laundering, in China it is just at the initial stage. There is little experience, and the fundamentals have yet to be put in place. Thus, focusing on the financial institutions, which are most vulnerable to money laundering activities, is a realistic and sound policy, and a step forward in the fight against money laundering.

5.3.2 The Definition of Money Laundering

The definition of money laundering is provided under Article 2 of the Rules for Anti-money Laundering by Financial Institutions, "*Money laundering in these rules refers to any action that legalizes the ill-gotten income and yields generated from criminal activities like drug trafficking, gang violence, terrorist acts, smuggling or other crimes through various means in which the source and origin of such income and yields are disguised.*" It is obvious that the definition of money laundering in this rule is different from that under the Chinese Criminal Code. According to the Criminal Law, amended in 2001, "*predicate offences*" means drug-related crime, organized crime of an underworld nature, terrorist crime or smuggling. Under the Rules for Anti-Money Laundering by Financial Institutions, however, dirty money laundered through financial institutions also includes illegitimate proceeds and its yield from embezzlement, fraud, tax evasion, appropriation of state assets and other crimes. It is clearly stipulated in the Rules for Anti-money Laundering by Financial Institutions that money laundering refers to any action that legalizes the income and yields generated from criminal activities like drug trafficking, gang violence, terrorist acts, smuggling or other crimes through various means in which the source and origin of such income and yields are disguised. This change is fully compatible with the spirit embodied in several international conventions or soft laws, such as the Strasbourg Convention, the EC Directive and the FATF Recommendations. It must be remembered that an illegal act is not the same as criminality. At present, laundering the proceeds from the four kinds of crimes given in the criminal law is a criminal act, while it is only an illegal act if the laundering follows from other crimes, on the basis of the Rules for Anti-Money Laundering by Financial Institutions.

5.3.3 The Principles of Anti-money Laundering

The Rules have established three principles. The first principle is one of legality and prudence. That is to say, financial institutions and their employees must abide by these rules in order to fulfill their due and serious obligations to combat money laundering activities and to identify suspicious transactions in a painstaking manner, and they must not engage in any unfair competition that could run counter to their anti-money laundering obligations.

The second principle is one of confidentiality. Financial institutions and their employees must abide by the relevant rules and regulations and refrain from disclosing any information on anti-money laundering activities to their customers and/or other personnel.

The third principle is one of full cooperation with the judicial department and the administrative enforcement department. Financial institutions must aid the judiciary and/or law enforcement departments including the customs and taxation authorities in combating money laundering in accordance with the relevant laws and regulations by investigating, freezing or suspending the transfer of customers' suspicious deposits.

Overseas branch offices of Chinese financial institutions must abide by the anti-money laundering laws and regulations of their host countries or regions and provide assistance to departments involved in anti-money laundering operations in these countries or regions.

These three principles provide requirements for financial institutions to fight against money laundering. These requirements are not unique to China. In fact, similar requirements can be found in the Basel Statements and the 1991 EC Directive. It is acknowledged that the establishment of these three principles is attributed to the full use of international experience for reference purposes.

5.3.4 The Supervisory Authority for Anti-money Laundering Operations

In the long run, the establishment of a preventive system against money laundering will contribute to the security of financial institutions and the long-term interests of a country. However, it is also a fact that setting up such a system may result in increasing costs for commercial banks and a reduction of deposits. For this reason, commercial financial institutions may not have much interest in the fight against money laundering on the basis of their short-term interests. To deal with this situation, Article 7 of the Rules for Anti-money Laundering by Financial Institutions provides that the PBC is the supervisory authority for anti-money laundering operations. The bank is establishing a leading group to supervise the financial institutions' anti-money laundering operations, whose duties are as follows:

(1) Supervising and coordinating anti-money laundering procedures in financial institutions.

(2) Conducting research and formulating strategies, working out plans and policies on anti-money laundering for financial institutions, establishing working mechanisms for anti-money laundering operation and reporting systems for large-value and/or suspicious RMB fund transactions (the State Administration of Foreign Exchange is responsible for supervising reporting of large-value and/or suspicious foreign exchange transactions and will establish a reporting arrangement to monitor such transactions).

(3) Establishing a monitoring system for scrutinizing payment transactions.

(4) *Working out proper solutions for major difficulties encountered by financial institutions in combating money laundering.*

(5) *Cooperating in international anti-money laundering operations and providing guidance for international exchanges in the areas of anti-money laundering by financial institutions.*

(6) *Other anti-money laundering functions of the PBC.*

It can be concluded that the PBC, as a supervisory authority, provides leadership to and supervises the banking industry in their anti-money laundering efforts, which is of great significance for financial stability and security. However, the establishment of an overall preventive system against money laundering is a huge project that involves customs, tax authorities, industrial and commercial authorities, exchange control authorities, the courts, the prosecutorial office, in addition to the whole financial system. For this reason, the supervisory authority for anti-money laundering operations should not only be responsible for the financial system but should also set up an effective cooperative system with other relevant anti-money laundering departments for effective control.

5.3.5 Customer Identification

The obligation for customer identification is one of several important countermeasures against money laundering by financial institutions that has been formulated in Chinese, as well as international anti-money laundering documents. Article 10 of the Rules for Anti-Money Laundering by Financial Institutions reads, "*Financial Institutions shall establish a customers' identity registry system to verify the identities of customers who proceed with financial business including deposits and settlement with them. Financial institutions shall not be allowed to open anonymous accounts or accounts under obviously fictitious names for their customers, and/or provide financial services including deposits and settlement whose identities are yet to be clarified.*" After that, Article 11 and 12 respectively provide for the obligation for customer identification for both individuals and organizations. Article 11 reads:

"*When opening deposit accounts or providing settlement service for individual customers, financial institutions shall verify the customers' IDs and record the* names and ID numbers. If a customer is represented by another person to open a personal deposit account with a financial institution, the financial institution shall verify both the representative's and principal's IDs and record the names and ID numbers thereof."

Article 12 reads:

"When opening accounts or providing financial services including deposits and settlement for institutional customers, financial institutions shall abide by relevant rules of the People's Bank of China and ask the customers to show valid documents for verification and recording."

The obligation for customer identification by Chinese financial institutions is consistent with the contents of international documents. For example, the "*customer*" includes not only individuals but also organizations. Apart from representatives, principals' identity should also be identified. These contents are consistent with those of international requirements. However, under Chinese legislation, the provisions of customer identification are more abstract and general. In theory, every customer of all transactions should be identified. This practice is slightly different from that of other countries, which specify the time when financial institutions should carry out identification requirements[286] and when customer identification requirements are unnecessary.[287]

---

[286] Under the EC Directive, it is very clear that the institutions and persons subject to the Directive should identify a customer when: (a) they enter into a business relationship, such as opening an account or offering safe custody facilities; (b) they conduct a single transaction (or several connected transactions) with a customer for a large amount. Under the amendment to the 1991 EC Directive, the threshold is Euro 15,000; (c) in the event of doubt that a customer is acting on his own behalf in conducting a transaction, measures should be taken to seek to identify the person on whose behalf he is acting; (d) wherever there is suspicion of money laundering, customer identification measures must be carried out, even where the amount of the transaction is lower than the threshold.

[287] Under the 2001 Amendment to the EC Directive, customer identification obligation need not be carried out in the following circumstances: (a) life insurance policies where the periodic premium amount or amounts to be paid in any given year does not or do not exceed EUR 1,000 or where a single premium is paid amounting to EUR 2,500 or less; (b) insurance policies in respect of pension schemes taken out by virtue of a contract of employment or the insured's occupation, provided that such policies contain no surrender clause and may not be used as a collateral thresholds. In addition, identification obligation can be waived if the customer is a credit or financial institution situated in a third country which imposes, in the opinion of the relevant member states, equivalent requirements to those laid down by this Directive. It is also not necessary to perform the identification obligation, if the payment for the transaction is to be debited from an account opened in the customer's name with a credit institution subject to anti-money laundering requirements.

Considering the fact that it would be excessively onerous for financial institutions to identify each customer every time, it is essential to specify the occasions when there is a need to identify the customers and those who are exempt from customer identification requirements, so that financial institutions can focus on the ones who need to be checked, thus reducing the costs incurred in combating money laundering.

5.3.6 The Large-value Transaction Reporting System

In order to strengthen supervision over financial transactions, to standardize financial transactions reporting activities and to prevent financial institutions from being misused for money laundering and other law-violating and criminal activities, all of these three regulations establish the large-value transaction reporting system. Under the Rules for Anti-money Laundering by Financial Institutions, there are only general provisions to the effect that financial institutions shall abide by relevant rules and report any large-value transactions detected in the process of providing financial services to customers to the PBC and/or the State Administration of Foreign Exchange.[288] Branch offices of financial institutions must report large-value transactions to the local branch offices of the PBC or the State Administration of Foreign Exchange in line with relevant rules on procedures of reporting of fund transactions, and at the same time keep their supervising organizations informed of such transactions.[289] Financial institutions must carry out examination and analysis on large-value transactions, and report to the local public security department if criminal activities are detected.[290]

Under the Administrative Rules for the Reporting of Large-value and Suspicious RMB Payment Transactions, three kinds of large-value RMB payment transactions are particularly defined:

(1) Any single credit transfer above RMB 1m yuan between legal persons, other organizations and firms created by self-employed persons;

(2) Any single cash transaction above RMB 200,000 yuan, including cash deposit, cash withdrawal, cash remittance, cash draft, cash promissory note pay-

---

[288] See *Rules for Anti-money Laundering by Financial Institutions*, Article 3.
[289] Ibid., Article 15.
[290] Ibid., Article 16.

ment;

(3) Fund transfers above RMB 200,000 yuan among individual bank settlement accounts, and between individual settlement account and corporate bank settlement account.

Under the Administrative Rules for the Reporting by Financial Institutions of Large-value and Suspicious Foreign Exchange Transactions, the following foreign exchange transactions constitute large-value foreign exchange transactions:

(1) Any single deposit, withdrawal, purchase or sale of foreign exchange cash above US $ 10,000 or its equivalent, or the accumulated amount of multiple deposit, withdrawal, purchase or sale transactions of foreign exchange within one day above US $ 10,000 or its equivalent;

(2) Foreign exchange non-cash receipt and payment transactions made through transfer, bills, bank card, telephone-banking, internet banking or other electronic transactions or other new financial instruments in which a single transaction volume or accumulated transaction volume within one day exceeding US $ 100,000 or its equivalent by individual customers, and in the case of corporate customers, a single transaction volume or accumulated transaction volume within one day exceeding US $ 500,000 or its equivalent.

The provisions of the large-value transactions reporting system are not only very concrete but also comparatively scientific. There are various quantity standards on the basis of different transactions. Specifically speaking, according to the nature of money, transactions are divided into RMB large-value transactions and foreign exchange large-value transactions; according to the nature of customers, transactions are divided into individuals large-value transactions and institutions large-value transactions. And transactions can also be divided into cash large-value transactions and non-cash large-value transactions in terms of the means of payment.

The large-value transaction reporting system can be regarded as the "*objective model*", which means financial institutions are required to report certain types of financial transactions above a threshold to the PBC and/or the State Administration of Foreign Exchange, whether or not the transaction is felt to be suspicious. Such a system leaves less to the discretion of financial institutions, thus promoting uniformity and consistency in enforcement. However, the rigid transactions reporting practice will result in a large amount of indiscriminate information. Li Lian, a draftsman of these anti-money laundering rules, estimated that there are about 100 billion large-value transactions reported every year.[291] This reporting system is both costly and inefficient. Criminals can also easily circumvent relevant regulations through a practice called "*smurfing*", which means money launderers break up the whole transaction into segments to get under the threshold. For these reasons, a large-value transaction reporting system is not enough, so there is also a suspicious transactions reporting system.

5.3.7 The Suspicious Transactions Reporting System

Suspicious transactions refer to those transactions of an abnormal amount, frequency, source, direction, use or similar. The suspicious transactions reporting system is regarded as an important countermeasure against money laundering in Western developed countries. China has used their experience for reference. Under the Rules for Anti-money Laundering by Financial Institutions, a suspicious transactions reporting system is provided which reads:

"*Financial institutions shall abide by relevant rules and report to the PBC and/or the State Administration of Foreign Exchange of any suspicious transactions detected in the process of providing financial services to customers.*"[292]

Branch offices of financial institutions have to report suspicious transactions to the local branch offices of the PBC or the State Administration of Foreign Exchange in line with their relevant rules on procedures of reporting of fund transactions, and at the same time keep their higher authorities informed of any such transactions.[293] Financial institutions must examine and analyze suspicious transactions, and report to the local public security departments if criminal activities are detected.[294]

In addition, there are very concrete provisions about suspicious RMB payment transactions and suspicious foreign exchange transactions under the other two rules.

---

[291] http://www.china.com.cn/chinese/law/279139.htm, 19 February 2003.
[292] *Rules for Anti-money Laundering by Financial Institutions*, Article 14.
[293] Ibid., Article 15.
[294] Ibid., Article 16.

Under the Administrative Rules for the Reporting of Large-Value and Suspicious RMB Payment Transactions, 15 types of suspicious transactions are listed in Article 8. When a financial institution discovers from its customer any occurrence as listed in Article 8 in the processing of payment and settlement business, it must record it, analyze the suspicious payment transaction, and fill in the Suspicious Payment Transaction Reporting Form before reporting the case.[295] When a financial institution finds it necessary to further verify a case of suspicious payment transaction, it must report to the PBC in a timely manner.[296]

Under the Administrative Rules for the Reporting by Financial Institutions of Large-Value and Suspicious Foreign Exchange Transactions, 11 types of foreign exchange transactions constitute suspicious foreign exchange cash transactions and 20 types constitute suspicious foreign exchange non-cash transactions.[297] These must be reported monthly in both hard and electronic copy.[298] Additionally, three types of foreign exchange cash transactions and 24 types of non-cash foreign exchange transactions, if indicative of suspected money laundering, must be examined and reported promptly to superior authorities in hard copy with relevant documents attached.[299]

Obviously, it is hard work to formulate the indicators of suspicious transaction reporting, since the standard of the suspicious transaction is very complicated and varies with the circumstances. This work took Chinese anti-money laundering experts more than one year to draw up, on the basis of the experience of other countries and taking into account the realities of the China's economic development.[300] These standards offer guidance for financial institutions to follow and can help them to judge whether or not a transaction is suspicious. The indicators prescribed by these anti-money laundering rules are concrete and specific, but in the light of the complexities of money laundering activities, legislators are not able to exhaust the possible conduct

---

[295] See *Administrative Rules for the Reporting of Large-value and Suspicious RMB Payment Transactions*, Article 11.
[296] Ibid., Article 12.
[297] See *Administrative Rules for the Reporting by Financial Institutions of Large-value and Suspicious Foreign Exchange Transactions*, Articles 9 and 10.
[298] Ibid., Article 11.
[299] Ibid., Articles 12 and 13.
[300] See *The Full Spectrum of Money Laundering Strategies*, http://www.china.com.cn/chinese/law/279139.htm, 19 February 2003.

of suspicious transactions and these indicators are far from complete.

5.3.8 Account Information and Transaction Record Keeping

The account information and transaction record keeping system is also an important measure, which has been required since 1990 in the FATF Recommendations and in the 1991 EC Directive. The purpose of this system is twofold. On the one hand, collection, analysis and reporting of large-value and suspicious transactions is not a one-off practice and suspicious transactions need to be monitored on a continuous basis, given the growing sophistication of money laundering. On the other hand, judicial department need records of financial transactions in the investigation of money laundering and may need such record as evidence, so financial institutions are required to retain the account information and transaction record for a certain length of time. Chinese anti-money laundering rules use international experience for reference. Under the Rules for Anti-money Laundering by Financial Institutions, article 17 reads, "*Records of account information shall be kept for a minimum of five years from the date of closing the account; Transaction records shall be kept for a minimum of five years from the date of booking the transaction.*" Transaction records include information on the ownership of the account, amount of deposit or withdrawal effected through the account, time of transaction, source and destination of funds and the means of fund etc. This record keeping system is fully in line with relevant requirements of the international community, including the contents that should be preserved and the time during which they should be kept.

5.3.9 Legal Responsibilities for Offences against Rules

Legal responsibilities for offences against rules are all prescribed in the three rules; they include administrative and criminal responsibility. Administrative responsibility means warning, fining and disqualifying. The PBC will issue a warning, ordering a financial institution committing any irregularities in violation of these rules to take remedial steps within a specified period of time, and if the financial institution fails to make the necessary corrections, a fine may be imposed and its senior executives immediately accountable for such misconduct may be disqualified from holding any positions in the financial industry if the circumstances are serious. [301] In addition, a disciplinary penalty will be imposed on the staff of a financial institution who provides assistance with money laundering activities; and when the misconduct constitutes a violation of the criminal law, the case will be transferred to the judiciary authorities. [302]

5.4 Conclusions

Although the crime of money laundering had already been defined in a special criminal ordinance "*Decision on Suppressing Drug Dealing*" in late 1990, and amended in the 1997 Criminal Code, there were no administrative regulations to prevent money laundering for a long period. Considering the nature of criminal law, which should be regarded as the "*red warning*" or the last line of defense, compared with the "*yellow warning*"—civil laws and administrative laws, this phenomenon that criminal law is an isolated weapon cracking down on money laundering activities is not logical. As a matter of fact, the provisions of money laundering crime in criminal law exist in name only because nobody has been prosecuted up to the present in judicial practice in the history of anti-money laundering in China. This situation was partly due to the undefined nature of the administrative measures.

The above-mentioned three rules, namely the Rules for Anti-money Laundering by Financial Institutions, the Administrative Rules for the Reporting of Large-Value and Suspicious RMB Payment Transactions, and the Administrative Rules for the Reporting by Financial Institutions of Large-Value and Suspicious Foreign Exchange Transactions, fill a gap in this field with profound significance. These three rules draw fully on international experience for reference and provide guidance for Chinese financial institutions. Not only are the principles of anti-money laundering pre-

---

[301] See *Rules for Anti-money Laundering by Financial Institutions*, Articles 20—23; *Administrative Rules for the Reporting of Large-value and Suspicious RMB Payment Transactions*, Articles 22 and 23; *Administrative Rules for the Reporting by Financial Institutions of Large-value and Suspicious Foreign Exchange Transactions*, Articles 17—19.

[302] See *Administrative Rules for the Reporting of Large-value and Suspicious RMB Payment Transactions*, Article 24; *Administrative Rules for the Reporting by Financial Institutions of Large-value and Suspicious Foreign Exchange Transactions*, Article 20.

scribed, but also concrete obligations for financial institutions are formulated, such as customer identification, record keeping and large-value/suspicious transaction reporting and the like. Except for substantive obligations for financial institutions, procedural provisions are also provided. For example, the reporting procedures of suspicious transactions are concrete and clear. In addition, legal responsibilities are formulated for misconduct in financial institutions, which can be considered as warning lights for those potential irregularities. However, these three anti-money laundering rules are not perfect. The most obvious problems in these administrative legislations of anti-money laundering are outlined below.

First, obligations of preventing money laundering are not imposed on non-financial institutions but on financial institutions alone. But *"experience shows that money launderers will utilize almost any form of corporate and trust activity to launder their profits"*[303]. Financial institutions represented by banks are not the sole industry that can be involved in money laundering schemes. In fact, money-laundering activities are penetrating many other businesses, which can involve large amounts of currency. Criminals can conceal the illegal origin by means of purchasing cars, precious metals, valuable jewelry and antiques. Criminals also can disguise the nature of proceeds by means of operating restaurants, hotels, shops and casinos through which dirty money is integrated with legal earnings. To deal with this trend in money laundering schemes, the international community has already made relevant responses, such as the revised Forty Recommendations, the 2000 United Nations Convention against Transactional Organized Crime (the Palermo Convention), and the 2001 EC Directive, all of which require non-financial institutions to take the responsibility of anti-money laundering. For this reason, not only financial institutions but also dealers in high-value goods, real estate agents, lawyers, notaries and other independent legal professionals should all bear the responsibility of anti-money laundering in order to improve the legislative outcomes.

Second, there is no specialized financial intelligence unit (FIU) in China. The current three rules all provide that the large-value/suspicious transactions should be reported to the PBC or the State Administration of Foreign Exchange. This is a tempo-

---

[303] Tom Sherman, *International Efforts to Combat Money Laundering: the role of the Financial Action Task Force in Money Laundering*, Edinburgh University Press 1993, p. 14.

rary arrangement. Neither the PBC nor the State Administration of Foreign Exchange (SAFE) is a specialized information center that can play the role of the FIU in many developed countries, which can collect, analyze and distribute suspicious transactions reports and other intelligence quickly and effectively. Money laundering crime is very different from traditional crimes. China should establish an independent anti-money laundering institution, to work with the public security bureau, prosecutor's office, industrial and commercial bureau, customs, banks and other sectors, to utilize computer networks and to gather and analyze various unusual transactions reporting, to provide financial information for judicial authorities as well as to exchange information with different countries. Only in this way can China control money laundering activities properly and effectively.

Third, the above-mentioned rules do not fall under the hierarchy of national laws but are part of the rules of administrative agencies, which are enacted by the PBC. National laws and sectional rules vary in the scope of application, authority and importance because of different law-giving bodies. This situation indicates that money laundering deterrence in China is inadequate. Anti-money laundering legislation aims to fight money-laundering crime and other relevant crimes. That is to say it lays particular stress on both state and public interests, which come before personal interests. For example, the protection of individual privacy, to a certain degree, should give way to the fight against money laundering. In addition, in order to ensure that financial institutions carry out their relevant obligations, it can be provided that non-compliance by financial institutions is a crime. However, these problems concerning fundamental rights should only be addressed by national legislation. For this reason, it is necessary to enact special anti-money laundering laws at the national level.

Chapter 6

The Current Situation of Money Laundering Crime in China

6.1 Introduction

Money laundering offence was stipulated by Chinese Criminal Law more than ten years ago[304]. However the judicial situation is that no one has been prosecuted yet. Does money laundering exist in China in reality? This chapter first describes the phenomena which are closely related to money laundering, namely the current situation of predicate offence and other factors conducive to money laundering, such as corruption, underground bank shops and shell companies in China. Based on these facts, it infers that money laundering is a real problem in China. Then it explores the reasons why case examples of money laundering are not available. Finally this chapter presents the endeavors to be made to investigate money laundering.

6.2 Predicate Offences

Money laundering depends upon the existence of underlying crimes. There would be no money laundering offences without predicate crimes. Indeed, the more serious

---

[304] Money laundering was first ruled under the "*Decision on Suppressing Drug Dealing*" in 1990. Laundering illicit money acquired from drug-related crimes was definitely provided as a crime, though the term of money laundering did not exist at that time.

the predicate offences are, the more rampant the money laundering crimes will run. The predicate offences, namely drug trafficking, smuggling, organized underworld crimes and terrorism are serious in China due to such reasons as poverty[305], disparities in economic development[306] and lack of an effective supervising system[307].

6.2.1 Organized Underworld Crimes

Article 294 of the 1997 Criminal Code stipulates the crime of organizing, leading, or actively participating in a mafia-style organization, the crime of entering China and recruiting members of mafia-style organization, and the crime of harboring a mafia-style organization. In China, typical mafia doesn't exist. However, we do have the organizations with the nature of criminal syndicates, which organize illegal or criminal activities through violence, threats or other means, such as overrunning a place, perpetrating outrages, or cruelly injuring or killing people.[308] In order to make the concept of mafia-style organization more precise, the Standing Committee of the NPC issued a legislative interpretation on April 28 2002, which pointed out that a

---

[305] Since economic reform and opening up in China, the national economy has enjoyed a continuous and rapid development and people's living standards have risen a lot. However, due to its large population of 1.3 billion, there is still a big gap of national income between China and developed countries. In fact, the policy of reform and opening up has made some people rich and at the same time it also has resulted in a large number of poorly off people. According to the report of the National Labor Union in 2002, the number of employees who live under the line of the lowest urban living standard is about 18.28 million. (The line of the lowest urban living standard varies from city to city, ranging from 143 RMB to 319 RMB for a month.) The total number of urban poorly off people may be more than 25 million if the urban poorly off employees account for two thirds of all urban poorly off people. And the situation of the peasantry is worse. The average net income from agriculture is decreased during the three years from 1998 to 2000. In the opinion of former Premier Zhu Rongji, the spiniest problem is how to raise the income of peasants. In a governmental work statement in 2002, the second important work is to raise the income of peasants. It should be said that to some extent the life pressure from poverty produces crimes.

[306] The economic development is unbalanced in China between urban areas and rural areas, east and west, coastal areas and inland. This disparity results in a very serious social problem, unfair distribution. Even in the same area, there is still a big gap in residents' income because of trade monopolies or the other factors. According to a survey by the State Statistical Bureau in 2000, one-fifth people possess 42.5% wealth. China is gradually turning into a polar society and this situation causes the frequent occurrence of conflicts. Some people expect to gain social wealth through crimes and to change the situation of unfair distribution. See *South Weekend*, 15 March 2001.

[307] Power corrupts and absolute power corrupts absolutely. This is a famous dictum.

[308] See Wang Hanbin, The explanation of the Criminal Code of the People's Republic of China, *the Fifth Session of the Eighth National People's Congress*, March, 1997.

mafia-style organization should contain four elements. First, it is a relatively stable criminal organization formed by many persons, among whom there are obvious leaders with regular members. Second, it commits organized illegal or criminal activities to gain economic profits so that it can have strong economic strength to support its activities. Third, it frequently commits organized illegal or criminal activities through violence, threats or other means, perpetrating outrages, overrunning a place or cruelly injuring or killing people. Last, it exploits the people and illegally controls or has an impact in a particular area or in a particular trade, thus seriously disrupting economic order and people's daily activities by means of committing criminal activities or taking advantage of functionaries of a state organ.

Crimes of mafia-style organizations are quite serious although they are new types of crimes as defined in Chinese criminal law. Zhang Xinfeng, the Director-General of the Criminal Investigation Department of the Ministry of Public Security of the PRC, pointed out at the summit conference of international police, held in Hong Kong on 18 March 2002, that mafia-style organizations in China are growing so fast that they seriously damages the security of society.[309] In the year 2001, courts at all levels throughout the country tried 350 cases of organizational crime of the underworld, involving 1953 criminals, 6.3 times and 3.8 times respectively, rose than the previous year.[310]

6.2.2 Smuggling Crimes

Smuggling, as a crime aiming at seeking sudden huge profits, exists for two main reasons. First, goods prices differ considerably from country to country, from area to area. This stimulates criminals to go to the trouble of traveling a long distance to buy goods and sell them at a profit. Second, every country and area exercises foreign trade controls to varying degrees to protect national economic development. Thus, criminals have to escape supervision of customs to transport, carry and post the goods.

Due to the strict planned-economy system, the phenomenon of smuggling crime

---

[309] See *South Weekend*, 28 March 2002.

[310] See *The Bulletin of the Supreme Court* (*On the meeting of the Fifth Session of the Ninth People's Congress on 11 March 2002*).

was not a serious problem in China in the past. However, with the policy of economic reform and opening up in the 1980s, smuggling crime is getting more and more rampant. To deal with this ever-increasingly grave smuggling crime, the Standing Committee of National People's Congress issued the Decision Regarding the Severe Punishment of Criminals Who Seriously Sabotage the Economy on March 8 1982, which raised the maximum statutory punishment of smuggling-crime from ten-year's imprisonment to the death penalty. In addition, the Standing Committee of National People's Congress issued the Supplementary Provisions Concerning the Punishment of the Crimes of Smuggling on January 21 1988, which stipulates various smuggling crimes in terms of different objectives and provides diverse statutory punishment. Ten years later, the 1997 Criminal Code absorbed the main contents of the two decisions and formulated ten kinds of smuggling crimes. These various smuggling crimes are as follows: Crime of smuggling weapons and ammunition; Crime of smuggling nuclear materials; Crime of smuggling counterfeited currencies; Crime of smuggling cultural relics; Crime of smuggling precious metals; Crime of smuggling rare and precious animals and their products; Crime of smuggling rare plants and their products; Crime of smuggling pornographic articles; Crime of smuggling ordinary goods or articles and Crime of smuggling solid waste. The maximum statutory punishment of these smuggling crimes, with the exception of Crime of smuggling rare plants and their products, Crime of smuggling pornographic articles, and Crime of smuggling solid waste, is the death penalty. In fact, according to Article 157, whoever shields smuggling with arms can be sentenced to death, no matter what articles the criminals have smuggled.

It should be acknowledged that the Chinese Criminal Code has a very serious punishment on smuggling crimes. After all smuggling crimes fall under the category of economic crimes, and few countries impose capital punishments on economic crimes. In spite of this fact, the death penalty doesn't produce much deterrence on smugglers in China. It is unimaginable that there should be so many people, so many various commodities and so great quantities involved in smuggling crimes. And the two most distinguished characteristics of smuggling crimes in China are as follows: first, state organs disregard their responsibility and exercise their privilege to commit smuggling crimes unexpectedly. Second, many customs officials have worked hand in glove with smugglers and customs are nominal consequently.

Recently the notorious Yuan Hua smuggling case[311] involved more than 570 officials, among whom are Li Jizhou, the former Vice-Minister of the Ministry of Public Security of the PRC, Wang Leyi, the former Deputy Administrator of the General Administration of Customs of the PRC as well as many high-ranking customs officials. It was ironic that with the exposure of the Yuan Hua smuggling case, these officials fell one after another just like dominos. And this phenomenon is surely very unique.

6.2.3 Drug Crimes

With opium entering into China in the 17th century, the Chinese people suffered from drugs. After the foundation of the PRC in 1949, the Chinese government launched a nationwide anti-drug movement throughout the country. From 1949 to 1953, 220 thousand drug cases, involving 80 thousand criminals were tried and 800 criminals were subjected to the death penalty. After several years' efforts, drug crimes were almost eradicated and this situation lasted for nearly 30 years.[312] However er drug crimes were resurgent again since the 1980s and were getting even more serious. Taking dopes for example, the number of dopes registered in public security sectors accounts to 70 thousand in 1989, 148.5 thousand in 1991, 250 thousand in 1993, 520 thousand in 1995, and 680 thousand in 1999.[313]

To deal with the ever-increasingly grave drug crimes, the Standing Committee of the NPC issued the Decision on the Prohibition against Narcotic Drugs on 28 December 1990, which supplements several new kinds of drug crimes and increases statutory punishment. The 1997 Criminal Code eventually adopted these amendments. In addition, in the 1990s the Supreme People's Court gave notices that drug criminals subject to death penalty in Yun Nan, Guang Dong, Guang Xi, Si Chuan, Gan Su and Gui Zhou Provinces should be approved not by the Supreme People's Court but by high courts of these provinces.

Despite the fact that China has a strong control over drug crimes, drug crimes

---

[311] The crime culprit of the Yuan Hua smuggling case is Lai Changxing, who now shelters himself in Canada to escape punishment.

[312] See Ma Kechang, Bao Suixian, *The Current Situation, Reasons and Countermeasures of Drug Crimes in China. The Theory and Practice of suppression of Drug Crimes*, Publishing House of the China University of Political Science and Law 1993, p. 12.

[313] See *Law Yearbook of China 1989—1999*, Press of Law Yearbook of China 1999.

develop even more rapidly and seriously. According to the statistics from 1983 to 1990, courts at all levels throughout the country tried 18457 drug cases, involving 25394 drug criminals, and 1284 criminals among them were subject to life imprisonment or the death penalty.[314] In 1998 the public security sectors all over the country uncovered 184 thousand illegal or criminal drug cases, among which 119 cases involved more than 10 thousand grams of heroin. And also 4 tons of heroin, 1.6 tons of crystallized methamphetamine were confiscated, 1.34 times and 1.2 times respectively, more than the previous year.[315] In 1999, 5.3 tons of heroin and 16 tons of crystallized methamphetamine were confiscated, and 33 thousand drug criminals were punished.[316]

6.2.4 Terrorism Crimes

Terrorism crimes had been absent in China for quite a long period. But in recent years, terrorism crimes have been turning up now and then, along with ever-increasingly grave international terrorism. Especially since the 1990s, those who proposed to establish an independent "*East Turkey*"[317], organized a series of terrorism crimes in Xin Jiang, such as explosion, assassination, arson, raids and others. These terrorism activities seriously damaged the security of life and property of the people of various ethnic groups, as well as threatened the peace and stability of relevant areas. It was reported that from 1990 to 2001, more than 200 terrorism activities committed by "*East Turkey*" organizations arose in Xin Jiang, and 162 people were killed and 440 people were injured.[318]

In order to deal with terrorism crimes, Article 120 of 1997 Criminal Code stipulated the Crime of Organizing, Leading or Actively participating in an Organization

---

[314] See *The Work Section Points of the Supreme People's Court on Trying Drug Cases in Twelve Provinces*, 17 December 1991.

[315] See *Law Yearbook of China 1999*, Press of Law Yearbook of China 1999, p. 159.

[316] See *Law Yearbook of China 2000*, Press of Law Yearbook of China 2000, p. 184.

[317] "*East Turkey*" is a reactionary organization established in Xin Jiang in 1944, aiming at striving for the independence of Xin Jiang. In the 1950s the organizers went into exile to Europe. It was reported that these organizations-in-exile for the same purpose add up to more than 50 groups. Now these reactionary organizations are gradually transforming into terrorism groups.

[318] See *Disclosure on Terrorism of East Turkey in Xin Jiang Province*, http://news.163.com/editor/020201/020201_345398.html, 1 February 2002.

engaged in terrorist activities, which rules, "*Whoever forms, leads or actively participates in a terrorist organization shall be sentenced to fixed-term imprisonment of not less than three years but not more than 10 years; other participants shall be sentenced to fixed-term imprisonment of not more than three years, criminal detention and public surveillance.*" "*Whoever, in addition to the crime mentioned in the preceding paragraph, commits other crimes of homicide, explosion or kidnap shall be punished in accordance with the provisions on combined punishment for several crimes.*"

After the terrorist attack on 11 September 2001, the Security Council of the United Nations made a quick response and adopted Resolution 1373 on 28 September 2001, to call on member states to work together urgently to prevent and suppress terrorist activities, including through increasing cooperation and full implementation of the relevant international conventions related to terrorism. In order to meet the need to combat terrorist activities both at the national level and the international level, the Twenty-fifth Session of the Ninth Standing Committee of the NPC adopted the third Amendment to the 1997 Criminal Code, which increases the punishment of the Crime of Organizing, Leading or Actively Participating in an Organization Engaged in Terrorist Activities, which reads: "*Whoever organizes or leads a terrorist organization shall be sentenced to fixed-term imprisonment of not less than 10 years or life imprisonment, whoever actively participates in a terrorist organization shall be sentenced to fixed-term imprisonment of not less than three years but not more than 10 years; other participants shall be sentenced to fixed-term imprisonment of not more than three years, criminal detention or public surveillance or deprivation of political rights.*"

6.3 Other Factors Conducive to Money Laundering Crime

Money laundering crimes can be found in China, not only because predicate crimes of drug trafficking, smuggling, organized underworld crime and terrorism are very serious, as mentioned above, but also such relevant factors as corruption, shell-companies and underground money shops have an impact on money laundering crime.

6.3.1 Corruption

Due to insufficient control and weak supervision mechanisms, corruption has become a systematic social problem in China. Both experts and the public consider the corruption crime as the most serious problem in China at present. In order to crack down on corruption, a series of measures have been taken in China. The crime of holding a huge amount of property with unidentified sources was established in 1988.[319] The Rules on Income Declaration of Leading Party and Government Officials above the County (Division) Level was adopted in 1995.[320] Also in 1999 the Regulation of Individual Deposit Accounts Under Authentic Name was implemented. All these measures make it difficult for corrupt officials to conceal the nature and source of illicit funds from corruption. There is no doubt that corrupt officials would try every means to launder those proceeds. Although the predicate offences of money laundering crime only refer to four kinds of crimes and don't include corruption crime, the phenomenon is prevalent that Chinese corrupt officials launder money derived from embezzlement and corruption through all kinds of ways.

- Qi Huogui, the former secretary of Dongfang City in Hai Nan Province took a bribe of 230,000 RMB. Then somebody helped him to open a bank account of 230,000 RMB under a false name of Ye Kejian and with the password "*777777*" in Chinese Industrial and Commercial Bank.[321]

- Li Yushu, the former vice Mayor of Leshan City in Si Chuan Province, took a

---

[319] Under the Supplementary Provision Concerning the Punishment of the Crimes and Embezzlement and Bribery issued on 21 January 1988, Article 11 provides the crime of holding a huge amount of property with unidentified sources. And later this content was absorbed in Article 395 of 1997 Criminal Code, which reads: "*Any State functionary whose property or expenditure obviously exceeds his lawful income, if the difference is enormous, may be ordered to explain the sources of his property. If he cannot prove that the sources are legitimate, the part that exceeds his lawful income shall be regarded as illegal gains, and he shall be sentenced to fixed-term imprisonment of not more than five years or criminal detention, and the part of property that exceeds his lawful income shall be recovered.*"

[320] The Central Committee of the Communist Party of China issued the Rules on Income Declaration of Leading Party and Government Officials above the County (Division) Level on 30 April 1995, which requires that leading party and government officials above the county (division) Level should declare their income. Because this rule is issued by the Communist Party, it has no legal force and only limited officials are subject to this rule, it doesn't exert much effect on the fight against corruption.

[321] See Liu Jie, Chinese Banking Business: the Storm of Anti-Money Laundering Is Ongoing, *Reform and Theory*, July 2000.

bribe of 8.16 million RMB. Then he founded a company, which had assets of 6.58 million in the name of other people.[322]

- Lu Congyou, the former vice Mayor of Lian Yun Gang City in Jiang Su Province, registered a chemical industry with his illegal money in the names of his parents who are in their eighties.[323]

- Cong Fukui, the former vice Provincial Governor of Hu Bei Province, established Long Yin Company in the name of other people. Cong Fukui transferred his bribery funds to this company and made them look like profits from operation.[324]

- Cheng Kejie, the former Vice Chairman of the Standing Committee of the National People's Congress, together with his mistress Li Ping asked a businessman from Hong Kong, named Zhang Jinghai, to transfer RMB 41 million yuan from bribes to Hong Kong and paid Zhang Jinghai more than RMB 11 million yuan for the laundering cost. Cheng Kejie committed the most serious bribe crime among all the investigated high-ranking officials since the foundation of the PRC. Also he is the highest official who was subject to the death penalty for economic crimes.[325]

These examples show that corruption crime and money laundering are twin brothers. With the ever-growing gravity of corruption in China, money laundering is equally getting increasingly serious. Only after we have cleaned up money laundering, can we effectively get corruption under control. Conversely, it will be difficult to eliminate corruption if money-laundering activities are rampant.

Although due criminal punishment has been meted out to the above-mentioned criminals, these criminals haven't been indicted of money laundering and punished because laundering the money from corruption and embezzlement isn't a crime in China. We have to admit it is a loophole of legislation in the criminal law, especially when the predicate offences are being widened at the international level.

6.3.2 Underground Money Shop

The underground money shops in China are always located in coastal areas,

---

[322] See *The Newspaper of Democracy and Legal System*, 15 January 2002.
[323] See *South Weekend*, 23 March 2001.
[324] See *Cities' Finance and Economics*, 18 November 2002.
[325] See *South Weekend*, 23 March 2001.

which have comparatively stronger economies. It is often the enterprises that will conduct illegal transactions in underground money shops. This is because enterprises in the coastland have a large demand for foreign exchange, while China has strong controls over foreign exchange, so not only are complicated procedures involved but also the amount of Chinese currency convertible into foreign exchange through normal channels is quite limited. Underground money shops need only simple procedures as well as cheap service charges, usually the commission being only about 1% ~ 2%. In order to rectify the financial order, competent authorities organized a continuous fight against underground money shops. In 2001, Guang Dong Province banned 60 underground money shops, involving 250 people and 59 million RMB. Fu Jian Province banned 15 underground money shops, involving 0.4 billion RMB.[326] Besides, the operator of underground money shops may also shoulder criminal responsibility. Article 174 of the Chinese Criminal Code includes the Crime of Establishing a Financial Institution without authorization[327], and Article 176 includes the Crime of Illegal Pooling of Public Deposits.[328]

However, the continuous attacks upon underground money shops haven't had a satisfactory result. Moreover, many underground money shops indeed have a close relation with smuggling, money laundering and other crimes. In China, where there are rampant smuggling crimes, there are also underground money shops. In the Yuan Hua smuggling case, from 1996 to 1998, the 12 billion RMB, the proceeds from smuggling crimes were transferred to "*Dong Shi-li*" underground money shop. Then "*Dong Shi-li*" notified its co-partner in Hong Kong to remit foreign exchange to Yuan Hua accounts opened in Hong Kong.[329] Thus underground money shops gradually be-

---

[326] See *Economic Report in 21 Century*, 5 November 2001.

[327] Article 174 reads: "*Whoever establishes a commercial bank or any other banking institution without the approval of the People's Bank of China shall be sentenced to fixed-term imprisonment of nor more than three years or criminal detention and shall also, or shall only, be fined not less than 20,000 yuan but not more than 200,000 yuan; if the circumstances are serious, he shall be sentenced to fixed-term imprisonment of not less than three years but more than 10 years and shall also be fined not less than 50,000 yuan but not than 500,000 yuan.*"

[328] Article 176 reads: "*Whoever illegally takes in deposits from the general public or does so in disguised form, thus disrupting the financial order, shall be sentenced to fixed-term imprisonment of not more than three years or criminal detention and shall be, or shall only, be fined not less than 20,000 yuan but not more than 200,000 yuan; if the amount involved is huge, of if there are other serious circumstances, he shall be sentenced to fix-term imprisonment of not less than three years but not more than 10 years and shall also be fined not less than 50,000 yuan but not more than 500,000 yuan.*"

[329] See *Economic Report in 21 Century*, 5 November 2001.

come the arena where turn illicit money into *"legal money"*. It was reported that the illicit money laundered by the underground money shops count up to 200 billion every year, accounting for 2% of gross domestic product (GDP).[330]

That is to say the underground money shops are closely related with money laundering crime and this situation draws attention from the competent authorities. In July 2002, the State Administration of Foreign Exchange as well as the Ministry of Public Security established an emphasis in fighting against illegal foreign exchange transactions, together with the fight against money laundering, decided to go a step further for the attack on the underground money shops, and planed to establish corresponding systems of information collecting and early warning.

6.3.3 Shell Companies

According to the Company Law of the PRC, for the incorporation of a limited liability company, the capital contributions of the shareholders must reach the statutory minimum amount of capital. Each shareholder shall make in full the amount of the capital contribution. After all shareholders have made their capital contributions in full, such contributions must be verified by a statutory capital verification institution, generally referred to as an accounting firm.[331] As to the incorporation of a joint stock limited company, the share capital subscribed for by the sponsors and raised from the general public shall reach the statutory minimum amount of capital. After payment in full of the subscription money for all shares is made, a statutory capital verification institution shall be commissioned to conduct a verification of the funds and produce a verification certificate.[332] However, in China, those who apply for company registration often obtain the registration by deceiving the competent company registration authority through falsely declaring the capital to be registered with falsified certificates or by other deceptive means. Or, sponsors or shareholders of a company frequently make a false capital contribution by failing to pay the promised cash or tangible assets or to transfer property rights, or surreptitiously withdraw the contributed capital after the incorporation of the company. These companies, which don't have funds or e-

---

[330] See *Finance*, Vol. 13, 2002, p. 9.
[331] See *Company Law of the People's Republic of China*, Articles 19, 25, 26.
[332] Ibid., Articles 73, 91.

Chapter 6 The Current Situation of Money Laundering Crime in China

nough funds required by law, or don't have organizational structure or fixed premises and necessary conditions for production and operation, are called shell companies. Shell companies have existed in China since the implementation of the market economy.

Shell companies have a close relation with money laundering crime. It is the frequently used-means for criminals to set up a shell company, compile false financial statements, report business turnover and profit untruthfully and then pay all kinds of taxes, in order to cover up or conceal the source or nature of the illicit funds. For example, Shao Jun, the former manager of the Shipping Company in the Capital Steel Factory, established a shell company in Britain and open accounts with Hong Kong's American Bank and HSBC to launder dirty money, which was from bribery.[333]

Not all shell companies are used by criminals to commit money-laundering crime. However, it is also a fact that many shell companies indeed provide a secure and protective screen for money launderers. The problem is that shell companies are widespread in China, especially during the period of transition of economic systems. It was reported that in Nan Jing, criminals counterfeited bank documents and helped those who apply for company registration to be registered with falsified certificates. With the help of these criminals, 23 shell companies defrauded business licenses.[334] It is regrettable that all accounting firms didn't examine and verify relevant certificates carefully so that the schemes of criminals easily succeeded. In June 2001, 219 shell companies were investigated by Shanghai Industrial and Commercial Administrative Bureau. It is surprising that all of the 219 shell companies registered and opened for business with the aid of the same accounting firm, which advanced capital, provided false reports on the verification of capital and falsified business licenses for these companies in six months.[335]

The problem of falsification of account from Chinese accountants is getting more and more serious. In the first half-year of 2001, the Chinese Associate of Registered Accountants carried out an inspection into accounting firms and there were more than

---

[333] See Shao Sha-ping, The New Criminal Law and Control on Money Laundering, *The Frontier of Law*, Vol. 1, Law Press, 1997.

[334] See *Legal Daily*, 13 October 2000.

[335] See *Li Yong Le, Various Shell Companies in Shanghai*, http://www.zaobao.com/stock/pages8/china260102.html, 26 January 2002.

100 accounting firms and 400 registered accountants that were investigated as a result of their bad faith and false accounting. It is obvious that the situation of falsification of account is not unusual.[336]

Intermediary organizations such as accounting firms are the first line of defense against economic crimes. But in China, intermediary organizations don't act as watchdogs but serve as umbrellas frequently. No wonder Premier Zhu Rongji inscribed "*No false account*!" as a motto for the Shanghai State Accounting Institution.[337] It is grieving that this self-explanatory professional ethics should need to be required by Premier Zhu.

6.4 The Judicial Situation of Money Laundering Crime: Few Has Been Prosecuted Yet

Money laundering crimes can be found in China. On the one hand, the crimes of drug trafficking, smuggling, organized underworld crime and terrorism are very serious in China. It is a normal practice for criminals who have committed predicate offences to launder illicit proceeds so that they can flee from justice and use the dirty money freely and unrestrainedly in economic activities. On the other hand, as Chinese economic system is in transition, legislation of anti-money laundering is not very perfect and financial supervision is relatively weak. Compared with developed countries, it is safer for criminals to launder dirty money in a country in which strict preventive measures haven't been established or are not very mature. In addition, money-laundering crimes for the moment are on the increase with an ever-growing scale, and also it is a typical international crime. With the globalization of economic systems, criminals can launder money in every corner in the world. So it is difficult for China to have a narrow escape.

Although it is difficult to estimate the scope of money laundering crime in China, we can pinpoint its severity through other related facts. According to the statistics of the State Administration of Foreign Exchange, the flight capital[338] in China from 1997

---

[336] Ibid.
[337] See *Beijng Youth Paper*, 30 October 2001.
[338] Flight capital = positive trade balance + net capital influx − increased foreign exchange reserve.

to 1999 amounted up to $ 52 billion, about $ 16 billion to $ 17 billion every year. Some economists estimated that the figure might be ever larger because much flight capital hadn't been included in the record, while the amount of introduction of foreign capital is only about $ 40 billion every year. Some experts speculated that there is some former flight capital and some international dirty money among the $ 40 billion.[339] It was also reported by overseas media that foreign direct investment in Hong Kong in 2000 was as high as 64.3 billion dollars, while it was only 38 billion of dollars in the mainland of China. It is unbelievable that the tiny area of Hong Kong has actually become a competitor of foreign investment with the mainland of China. A usual surmise is that Hong Kong has turned into the money-laundering base of the mainland. This surmise is being verified recently. The Commission against Corruption in Hong Kong found out that some of the criminals who committed smuggling, embezzlement, tax evasion and other crimes in the mainland of China laundered their dirty money via the largest money-laundering criminal gang throughout the history of Hong Kong. Among those criminals in the mainland of China, Lai Changxing, the prime culprit of the Yuan Hua smuggling group was one of the major customers.[340]

Money laundering crime exists indeed in China. However nobody has been prosecuted up to the present in judicial practice. For this reason, somebody even wrote an article entitled *"when will the court in China hear the first money-laundering case"* in the magazine *Chinese Lawyer* in the third issue of 2000. The fact that money-laundering crime is not easily investigated rests with the nature of money laundering crime. Money laundering is often masked by legal business activities. It is not as easy to be discovered as traditional crimes are by the public authorities. And also money-laundering crime has no direct victims. It is more secret as few people will report a case to the security authorities. Additionally, money laundering crime differs from *"street crimes"*. Those who commit money-laundering offences often have professional skill and knowledge. They make use of their talent not only to commit money-laundering crime but also to gloss over evidence of crime. On the contrary, investigative authorities are often good at dealing with traditional street crimes and lack superb inves-

---

[339] See *The Economic Observer*, 22 July 2002.
[340] See *State Administration of Foreign Exchange*, http://www.jcrb.com.cn/yfw/shownews.asp? id = 2919, 19 November 2001.

tigative capability for complicated white-collar crimes. Due to these factors, it is very difficult for judicial authorities to detect money-laundering crime.

In fact, it is not easy to detect money-laundering crime in both developing countries, which lack perfect preventive systems, and developed countries, which have taken many steps responding to money laundering. From 1987 to 1997, there were only about three or four cases of money laundering that had been successfully dealt with in the United Kingdom. Moreover the amount of money was only about 1400 pounds. Compared with 300 billion pounds, which is suspected of being laundered through British financial institutions every year, this figure is very small. And the criminals who have been sentenced are not big shots but small potatoes.[341] Another example, among more than 3000 cases investigated in Hong Kong in the past four years, only 49 cases were determined to be money-laundering crimes.[342] Taking the world as a whole into consideration, money laundering is not easy to detect, which is determined by its innate attributes.

Of course there are special reasons for the lack of cases of money laundering crime in China. Money-laundering crime was not provided in the Chinese Criminal Code until 1997. We couldn't charge somebody with money laundering crime, although the phenomenon of money laundering did exist according to the investigative practice of public security organization in China.

- In March 1989, Zhang, a resident of Hong Kong was desirous to transfer proceeds, which were derived from his smuggling activity, from mainland of China to Hong Kong. He consulted with Qiuyi Company in Hong Kong about his payment on behalf of the latter to another company in Jiang Su Province, which sold cotton yarn to QiuYi Company. This sum of payment is about 830,000 RMB. After that, Qiuyi Company remitted Hong Kong dollars to the account of Zhang in Hong Kong.[343]

- In 1989, Wu Dapeng, an employee in the Beijing branch of the Bank of China, colluded with a businessman in Hong Kong and Tai Wan and stole 4 bills of exchange by taking advantage of his position and remitted one draft, with the amount of

---

[341] See Barry A. K. Rider, The Control of Money Laundering Crime, *Peking University Law Journal*, Volume 5, 1999.

[342] See *Economic Report in 21 Century*, 5 November 2001.

[343] See Ding Muying, The Research on Money Laundering, *Chinese Criminal Law Journal*, Vol. 38, 1998, p.33.

$870,000, to several foreign financial institutions, with the purpose of investing in China with these booties.

- In February 1993, Dong, a Chinese American, and Zheng, an overseas Chinese, entered our country with $1.4 million, which was derived from drug dealing. They attempted to launder the proceeds via Chinese financial institutions. [344]

In 1997, money-laundering crime was formulated in the Criminal Code. However, the blemished criminal legislation restrains judicial activity. According to Chinese criminal law it is impossible to decide the owner of the criminal money as a money launderer. That is to say, the subject of money laundering shouldn't be the executor or accomplice of the predicate crime. This kind of criminal legislation undoubtedly reduces the scope of fighting money-laundering activities. Besides, the defendant who is accused of money-laundering crime should be proved that he knows the funds are derived from drug crimes, organizational crime of the underworld, terrorism or smuggling. It is very difficult for public prosecutors to assume the burden of producing evidence. And also the scope of predicate offences is quite narrow. The predicate offences only refer to smuggling, drug crime, terrorism and Mafia. As a matter of fact, there are many other severe crimes, such as crime of trafficking in people, crime of kidnapping, crime concerning securities, crime of financial fraud, etc, generating a large amount of wealth, which criminals have an urgent need to launder. It can be concluded that the shortage of money-laundering cases in judicial practical work are really linked to the loopholes of legislation in the criminal law.

In addition, money-laundering offence is a new type of crime provided in Chinese Criminal Code after all. Theoretical research on it is far from enough and also judicial authorities lack practice experiences on combating money laundering. Some cases that have been discovered in China really coincide with the elements of money laundering. Judicial authorities, however, did not investigate these cases from the angle of fighting money laundering. For example, Ye Jihuan, the second personage in the famous organized underworld crime of Zhang Zhiqiang, kidnapped a merchant from Hong Kong and extorted 4 million RMB, among them he was distributed 2 million RMB. After that, he purchased shops and casinos in the name of his brothers

---

[344] See Wang Deqing, The Present Conditions of Money Laundering Crime and Preventive Counter-measures in China, *Tian Jing Politics Science and Law*, Vol.4, 1997. p.9.

and sisters with these proceeds and had these relatives manage the shops and casinos. It is a typical means of money laundering to invest with the dirty money derived from crimes committed by Mafia. These relatives of Ye Jihuan committed the crime of money laundering obviously, but no one was charged with the crime of money laundering.[345]

In this regard, not only China but also other countries are the same. For example, the Privacy Act of Bank was enacted in 1970 in America. Banks are imposed the obligations of suspicious transactions reporting and record keeping under this act. But many banks didn't implement these relevant obligations fully in the following ten years. Relevant authorities hadn't paid much attention to whether the act was implemented well in America until Boston Bank was involved in a criminal investigation in February 1984. And at last this incident resulted in the enactment of the Money Laundering Control Act in America.[346]

6.5 The Endeavors to Be Made to Investigate Money Laundering Crime

The investigation of money laundering crime is arduous work. As indicated before, money laundering is such a crime with high secrecy, unusual professionalism and extraordinary complicacy. Besides, money laundering activity has no direct victims. Therefore, it is said that the dark figure of money laundering crime is considerably high. If money laundering crime hasn't been detected, "*there will be little chance of a successful prosecution resulting in convictions, much less of the forfeiture of proceeds*"[347]. Thus it can be seen how important the successful investigation of money laundering crime is. It is no denying the fact that not all money laundering activities could be investigated. However, if we conduct fundamental work diligently we could find some money laundering cases. And also we can prevent those vulnerable professions from associating with dirty money as well as can effectively restrain the

---

[345] See Ruan Fangming, *Comparative study on Money Laundering*, Press of the Chinese University of Political Science and Law, 2002, p.76.

[346] Ibid., p.77.

[347] Ernesto U. Savona, *Responding to Money Laundering*, *International perspective*, Harwood academic publishers 1997, p.200.

momentum of money laundering crime. To investigate money laundering crime, the following points are essential:

6.5.1 The Weakest Link in the Process of Money Laundering Should Be Recognized

Knowing about the process of money laundering will be helpful to see through money laundering schemes and eventually to detect these crimes. According to theoretical research, a complete process of money laundering includes three stages: placement stage, layering stage and integration stage.[348]

Placement stage is the process by which the dirty money is first placed either in a financial institution or used to purchase insurance and buy stocks or thrown into an underground bank shop. The way of placement stage varies rather widely due to different sources of dirty money and various responses to money laundering. In this stage, money launderers run the biggest risk and it is comparatively easy for investigators to detect money laundering activities. Layering stage is the second process where criminals conduct complicated transactions to conceal or disguise the source of the dirty money or the ownership of the funds. As a result of the circuitous movement of dirty money between different financial institutions or even between different countries, it is more difficult for competent authorities to identify and to trace the proceeds from criminal activities. Integration stage is the last one which means the dirty money is successfully integrated into the legitimate economic and financial system. Thus criminals can freely and safely use these proceeds which seem to be legitimate earnings. In this stage there is little chance for investigators to make a distinction between the dirty money and the legitimate profit.

From this simple overview of the money laundering process, it is obvious that investigators should give a high priority to the placement stage, which is the weakest link during the whole process. It is obvious that banks are vulnerable to money launderers. However, many other business areas are also penetrated with money laundering activities. Therefore, it is equally essential to put stress on non-bank financial

---

[348] See William C. Gilmore, *Dirty Money*, *The Evolution of Money Laundering Counter-measures*, Council of Process, 1995, p. 37.

institutions and non-financial institutions to prevent them from being used by money launderers and try to investigate money laundering activities which make use of non-bank financial institutions or non-financial institutions. For example, the securities market is vulnerable to money launderers in china. The Regulations of Securities Account came into force on 1 June 2002, which has strong control over opening securities account. It requires that a virtual certificate is necessary when opening a security account. However, opening accounts under an authentic name is not equal to trading under true identification. Besides, commission businesses through Internet, telephone and other non-face to face transactions are growing fast. It is hardly possible to require shareholders to deal with securities under authentic identification. Thus criminals may make use of the securities market to launder money. Therefore investigators should pay much attention to this problem.

Another example, Chinese pawnbroking, as a non-financial service, is not under the supervision of the People's Bank of China. Many pawnbrokers can start collateral loan. Thus, pawnshops are likely to be exploited by money launderers. Therefore, pawnshops should also set up preventive measures against money laundering, using the regulations of the People's Bank of China for reference on the one side, on the other side, investigators should also pay close attention to this phenomenon.

6.5.2 Financial Institutions Should Truly Implement Relevant Obligations

It is widely accepted that financial institutions are the most vulnerable industry for money launderers. For this reason, the most important international documents on combating money laundering activities all agree that financial institutions should play a significant role to keep away money laundering crimes, such as the 1988 Basle Committee Statement, the Recommendations of Financial Action Task Force, and the EC Directive. These documents all emphasize that financial institutions should assume such obligations of anti-money laundering crimes as customer identification, record keeping and suspicious transaction reporting. In the 20 century, we imposed fragmentary and indirect obligations on financial institutions in several documents, where the provisions, unfortunately abstract and obscure, were hard to manipulate. Besides, if somebody violates obligations, we either had no penalties or have no virtu-

Chapter 6 The Current Situation of Money Laundering Crime in China

al penalties. That is to say, we didn't have punishment and compulsion for financial institutions and employees who went against their obligations at the time. Since the 21 century, under the guidance of the People's Bank, Chinese financial institutions have started the campaign of fighting against money laundering crime and stipulated such rules as "*The Provisions on Anti-Money Laundering For Financial Institutions*", "The Regulations on Reporting Large Amount and Suspicious Transactions of RMB", "The Regulations on Reporting Large Amount and Suspicious Transactions of Foreign Funds" and the like. However, we should not be complacent over just formulating several rules but should make great efforts on how to truly implement these rules. Only in this way can we turn the regulations on paper into virtual instruments in the fight against money laundering.

6.5.3 Financial Intelligence Unit (FIU) Should Really Play Its Role

Professional money laundering necessitates professional institutions specializing in the fight against money laundering. An FIU, as a national information center for the collection, analysis, and dissemination of information regarding potential money laundering, is of great importance in combating this crime. In 2000, the United Nations Conventions against Transnational Organization Crime expressly pointed out the need for an FIU. Many countries have already established FIUs, which are helpful to facilitate the reporting of suspicious money laundering activities and to coordinate the investigation of these suspicious activities when warranted. China didn't set up an FIU until June 2004. In the days without an FIU, it was difficult to investigate money laundering activities. Furthermore, even though suspicious transactions were reported to the People's Bank on the basis of corresponding regulations, it was still hard for authorities to analyze these suspicious reports, and it was out of the question to collect evidence to verify money laundering activities. For this reason, the establishment of an FIU in China was necessary. However, due to its recentness in China, the effort of the FIU is just at the initial stage. Although the FIU has received some suspicious transactions reporting, the feedback for suspicious transactions reporting is not sufficient. Therefore what is more important is that the FIU should really play its role in the fight against money laundering.

6.5.4 Special Investigative Techniques Should Be Used

Conventional police methods, such as searches, seizures, arrests, and interrogations, could be characterized as "*necessary evils*" since they involve some use of the state's coercive power and therefore some infringement of liberty. Special investigative techniques differ from conventional techniques because they substitute one "*necessary evil*" (deception) for another "*necessary evil*" (coercion).[349] To investigate tricky and covert money launderers may need special investigative techniques. Competent authorities may consider the use of undercover agents, civilian informants, electronic interception of conversations through telephone wiretaps and ambient microphones to detect the money laundering crimes. Of course there will be a conflict between the demands of fight against crime and the protection of freedom and democracy. Therefore covert methods should be quarantined in specialized units, such as frontier, enter and exit port, special sea area or other special sites.

6.6 Conclusions

In China, the largest criminal problems are drug crimes, smuggling, corruption and other organized crimes. All of these involve money laundering. Besides, underground bank shops and shell companies, which can be considered as conducive factors to money laundering, are rampant in China. However, few case examples of money laundering are available in China. The lack of money laundering case examples is not considered a sign that criminals are not taking advantage of China to launder money frequently. Rather, we admit that adequate means of detecting money-laundering crime have not yet been fully developed in China. Therefore, China should make greater efforts to investigate money laundering crime successfully. Actions speak louder than words. Successful investigation and prosecution is the best proof of the effectiveness of the anti-money laundering regime.

---

[349] See Jacqueline E. Ross, Tradeoffs in Undercover Investigations: A Comparative Perspective, *University of Chicago Law Review*, Summer, 2002.

Chapter 7

Comparison of Anti-money Laundering System between the EU and China

7.1 Introduction

Money laundering, as an increasingly serious crime, needs strict criminal measures to fight against on the one hand, on the other hand, administrative preventive measures are no less important than criminal measures. Suppression and prevention are always two parallel approaches to deal with crimes. In EU countries, both criminal measures and administrative measures are elaborated well to cope with money laundering problems and have exerted significant efforts in the fight against money laundering. In China, the deterrence of money laundering is just at the initial stage, many problems are still waiting to be overcome and solved.

In this chapter, six issues involved in criminal measures and preventive measures, which are money laundering offence, confiscation system, coverage of anti-money laundering measures, customer identification, suspicious transactions reporting, awareness raising, training and supervision, will be discussed both in EU levels and in China and some comparison will be made to find out what the existing problems are in the fight against money laundering in China and what China should learn from EU countries so that China can improve its comprehensive competence in combating money laundering.

7.2 Criminal Measures

7.2.1 Money Laundering Offence

Money laundering crime is a highly international phenomenon and takes little account of borders. Given its global nature, the legal systems against money laundering crime in various countries, especially the arrangement of its constituent elements should be as similar as possible, if identical elements are impossible. Due to different social backgrounds and legal systems of every country, the constituent elements of money laundering crime vary considerably from country to country.

7.2.1.1 Money Laundering Offence in the EU

The 1988 Vienna UN Convention and the 1990 Strasbourg Convention undoubtedly have played a significant role in establishing the elements of money laundering offence. All of the member states of EU have signed and ratified these two conventions and their criminal laws concerning money laundering offence are primarily based on them. Therefore, many aspects of anti-money laundering law in EU countries are analogous to each other, though differentiation is inevitable.

According to the Second Commission Report to the European Parliament and the Council on the Implementation of the Money Laundering directive, all the EU countries except Luxembourg have extended the predicate offence to a wide scope, other than drug trafficking. Only Luxembourg covers offences linked to drug-related money laundering. In fact, the Act of 11 August 1998 also supplements the expanded definition of the laundering offence.[350] Therefore, all of the EU members have already applied the crime of money laundering to a comparatively wide scope. Overall, the approach that has been taken with regard to the scope of predicate offences can be divided into four broad categories:

  —All predicate crimes e. g. France, Finland, Ireland, Italy, the United Kingdom, the Netherlands;

---

[350] See *Financial Action Task Force on Money Laundering Annual Report 1998—1999*, 2 July 1999, pp. 11—13.

Chapter 7 Comparison of Anti-money Laundering System between the EU and China

—*Crimes with a specified minimum period of imprisonment e. g. Austria (greater than 3 years); Sweden (greater than 6 months);*

—*A list of predicate offences e. g. Greece (20 crimes), Belgium (near 20 crimes), Denmark (almost 10 crimes), Spain (3 crimes), Portugal (near 10 crimes);*

—*Hybrid system, a combination of the second and the third mode e. g. Germany, Luxembourg.*

All members of the EU except Austria provide that tax fraud is a predicate crime for money laundering. In addition to money laundering offences which are based on laundering the proceeds of certain crimes, many countries e. g. France, Germany, Luxembourg also have provisions making it an offence to launder money for a criminal organization. Furthermore, in almost all countries, the laundering of the proceeds of a foreign offence is as much a crime as the laundering of the proceeds of the same domestic offence.[351]

What is satisfactory is that in more and more countries laundering proceeds of one's own also allows a prosecution of money laundering crime. Take the Netherlands for an example. In the past it was impossible to sentence the owner of the criminal money as a money launderer. It was only possible to convict him of the crime through which he obtained the money.[352] However, since the new legislation, which came into force in December 2002, money laundering no longer is considered as an example of favor, but as an independent and autonomous crime. That is to say, if a drug dealer laundered his money, it should be possible to prosecute and sentence the drug dealer for not only dealing drugs, but also for money laundering.

The mental element of the money laundering offence is a knotty problem. Some countries require knowledge or intent, but many others have extended the mental element of the offence to a wider level. Broader concepts of mens rea include "*belief*", "*suspicion*" or "*reasonable suspicion*" (mostly in common law countries) or reckless-

---

[351] See Financial Action Task Force on Money Laundering, *Review of FATF Anti-Money Laundering Systems and Mutual Evaluation Procedures 1992—1999.*

[352] See Bert Ravenstijn, The Netherlands: Anti Money-Laundering Programs—The Case of ING, *Journal of Money Laundering Control*, Vol. 3 No. 4, 2000. p. 360.

ness, *gross negligence or negligence* (*in certain civil law countries*).[353] For instance, the Netherlands has both intentional and negligent money laundering crimes. And the negligent offence has a lower penalty than the intentional one.[354] Similarly, Sweden also has a negligent money laundering offence.[355]

Within the elements of money laundering offence, one important issue is whether corporate criminal liability exists. There are heated controversies about the constitutional appropriateness of imposing corporate criminal liability. This has been the case especially in civil code countries. The central point is whether an inanimate corporate possesses an evil mind. However, the Netherlands and Denmark, for example, do not seem to have this problem. And in recent years, Belgium and France have adopted corporate criminal liability too. While in Germany, corporate liberality is only an administrative one, carrying no penalty more serve than a fine and no registration as a "*criminal*" in the national records.[356]

7.2.1.2 Money Laundering Offence in China and Comparison between the EU and China

Under the 1997 Chinese Criminal Code and the 2001 Amendments to the Criminal Code, the scope of the predicate offence is confined to four kinds of crimes: drug-related crimes, organizational crime of the underworld, smuggling and terrorism. It should be acknowledged that, in addition to these four kinds of crimes, proceeds are also generated from corruption, embezzlement, loan sharking, extortion, fraud, kidnapping, trafficking in human beings, and a host of other offences. Compared with the money laundering legislation in EU countries, it is apparent that EU countries have a wider scope, though improvement still needs to be made. In fact, we must recognize that money laundering is associated with all types of crimes. It is not appropriate to limit money-laundering offences to drug-trafficking proceeds; neither is suit-

---

[353]　See Financial Action Task Force on Money Laundering, *Review of FATF Anti-Money Laundering Systems and Mutual Evaluation Procedures 1992—1999*.

[354]　For an ordinary intended money launderer, the maximum statutory punishment is 4 years, for a habitual launder, the maximum punishment s 6 years. While for a negligent money launderer, the maximum punishment is only 1 year.

[355]　See William C. Gilmore, *Dirty Money, The evolution of money laundering counter-measures*, Council of Europe Press, 1995, p.142.

[356]　See Michael Levi, New Frontiers of Criminal Liability: Money Laundering and Proceeds of Crime, *Journal of Money Laundering Control*, Vol.3 No.3, 2000, p.224.

able to limit it to any type of criminal offences.

As to the mental element of money laundering crime, the Chinese Criminal Code doesn't provide the negligent laundering but merely willful laundering. The mens rea, which prosecutors must prove in connection with money laundering, is knowledge. Specifically speaking, the defendant needs to be proved to know the funds were derived from drug crimes, organizational crime of underworld, terrorism or smuggling. In practice, proving knowledge is very difficult, let alone proving knowing that the proceeds were generated from four kinds of crimes. Moreover, usually there will be no admissions that knowing the money is derived from crimes. In order to prosecute criminals effectively and efficiently, clarity should be provided that knowledge could be inferred form objective circumstances. In addition, taking the experience of some EU countries for reference, negligent money laundering should also be taken into account by legislators. That is to say, the mens rea regarding money laundering offence could be amended so that money laundering offences might be committed if the defendant either knew or ought to have known that the money in question was the proceeds of crime.

Besides, there are some other improvements that could be made in the Chinese criminal code. It should be made clear that no matter which national jurisdiction the predicate offence is committed and whether criminal proceeds are the proceeds of the defendant's offences or of a third party's offences, it will constitute the offence of money laundering.

Though Chinese legal system falls into the civil code system, it is desirable that according to the Chinese Criminal Code, it is possible for an organization to shoulder criminal responsibility. Where an organization commits a money laundering crime, it shall be fined, and the persons who are directly in charge and the other persons who are directly responsible for the crime shall be given criminal punishment. In respect of this issue, corporate criminal liability, it seems that some EU countries have fallen behind. Only administrative fines to a corporate which has committed a serious offence, no other punishment to the leaders of a corporation, is obviously not enough.

7.2.2 Confiscation and Provisional Measures

In most cases, criminals committing crime is to pursue profit. Profit derived from crime not only can be used to finance criminal activities, but also to infiltrate into the legitimate economy. It has been said that criminals don't mind convictions or prison sentences provided they are able to retain their ill-gotten gains. Therefore an effective confiscation system is a very important deterrent to criminal activities. Moreover, an effective confiscation system can take away from criminals the capital to commit further crime and prevent criminals from infiltrating and corrupting the legitimate economy.

7.2.2.1 Confiscation Measures in the EU

All member countries of the EU have legislation concerning the confiscation of the proceeds or instrumentalities of crimes, as well as provisions providing for the seizing or freezing of assets, which may be subject to future confiscation. Generally those provisions worked well, though they vary widely from country to country.

In the EU, all member states except Italy and Spain have systems of value confiscation so that proceeds or instrumentalities cannot escape confiscation despite the fact that their forms have been changed or they have been commingled with other property. Unquestionably, the value confiscation system of EU members is coincident with the requirements under the 1988 Vienna UN Convention, 1990 Strasbourg Convention and the 2000 Palermo Convention as well.

As EU members have a comparatively long history to pay much attention to protecting individual rights, the rights of bona fide third party should be protected during the process of law enforcement. However, a large majority of members have laws that allow the confiscation of the proceeds of crime, or property of equivalent value from third parties who are non-bona fide third parties. These situations are as follows: the person knew that the property was derived from crime; the property was a direct or indirect gift from a defendant; or the property was still subject to the effective control of the defendant, even if held nominally in others' names.[357] For example, in the Netherlands, when dealing with "*the BUCRO case*", the court ruled the seizure and confiscation was barred when the property and assets alleged to be proceeds of crime was owned by a third party legal entity, even if the perpetrator of the criminal offence had

---

[357] See *Financial Action Task Force on Money Laundering Annual Report 1996—1997, Evaluation of laws and systems in FATF members dealing with Asset Confiscation and Provisional measures.*

Chapter 7　Comparison of Anti-money Laundering System between the EU and China

actual control of the assets through the legal entity. This required a subsequent legislative amendment by the Dutch government.[358]

What is very important about the confiscation system is that the confiscated assets sharing measures. Despite the fact that all EU members have criminalized money laundering and have confiscation capabilities, the confiscated assets sharing system is underdeveloped. In a large majority of these countries there is no specific law which allows this, though there is nothing to prohibit it. Most countries require such sharing or receipt of confiscated assets to be made pursuant to a mutual legal assistance agreement. It was reported that there has been little actual experience of asset sharing, though Luxembourg, the United Kingdom and Switzerland have received and shared assets. For most members, there is a restriction that sharing and receipt of assets applies only to cases where the assistance is pursuant to a request to freeze/seize or confiscate assets. It does not extend to situations where the only assistance provided is investigative assistance. However, the Netherlands does share for cases of both judicial and investigative assistance.[359]

As to the burden of proof, for the majority of members the burden of proving that assets are the proceeds of crimes is placed on the government. But it is possible for the court to reverse the burden of proof in some cases in several countries. For instance, in France a provision was introduced in May 1996 that makes it a criminal offence for a person who carries on habitual relations with a drug trafficker or user to be unable to provide evidence of a legitimate source of funds commensurate with his lifestyle. If convicted, then the person's property would be subject to confiscation. In this case the burden of proof is thus reversed for the criminal offence itself.[360] In Italy, Law 356/92 provides that the property of a person who has been convicted of certain offences which relate to the Mafia, such as drug trafficking or extortion, can be liable to confiscation if the person cannot justify the origin of the property and it is disproportionate to the person's legitimate income.[361] In Denmark, a Bill in Novem-

---

[358]　See Financial Action Task Force on Money Laundering, *Review of FATF Anti-Money Laundering Systems and Mutual Evaluation Procedures 1992—1999*.

[359]　See *Financial Action Task Force on Money Laundering Annual Report 1996—1997, Evaluation of laws and systems in FATF members dealing with Asset Confiscation and Provisional measures*.

[360]　Ibid.

[361]　See Financial Action Task Force on Money Laundering, *Review of FATF Anti-Money Laundering Systems and Mutual Evaluation Procedures 1992—1999*.

ber 1996 amended the confiscation legislation and created a measure of reversal of the burden of proof for serious offences.[362] In Austria, reversal of the onus of proof is primarily linked to situations where the defendant is a member of a criminal organization, and if the organization controls the property, it can be confiscated regardless of whether it is legitimately derived or not.[363] Sweden also has similar provisions.

Additionally, some countries applied an easier standard of proof for certain offences than the normal criminal standard to the confiscation proceedings, though the onus has not been reversed. Germany has a concept of extended forfeiture whereby for certain offences, property of the defendant that is not directly linked to a specific offence can be forfeited, if there is a justifiable assumption that it was acquired for or from illegal activity. In Netherlands, the court can take into account proceeds of similar activities to that for which the defendant was convicted if there is reasonable evidence.[364]

7.2.2.2 Confiscation Measures in China and the Gaps between the EU and China

Provisional measures, to seize or freeze property that may be used to prove a criminal suspect's guilt, as well as ultimate confiscation measures have been in the Chinese legal system for many years. Provisional measures are provided under the Chinese Procedure Criminal Code and the power of exercising provisional measures rests on investigative organizations, the public security organs and the people's prosecutor offices, while confiscation measures are parts of the Chinese Criminal Code. The power to confiscate proceeds or instrumentalities of a crime is placed on the people's court. The list of the confiscated property and the reason why the property should be confiscated are stated in the final criminal judgment.

According to the Chinese Criminal Code, the articles that should be confiscated not only include money and property illegally obtained by a criminal, but also contrabands or possessions used in the commission of a crime. Contrabands refer to the articles that are forbidden to be held by citizens, such as drugs, pornography and phony

---

[362] See *Financial Action Task Force on Money Laundering Annual Report 1996—1997*.
[363] See *Financial Action Task Force on Money Laundering, Review of FATF Anti-Money Laundering Systems and Mutual Evaluation Procedures 1992—1999*.
[364] Ibid.

money. Possessions used in the commission of the crime often refer to guilty tools, such as the vehicles for carrying drugs, and deposit for purchasing counterfeit money.

Generally speaking, the Chinese confiscation system is a comparatively traditional and conservative one, which is able to handle simple cases and is not enough to deal with complicated and modern crimes, such as money laundering and other transnational organized crime.

Compared with the EU countries, it is clear that the existing confiscation system of China still has substantial room for improvements. The major deficiencies of the Chinese confiscation system are as follows:

First, there is no special confiscation law dedicated to dealing with money laundering crime or other serious crimes. Just as stated above, the general confiscation system is not enough to cope with these extraordinarily sophisticated crimes.

Second, a value confiscation system has not been set up yet so that criminals have every chance to escape confiscation measures simply by converting the proceeds into other property or intermingling the proceeds with property acquired from legitimate sources.

Third, there are no provisions about protecting the rights of bona fide third parties in confiscation system, nor are there provisions concerning in what cases the assets alleged to be proceeds of crime while owned by a third party should be confiscated. This situation creates double negative results. As China doesn't have a good tradition of respect of human rights, the legitimate rights of a bona fide third party may be sabotaged by the intrusive measures of law enforcement on one side, on the other side, the assets possessed by a non-bona fide third party may eventually escape the confiscation measures.

Fourth, according to the current Chinese Criminal Code, "*all the confiscated money and property and fines shall be turned over to the State treasury, and no one may misappropriate or privately dispose of them*". That is to say, the mechanism of confiscated assets sharing is not put in place in China. This situation will impede the activeness and enthusiasm of competent authorities of other countries or the international organs specializing in the fight against transactional crimes. Therefore, the Chinese government should improve its capability to fight against money laundering on the one hand, and on the other hand, special consideration should be given to contributing the confiscated money and property to intergovernmental bodies specializing in the fight against money laundering crimes or sharing the confiscated money and property with other states. In the same way, at the national level, the institutions which have outstanding achievement in combating money laundering crimes should also be given compensation or economic awards.

Fifth, as to the reversal of the burden of proof, China does have a similar provision under the Crime of Holding a Huge Amount of Property with Unidentified Sources. Article 395 of the 1997 Criminal Code reads: *"Any State functionary whose property or expenditure obviously exceeds his lawful income, if the difference is enormous, may be ordered to explain the sources of his property. If he cannot prove that the sources are legitimate, the part that exceeds his lawful income shall be regarded as illegal gains, and he shall be sentenced to fixed-term imprisonment of not more than five years or criminal detention, and the part of property that exceeds his lawful income shall be recovered."* Since this crime only can be applied to state functionaries, the reversal of the burden of proof is not permissible in most cases. In those cases that have readily identifiable victims, it might not be very difficult to prove to the criminal standard that the defendant has engaged in prior criminal conduct from which he has profited or obtained certain property and linking the proceeds to specific prior criminal activity. But money laundering crime, drug trafficking offences and many other serious offences have no direct victims who can give evidence. And these crimes often create a large amount of wealth. In the case that offenders have a large amount of wealth while it is hardly possible for judicial authorities to sufficiently demonstrate that the possession of the criminals are proceeds from crimes, it should be considered to require an offender to demonstrate the lawful origin of these assets.

7.3 Preventive Measures

7.3.1 Coverage of the Anti-money Laundering Measures

7.3.1.1 Coverage of the Anti-money laundering Measures in the EU

The EC Directive and the 40 Recommendations of FATF, as two preventive approaches, are the leading international instruments in the field of preventing money laundering offences. All the EU countries are members of FATF. Under the influence of the EC Directive and the 40 Recommendations of FATF, the overwhelming majority of EU countries update their preventive measures against money laundering ceaselessly so that they can keep up with the international requirement in the fight against money laundering crime.

As to the coverage of anti-money laundering measures, great progress has been made in EU countries. In the early 1990s, EU members were required to apply the full range of money laundering counter-measures to banks and non-bank financial institutions. Non-bank financial institutions refer to securities firms (stockbrokers), insurance companies, bureaux de change (money changing offices), money remittance services, credit card companies, leasing companies, futures brokers, pensions funds or similar investment companies. According to the second Commission Report to the European Parliament and the Council on the implementation of the Money Laundering Directive, all of the member states not only brought bureaux de change under their anti-money laundering legislation, but also subjected them to some sort of official supervision. Besides, much attention has been paid to the anti-money laundering measures taken by securities firms (stockbrokers), insurance companies and money remittance services.

In the late 1990s, non-financial businesses and professions were required to be subject to anti-money laundering legislation. Non-financial business and professions include casinos and other gambling businesses, dealers in real estate and high value items, lawyers, notaries, accountants and auditors. In order to be in compliance with these requirements, many EU members did make great efforts to make non-financial sector activities be covered by anti-money laundering legislations.

For example, in the United Kingdom, the money laundering regulations cover all persons and institutions, including lawyers and accountants, when undertaking banking, investment or insurance-related business. In France, all persons who professionally advise upon, execute or control operations involving capital movements are obliged to notify the authorities of any transactions which they know to be related to money laundering. In Portugal, anti-money laundering legislation covers casinos, real estates agents (brokers and dealers), real estate management companies, companies organizing gambling or lotteries, antique/art dealers, jewelers, aircraft, boat and car dealers. In Spain, casinos, real-estate management companies, estate agents, jewelers, antique dealers, institutions involved in numismatics and philately are covered by anti-money laundering legislation. In Italy, new legislation adopted in 1997 provides non-financial activities can be brought under the anti-money laundering legislation. In the Netherlands, notaries have announced a voluntary scheme to report very suspicious transactions indicating serious cases of money laundering. Lawyers and accountants already have a similar arrangement.[365] Moreover, since December 2001, large business dealers are also under an obligation of anti-money laundering.[366] On 20 June 2002, Germany enacted broad new money laundering legislation. Under the new law, attorneys, accountants, real estate agents, tax advisors and notaries are brought within its coverage and are required to comply with the anti-money laundering obligations that banks and insurance companies must follow.[367]

7.3.1.2 Coverage of the Anti-money Laundering Measures in China and the Gaps between the EU and China

As mentioned above, in January 2003, the PBC promulgated three rules concerning the measures to be taken by Chinese financial institutions to fight against money laundering. These three rules are primarily to get financial institutions involved. In Article 2 of the Rules for Anti-money Laundering by Financial Institutions, financial institutions are defined as institutions legally established and engaged in financial business within the territory of the PBC, which include banks, credit cooperatives, postal savings institutions, non-bank financial institutions and foreign capital financial institutions.

It is clear that in China, at present, banks and non-bank financial institutions should bear the responsibility of preventing money-laundering activities. It should be recognized that there is a big gap between Chinese legislation and international requirements for this issue. Compared with the situation of anti-money laundering in the EU, not only banks and non-bank financial institutions, but also non-financial persons or entities, such as auditors, external accountants and advisors, real estate agents, notaries and other independent legal professionals, dealers in high-value goods and casinos are covered by the anti-money laundering legislation. This gap is due to

---

[365] See *Second Commission Report to the European Parliament and the Council on the Implementation of the Money Laundering Directive*, Annex 6.

[366] http://www.minjust.nl:8080/c_actual/persber/PB0863, 22 June 2002.

[367] http://www.moneylaundering.com/news.htm#Top, 20 June 2002.

the short history of anti-money laundering campaign in China. While Western countries already have a history of dozens of years of fighting against money laundering, the deterrence of money laundering of our country is just at the initial stage. That is to say, because we don't have much experience in the fight against money laundering, what we should do now is to have the fundamental work done in the first place. Thus focusing on the financial institutions, which are most vulnerable to money laundering activities, is a realistic and sound policy. Certainly, with the experience accumulated, we should take a further step to deter money laundering.

7.3.2 Customer Identification

7.3.2.1 Customer Identification in the EU

Customer identification measures are fundamental parts of any anti-money laundering system. EU members have made considerable progress in implementing customer identification measures and on the whole the identification regimes in EU members are deemed satisfactory.[368]

EU countries recognized that a customer refers to a person as well as an entity. A customer not only means a nominal customer but also refers to a beneficial owner of an account (or the person on whose behalf a transaction is conducted). In general, it is necessary to identify a customer when a new business relationship is established, such as opening an account or saving accounts, or when offering safe custody facilities. However if a transaction involves a large sum, the customer shall be identified. If a relevant institution has reason to suspect that the transaction is an attempt to launder money or is associated with the proceeds of an illegal activity, customer identification shall also be carried out even if the amount of the transaction is lower than the thresholds. In addition, with the development of money laundering schemes, the institutions assuming the obligation of customer identification cover not only banks, non-banks financial institutions, but also non-financial persons and entities.

Due to the influence of the EC Directive and FATF recommendations, identification regimes in EU members are similar, though not identical. For example, cash

---

[368] See *Second Commission Report to the European Parliament and the Council on the implementation of the Money Laundering Directive*.

thresholds for identification in EU members have been fixed at amounts between USD 8000 ~ 15,000. Specifically, France is 8,000; Belgium, Italy is 10,000; the Netherlands is 11,000; Ireland, Portugal is 12,000; Luxembourg, Sweden is 13,000; Denmark, Finland, Germany, Greece, Spain, and United Kingdom is 15,000.[369]

In order to prevent money launderers from structuring large cash transactions (smurfing practices) to invade the threshold, EU members also adopted several measures. For instance, Sweden and United Kingdom have included an interval of time (e.g. within three months) between transactions for smurfing control. In Germany, the Federal Banking Supervisory Office has introduced regulations on the use of automatic cash in-payment machines to combat smurfing.[370]

In view of the facts that, on the one hand, it would be excessively onerous for relevant persons or entities to identify each customer every time, on the other hand, it would be better to allow relevant persons or entities to focus on those customers who really need to be checked, most members provide exemptions for customer identification. Some exemptions are related to particular types of transactions. And some are related to particular types of customers. Unfortunately, the exemptions are not uniform. For example, in Germany, there is no duty of identification if: the transaction takes place between two institutions; a company or its employees regularly pay into or withdraw cash from a company account; or cash is deposited in a night safe.[371] In Italy, the identification obligations do not apply where: the foregoing transactions and business relations take place between approved intermediaries; payments are effected by or to the benefit of the state or public entities; or payments are made to the bailiff in the context of execution proceedings pursuant to article 494 of the Code of Civil Procedure.[372] In addition, Finland, Ireland, and the United Kingdom also give exemptions where payments or transfers for particular purposes, e.g. to pay insurance

---

[369] See Financial Action Task Force on Money Laundering, *Review of FATF Anti-Money Laundering Systems and Mutual Evaluation Procedures 1992—1999*, 16 February 2001, p. 16.

[370] See *Financial Action Task Force on Money Laundering Annual Report 1996—1997, Evaluation of Measures Taken by FATF Member Dealing with Customer Identification.*

[371] See Richard Parlour, *International Guide to Money Laundering, Law and Practice*, Butterworths, 1995, p. 78.

[372] Ibid., p. 101.

premiums, are received from foreign financial or other institutions. [373] In a word, the scope of the exemptions varies from member to member. What is commendable is that for several members, e. g. Denmark, Spain, United Kingdom, the exemptions do not apply where there is any knowledge or suspicion of money laundering. [374]

On the whole, EU members implement customer identification measures quite well. However, it was a fact that passbooks could be opened anonymously by Austria residents in the past. This was the most important and serious exception to identification requirements. Under the pressure both from the European Commission and FATF Group, the Austria government implemented a series of measures that are intended to facilitate the full elimination of the anonymous passbooks, and to prevent any subsequent misuse of passbooks where the holder has not been identified.

Overall, much has been done in the area of customer identification in EU members, but the measures in place still need to be kept under review and improved. For example, when implementing customer identification measures, EU members realized the difficulties for financial institutions to verify the identification of certain types of customers or transactions such as: legal entities, especially overseas private companies; shell companies, trusts and nominee accounts. [375] In recent years, with the rapid development of electronic transactions and financial services through new technology, EU countries also recognized the difficulties in implementing customer identification measures for non-face to face customers. Several members have addressed this issue in their guidance notes, circulars or instructions. Since the problems have been raised, it can be deduced that EU members would make greater efforts to solve the existing knotty problems.

7.3.2.2 Customer Identification in China and Comparison between the EU and China

For a long period of time, Chinese enterprises or institutions should use authentic names to open accounts, but the individuals needn't do so. Because of this, it

---

[373] See Financial Action Task Force on Money Laundering, *Review of FATF Anti-Money Laundering Systems and Mutual Evaluation Procedures 1992—1999*, 16 February 2001, p. 18.

[374] See *Financial Action Task Force on Money Laundering Annual Report 1996—1997, Evaluation of Measures Taken by FATF Member Dealing with Customer Identification.*

[375] Ibid.

was very common for individuals to use false names to open accounts and deposit money. The opening of anonymous accounts has been prohibited since the Regulation of Individual Deposit Account Under Authentic Name Registered came into effect on 1 April 2000. Except this regulation, there was no formal customer identification requirement for financial institutions before 2003.

In 2003 when the customer identification system of EU members already had been in place for more than ten years, the obligation of customer identification in China was formulated under the Rules for Anti-money Laundering by Financial Institutions. Major contents include:

- Financial institutions should verify the identity of a customer when processing financial business including deposits and settlement. For individual customers, financial institutions shall verify the customers' IDs and record the names and ID numbers. For institutional customers, financial institutions shall abide by relevant rules of the PBC and ask the customers to show valid documents for verification and recording.

- Financial institutions are prohibited from providing deposit and settlement services to customers whose identity is yet to be clarified or opening anonymous account or account with a fictitious name.

- If a customer is represented by another person to open a personal deposit account with a financial institution, the financial institution shall verify both the representative's and principal's IDs and record the names and ID numbers thereof.

It is obvious that the customer identification system in China absorbs the minimum requirements of EU members. For example, the customer includes not only individuals but also organizations. Apart from representatives, principals' identity should also be identified.

However, the legislation relating to customer identification in China came into existence only a couple of years ago. A *"culture"* of conducting customer identification is still in the developing stages. Specific issues relating to customer identification and due diligence are only addressed in a general way.

Besides, according to the legislation, it seems that every customer of all transactions should be identified. This practice is different from that of EU countries, which specify the time when financial institutions should perform identification and when customer identification need not be carried out. Considering the fact that it would be excessively onerous for financial institutions to identify each customer every time, it is really essential to specify occasions on which there is a need to identify the customers and what occasions are exempt from customer identification, so that financial institutions can focus on those customers who need to be checked, thus reducing the costs incurred by the efforts to combat money laundering.

In addition, many knotty practical issues haven't been touched by Chinese legislation, such as how to control smurfing practices, how to implement customer identification measures in case of non-face to face contact, how to identify overseas private companies, shell companies and the like. These problems surely will come forth in the process of implementing customer identification measures. Therefore, many problems are still waiting to be overcome.

7.3.3 Suspicious Transaction Reporting[376]

There is no doubt that a large-value/suspicious transaction reporting system has a substantial deterrent effect. And this system *"can be considered as the driving force in anti-money laundering regimes. The result of the system can have an important bearing on how effective a country is combating money laundering"*[377].

7.3.3.1 Suspicious Transaction Reporting System in the EU

Under the influences of the EC Directive as well as the Forty Recommendations, by the end of 1999, all members of the European Union except the Netherlands had a suspicious transaction reporting system for financial institutions, although the precise extent and form of the obligation vary from county to country.[378] The Netherlands has a system based on the reporting of unusual transactions, rather than suspicious transactions. Initially, financial institutions are required to report unusual transactions on the basis of objective or subjective indicators, and the FIU (MOT) then decides if

---

[376] The term "suspicious transaction reporting" is widely accepted by many international documents. In fact, the Netherlands has an unusual transaction reporting system. Besides, in many countries not only suspicious transactions, but also large-value transactions should be reported, such as China. In addition, with the development of the reporting obligation, professionals are now covered by the reporting obligation. Thus it may be better to say "*suspicious activities*" rather than "*suspicious transactions*". For the sake of conciseness, however, this article uses the term "*suspicious transactions reporting*".

[377] Financial Action Task Force on Money Laundering, *Review of FATF Anti-Money Laundering Systems and Mutual Evaluation Procedures 1992—1999*, 16 February 2001, p. 16.

[378] Ibid., p. 18.

the report is suspicious and should be forwarded on to law enforcement. The rationale behind the system of reporting unusual transactions lies in the fact that, *"the staff of financial institutions could not be asked to assess with certainty whether a transaction is suspicious or not. A bank employee's training is not the same as that of a policeman"*.[379]

At present not only financial institutions but also non-financial institutions are required to assume the obligation of suspicious transactions reporting in most EU countries. For example, in the Netherlands, large business dealers are under an obligation of reporting since December 2001. As a result, 63 dealers in vehicles, one ship dealer, four jewel dealers and two art dealers reported a total of 153 unusual transactions to the Dutch National Disclosure Office (MOT) in the first quarter of 2002.[380]

It is hard work to make certain whether transactions are suspicious. Many EU countries adopted the hybrid system, which combines the transaction size reporting systems (objective model) and suspicious transaction reporting systems (subjective model). Germany, Italy and the Netherlands are good examples of this kind of reporting system.

Due to the fact that the subjective criteria is very complicated and varies with the circumstances, as an aid to making this assessment, certain subjective indicators have been published in the Netherlands. The indicators not only serve as criteria for financial institutions to perform duties but also serve as a mechanism to prosecute institutions that have failed to report transactions that meet the criteria. However, in Germany, the Federal Banking Supervisory Authority refused to give an official catalogue of suspicious transactions because it thinks that the publication of such a catalogue might be useful to money launderers for planning action to avoid the detection of money laundering transactions.[381] In Italy, guidelines on various indications may be found in the instructions issued by the Banca d'Italia with the contribution of the Italian Banking Association. These instructions have not been published and are only a-

---

[379] Bert Ravenstijin, The Netherlands: Anti-Money-Laundering Programmes—The Cases of ING, *Journal of Money Laundering Control*, Vol. 3 No. 4, 2000.

[380] http://www.minjust.nl:8080/c_actual/persber/PB0863, 22 June 2002.

[381] See Richard Parlour, *International Guide to Money Laundering, Law and Practice*, Butterworths, 1995, p. 80.

vailable to authorities on request.[382] It can be concluded that whether the subjective indicators should be open to the public varies from country to country in the European Union.

It is clear that the Financial Intelligence Unit (FIU) is a substantial part of a suspicious transactions reporting system. It is commendable that every member of the EU has an operational FIU, though the status of the FIUs varies slightly. Specifically speaking, the three main categories are administrative, police and judicial authorities, though some may be mixed policy/judicial authorities. The breakdown of these FIUs is as follows:[383]

——*Administrative body*: *Belgium, Finland, France, Greece, Italy, the Netherlands, Spain*

——*Police authority*: *Austria, Finland (MILD), Germany, Ireland, Sweden, the UK*

——*Judicial authority*: *Luxembourg, Portugal*

——*Mixed police/judicial authority*: *Denmark*

An administrative body plays the role of a "*buffer*" between the private financial sector and law enforcement and judicial/prosecutorial authorities. This kind of FIU pays much attention to preventing the unnecessary violation of the privacy of citizens and the disruption of relations between financial institutions and their clients. The police authority model facilitates the gathering, exchanging and analysis of information within a specialized police framework, but it may be likely to override individual privacy. And the judicial authority FIU combines the facilities on information access and analysis that the police model provides, with the speed of action both in receiving notice of suspicious activities and prosecuting offences that the judicial authorities offer. However, the perils to civil liberties in the police model are reinforced by the intervention of the judiciary.[384]

Although differing in nature, all FIUs share a common purpose in the fight a-

---

[382] Ibid., p. 103.

[383] See Paolo Clarotti, EU: The Perspective of the European Commission, *Journal of Money Laundering Control*, Vol. 2 No. 2, p. 169.

[384] See Valsamis Mitsilegas, New Forms of Transnational Policing: The Emergence of Financial Intelligence Units in the European Union and the Challenge for Human Rights: Part 1, *Journal of Money Laundering Control*, Vol. 3 No. 2, 1999, pp. 148—154.

gainst money laundering. As a matter of fact, FIUs in EU countries do play a special role in the fight against money laundering, though it should be acknowledged that problems of cooperation and exchanging information do arise due to the different legal nature of the FIUs.

Despite the fact that in general the mechanism of reporting suspicious transactions is well established in the member states of the European Union, there are some problems concerning the implementation of suspicious transactions reporting which need to be taken into account at present. In a large majority of the mutual evaluation reports, the number of suspicious transactions reporting from non-bank financial institutions was only a small percentage of the total number, with the securities and insurance industries making only a small contribution. Some jurisdictions lack an obligation to report when a financial institution choose not to enter into a transaction which is suspected to be linked with money laundering, i. e. attempted money laundering. And the mechanism on how to keep suspicious transactions reporting confidential and how to protect their staff has not been established well in several members. In addition, feedback for suspicious transactions reporting is not sufficient.[385]

7.3.3.2 Suspicious Transaction Reporting System in China and Comparison between the EU and China

Since the suspicious transaction reporting system (including large-value transaction reporting system) in China is a recent legal concept, it is not possible to judge the effectiveness of this system at present. From the legal provisions on paper, the general measures of Chinese reporting system largely comply with the internationals requirements and are similar to the normal standard of EU countries.

The Chinese reporting system combines a large-value transaction reporting system, which is deemed as an objective model, with a suspicious transaction reporting system, a subjective one. As mentioned before, in terms of the large-value transaction reporting system, various quantity standards are designed on the basis of different transactions. RMB large-value transactions and large-value foreign exchange transactions, individuals' large-value transactions and institutions' large-value transactions,

---

[385] See Financial Action Task Force on Money Laundering, *Review of FATF Anti-Money Laundering Systems and Mutual Evaluation Procedures 1992—1999*, 16 February 2001. p. 19.

and cash large-value transactions and non-cash large-value transactions, all of them have different quantity standards of "*large value*". Thus it can be said the provisions of large-value transaction reporting system is scientific and practical.

As to the suspicious transactions reporting system, Chinese legislators offered some very concrete indicators of suspicious transactions in those administrative rules. Suspicious transactions are divided into RMB suspicious transactions and foreign exchange suspicious transactions; cash suspicious transactions and non-cash suspicious transactions. All indicators are provided publicly. These indicators are useful for financial institutions to follow and can facilitate financial institutions to judge whether the transaction is suspicious or not. However, with public indicators available, potential criminals might take advantage of legal loopholes and circumvent relevant countermeasures.

According to those rules which came into effect in March 2003, the PBC and the State Administration of Foreign Exchange (SAFE) shall receive and analyze the report of large-value and suspicious transactions, and shall hand over the report and other related materials to the judiciary departments if criminal activities are suspected after conducting a review of such report and related materials. In addition, failing to report a large-value or a suspicious transaction will result in administrative responsibility. Administrative responsibility includes warning, fining and disqualifying. When the misconduct constitutes a violation of the criminal law, the case shall be transferred to judiciary authorities and criminal responsibility is inevitable.[386]

Compared with EU member states, there are some obvious deficiencies with the Chinese reporting system. First, the obligation of large-value/suspicious transaction reporting hasn't been imposed on non-financial institutions but only on financial institutions alone. Since money laundering can be carried out not only through financial institutions but also through other types of professional services and categories of undertakings, with the fight against money laundering deepening in China, non-financial institutions should also shoulder the obligation of large-value/suspicious transaction reporting. Second, an FIU hasn't been established in China. Since an opera-

---

[386] See *Administrative Rules for the Reporting of Large-value and Suspicious RMB Payment Transactions*, Article 24; *Administrative Rules for the Reporting by Financial Institutions of Large-value and Suspicious Foreign Exchange Transactions*, Article 20.

tional FIU is a necessary part of a large-value/suspicious transaction reporting system, the effectiveness of reporting system is likely to be severely limited by the lack of an FIU. Thus, an FIU is indispensable in China. Third, some sensitive issues, such as whether to report attempted money laundering, how to keep suspicious transactions reporting confidential and to protect their staff, and how to make feedback for suspicious transactions reporting sufficient, all haven't attracted much attention from Chinese legislators as well as law-executors. These problems encountered by EU members certainly will have an influence on the implementation of the Chinese suspicious transaction reporting system. For this reason, it is better to agree upon solutions for these issues in the beginning of the implementation of the reporting system.

7.3.4 Awareness Raising, Training and Supervision

Awareness of money laundering problems, such as what is money laundering, how criminals launder money and what are vulnerable links to money laundering, is the precondition of winning the fight against money laundering. Appropriate training programs can help staff recognize operations which may be related to money laundering as well as to instruct them as to how to proceed in such cases. Strict supervision carried out by competent authorities is the guarantee of the effectiveness of an anti-money laundering system. Although they fall into complementary measures, other substantial measures could become ineffective without these supplementary measures.

7.3.4.1 Awareness Raising, Training and Supervision in the EU

EU member states paid much attention to these issues ten years ago. In the middle of the 1990s, there were guidelines and training programs in place for banks in almost all EU countries. Guidelines for banks are generally very satisfactory. However, for non-bank financial institutions, the level of awareness of money laundering issues was generally much lower than for banks. Some countries such as Italy, Portugal and Sweden were encouraged by the FATF to realize that the use of guidelines developed for banks is neither useful nor appropriate for insurance companies, bureaux de change etc.[387]

---

[387] See *Financial Action Task Force on Money Laundering*, *Review of FATF Anti-Money Laundering Systems and Mutual Evaluation Procedures 1992—1999*, 16 February 2001. p. 24.

The Netherlands is a good example in raising awareness of money laundering problems for non-bank financial institutions. In the insurance and securities sectors, reports were published on measures that could be taken to improve the identification of unusual transactions and possible examples of how money laundering might take place. These reports were good examples of seeking to identify the potential risk areas and agree upon solutions before the problems arose in real life.[388]

Apart from official guidelines providing education and training for financial institutions and other bodies, a number of resources concerning money laundering and anti-money laundering measures are available in EU members, such as information circulars, guidelines, annual reports, videos, newsletters, brochures, fliers and posters. Some member states operate a website on which all this information is readily available.

As to the question of supervision, whether supervision for money laundering purposes is adequate is closely linked to the issue of whether adequate measures have been taken to prevent credit and financial institutions from being acquired or controlled by criminals. It is also linked to whether there is a requirement to register or license financial institutions. In all EU member countries, there are checks on the shareholders and senior management of credit institutions, securities brokers and insurance companies, and this is a part of a prudent supervision regime. A positive suggestion in this area was made in a Norwegian report, where it is recommended that, if supervisory authorities have responsibility for checking fitness and properness, they should be able to obtain assistance from law enforcement authorities. This could help determining whether a person has a record or whether there may be other intelligence on him.[389]

In addition, EU members conduct direct supervision for banking, insurance and securities sectors. Most supervisors check the anti-money laundering controls and procedures that the financial institution has in place. However, some also do random spot checks on individual files to determine whether the rules are being applied. Usually, money laundering checks are just a part of the regular overall prudent supervision, but some members also conduct specific anti-money laundering audits. These

---

[388] Ibid.
[389] Ibid., p.25.

mechanisms help to ensure that financial institutions have strong controls in place. Some members also issue questionnaires as a means of seeking further information on the controls in place.[390]

Although the complementary measures, awareness raising, training and supervision in EU members are generally satisfactory, there is an absolute need for continuing action to deepen and widen these measures. Non-bank financial institutions, securities firms, insurance companies, bureaux de change, money remittance services, credit card companies, need to be educated and regulated as strictly and effectively as banks have been. Besides, with the expanded coverage of anti-money laundering obligations, not only financial institutions but also non-financial institutions, such as casinos and other gambling businesses, dealers in real estate and high value items, lawyers, notaries, accountants and auditors, all need good education, enough training and strict supervision. Due to the various natures of these professions, different trade associations shall be heavily involved in promoting education, training and supervision.

7.3.4.2 Awareness Raising, Training and Supervision in China and Progress Yet to Be Made

Article 7 of the Rules for Anti-money Laundering by Financial Institutions provides that the PBC is the supervisory authority for anti-money laundering operations by financial institutions. The PBC shall establish a leading group supervising the work of anti-money laundering by financial institutions. Besides, Article 19 reads, the PBC shall provide guidance and organize training activities on the subject of anti-money laundering for financial institutions. Financial institutions shall launch anti-money laundering publicity among their customers and provide training for their staff on anti-money laundering so as to familiarize them with laws, administrative rules and regulations on anti-money laundering and strengthen their competence in combating money laundering activities.

It is obvious that general provisions about the supplementary measures have been formulated. These provisions designate the supervisory authority for anti-money laundering operations and make clear the role and responsibility of the PBC as well as fi-

---

[390] Ibid., p. 26.

nancial institutions. However, much work needs to be done. Since financial institutions cover a wide scope, which include policy banks, commercial banks, credit cooperatives, postal savings institutions, finance companies, trust and investment companies, financial leasing companies and foreign-funded financial institutions etc., guidelines and training programs developed for banks may not suitable for non-bank financial institutions. Thus it is important to suit the remedy to the case. Besides, the way to raise awareness within financial institutions of money laundering problems and provide training for their staff should be as multifarious as possible. Apart from official guidelines, annual reports, videos, newsletters, brochures, fliers, and posters concerning money laundering problems should be available.

In regard to supervision, most importantly, measures should be put in place to prevent criminals from acquiring and controlling financial institutions. Thus a rigid registration or licensing regime for financial institutions should be established. Underground money shop should be banned completely. And shareholders and senior management of financial institutions should be scrutinized. Besides, supervisory authority—the PBC should conduct both off and on-site inspections to ensure that financial institutions have strong control in place. Examinations conducted by the PBC may constitute a part of the regular overall prudent supervision, but specific anti-money laundering audits should also be conducted frequently. If these fundamental works have been conducted well, the next step how to guarantee enough and effective education, training and supervision for non-financial institutions should be taken into account.

7.4 Conclusions

With the fight against money laundering deepening in the international community, China has made significant progress in combating and preventing money laundering in recent years. In other words, it has established a money laundering offence for several serious crimes; it already has a confiscation system not only for money laundering crimes but also for other crimes; it has established identification requirements for customers and it has established a mandatory large-value/suspicious transaction reporting system. However, compared with the standards set up in EU countries, predicate offences of money laundering need to be widened and the confiscation system also should be improved to meet international standards. In addition, we should not be complacent over just formulating several rules but should endeavor to implement these rules, thus an FIU should be set up in China to facilitate the implementation of suspicious transaction reporting and customer identification measures should also be elaborated to respond to non-face to face transactions, smurfing practices and the like. To make these substantial measures effective, awareness raising, staff training and supervision of competent authority should also be actually put in place. That is to say, despite the notable progress made in the past, there is still an absolute need for continuing action in China to deepen and widen the fight against money laundering.

Chapter 8

Several Special Issues

8.1 Banking Secrecy and Money Laundering

8.1.1 Introduction

Money laundering is getting increasingly serious. The existence of banking secrecy provides a safe harbor for money launderers. This part first introduces the origin and foundation of banking secrecy. It then discusses the reasons why banking secrecy should be lifted in the fight against money laundering and in what cases banking secrecy should be lifted. Also it presents the conflict between retaliating against money laundering and protecting banking secrecy. Finally it points out that we should make a balance between fighting against crimes and protecting individual rights.

8.1.2 Origin and Foundation of Banking Secrecy

Although the meaning of banking secrecy is widely understood, there is no explicit definition at the international level. In respect of a financial institution, banking secrecy is a professional obligation and a right, which means financial institutions assume an obligation that they shall not, on the one hand, expose a customer's financial information acquired in the course of business, and on the other hand, financial institutions have the right to resist the third party's enquiries in order to protect the customers' interests. In respect of a customer, banking secrecy is a privilege, which means that the customer's financial information should be protected legally and should not be invaded by other parties.

The first effective banking secrecy statue was created in Switzerland and this case resulted form a particular episode in history. In the 1930s, the Nazi Government prohibited a German Jew's movement of assets out of Germany, in order to seize those assets. Because of the geographic proximity and Switzerland's then unofficial policy of confidentiality over banking deposits and transactions, Swiss banks were chosen for Jews to transfer their assets. In 1933, the Nazi Government enacted a decree, which stated, "*any German national who, deliberately or otherwise, activated by a base selfishness or any other vile motive, has amassed his wealth abroad or left capital outside the country, shall be punished by death*". One year after the law's enactment, three German Jews were executed. These executions, as well as the pressure put on Swiss Bank employees for information by German Gestapo agents, persuaded the Swiss Government to codify its practice of maintaining the confidentiality of its customers' accounts. Thus the first banking secrecy law came into being.[391]

At present, there are many reasons for a desire of such secrecy. According to one commentator: "*Secrecy laws have served to shield persons from financial loss in countries plagued by instability, weak currency and run-away inflation rate. Secrecy laws have also served to protect wealthy individuals or those who promote unpopular political causes by allowing them to hide their assets to avoid the threat of kidnapping or persecution.*"[392] In addition, banking secrecy can prevent commercial competitors from trying to discover financial information about their adversaries. And parents and grandparents can also make use of bank secrecy to avoid their potential heirs knowing about their inheritance in advance.

Although the notion of banking secrecy is accepted in most countries, the justifications differ widely. One view regards banking secrecy as a part of individual privacy

---

[391] See George J. Moscarino and Michael R. Shumaker, Beating the shell Game: Banking Secrecy laws and Their Impact on Civil Recovery in International Fraud Actions, *Journal of Money laundering Control*, Vol. 1 No. 1, 1997, p. 42.

[392] Ernesto U. Savona, *Responding to Money Laundering, International Perspectives*, Harwood Academic Publishers, 1997, p. 185, Note 344.

right.[393] It is a fact that banking secrecy is closely related to individual privacy. An individual's banking information directly reflects the individual's economic situations. Stocks, insurance, retirement funds, loan and mortgages are all discoverable from financial records. Banking information also mirrors an individual's personal interests. With access to banking records, the books and publications and the material items that the individual purchased all become visible. Furthermore, banking information can reflect an individual's political beliefs. With access to banking records, it becomes clear which groups and associations the individual belongs to, and which political party and causes the individual supported.[394]

One point of view considers banking confidentiality "*contractual in nature*"[395]. A financial institution, as one party to the transaction, should be loyal to customers in terms of the principle of good faith and should not disclose customers' financial information to others.

Another viewpoint deems banking secrecy to be professional secrecy. Some commentators have attempted to justify banking secrecy laws by analogy with the common law privileges of lawyer-client or doctor-patient.[396] Clients can disclose all information to lawyers without worrying about being denounced. In order to prescribe a suitable remedy, doctors should be told the whole truth about an illness. The relationship between financial institutions and customers is the same.

Due to the different justifications for banking secrecy, its legal protection varies from country to country. In some countries, there are no specific statutory provisions

---

[393] In the modern world, the individual's right to privacy is an international human right. It is not only fixed by most countries under their constitutional law, civil law or judge-made law, but also formulated in many international human rights agreements. For example, under the Universal Declaration of Human Rights, Article 12 reads, "*No one shall be subject to arbitrary interference in his privacy, family, home, or correspondence ...* " Under the International Covenant on Civil and Political Rights, Article 17 reads, "*no one shall be subject to arbitrary or unlawful interference with his privacy ...* " and Article 8 of the European Convention for the Protection of Human Rights and Fundamental Freedom also reads, "*everyone has the right to respect for his private and family life, his home and correspondence.* " Individual privacy is respected at a high priority, however, it is not absolute at any time, especially when individual privacy collides with national interest and social order.

[394] See Robert Pasley, Privacy Rights V. Anti-Money Laundering Enforcement, *2002 University of North Carolina School of Law Banking Institute North Carolina Banking Institute*, April 2002.

[395] Peter Maynard, Bahamas, Civil Liberties and Privacy—The Questions of Balance, *Journal of Money Laundering Control*, Vol. 1 No. 2, p. 177.

[396] See George J. Moscarino and Michael R. Shumaker, Beating the Shell Game: Banking Secrecy Laws and Their Impact on Civil Recovery in International Fraud Actions, *Journal of Money Laundering Control*, Vol. 1 No. 1, 1997, p. 47.

that impose a confidentiality obligation on banks or other financial institutions. The only obligation concerning secrecy is an assumed one, based on contract law, such as in the Netherlands.[397] The financial institutions have a contractual obligation of loyalty to uphold the banker-client privilege. In some countries, banking secrecy is covered by a series of laws and regulations. Banking secrecy is based on the right to personal privacy, which is a personal right. Thus banking secrecy can be considered an element within the sphere of personal privacy, as it is in the USA.[398] In some countries, banking secrecy is not only mandatory under the civil codes based on the right to personal privacy and contract laws based on the principle of good faith, but also protected by criminal laws. A violation of bank secrecy is subject to criminal sanctions. This "*public law*" strengthens and reaffirms the importance of the banker-client privilege established in the "*private laws*". For example, in Switzerland, both the intentional and negligent disclosure of secret banking information is punishable by criminal penalties.[399] As a result of the strict protection of banking secrecy, Switzerland is perfectly placed to attract foreign capital. Although Switzerland has less than 0.03 percent of the world's population, it is the world's third largest financial power.[400]

No matter which justification is relied on and which form is adopted for banking secrecy, it should be borne in mind that banking secrecy is not to be exploited to protect illegal interests but rather for its legal benefits. However, it is a fact that the existence of banking secrecy has indeed some negative influence. For example, the situation described above, where the enactment of the banking secrecy decree in Switzerland was proposed for protecting the Jewish legal assets. Because a large number of Jews were slaughtered and millions, possibly even billions, of dollars had been deposited in Swiss banks, the existence of banking secrecy prohibited family members of

---

[397] See Hans de Doelder, Vincent Mul, Marije van den Enden, Regulation of Financial Markets with Particular Reference to Market Abuse: A Perspective from the Netherlands. *Netherlands Reports to the Fifteenth International Congress of Comparative Law*, Bristol 1998.

[398] See John J. Byrne, Know Your Customer: What Happened and What Happens Next, *Journal of Money Laundering Control*, Vol. 3 No. 4, 2000, p. 348.

[399] See Marc G. Corrado, The Supreme Court's Impact on Swiss Banking Secrecy: Societe Nationale Industrielle Aerospatiale v. United States District Count, *1988 the American University Law Review*, Spring, 1988.

[400] See George J. Moscarino and Michael R. Shumaker, Beating the shell Game: Banking Secrecy laws and Their Impact on Civil Recovery in International Fraud Actions, *Journal of Money laundering Control*, Vol. 1 No. 1, 1997, p. 48.

those Jews who died in the Holocaust from discovering what funds had been deposited and the ultimate retrieval of those funds. In figurative terms, the shield that once protected the Jews' assets from the Nazis had now become a sword in the side of their successors.[401]

At present, nobody can deny that banking secrecy is the most significant weapon for money launderers. Switzerland, Luxemburg, Panama, Hong Kong, Grand Cayman Islands, Netherlands Antilles and Bahamas are all referred as notoriety "*bank secrecy heavens*" and these jurisdictions really make the crime of money-laundering much more serious and rampant.[402]

8.1.3 The Challenge of Anti-money Laundering Measures

In 1990, the FATF estimated that as much as $ 85bn per year in drug proceeds could be available for laundering in the USA and Europe.[403] In 1992, one US law enforcement agency put the total figure for US drug and non-drug-related money laundering at $ 300bn annually.[404] In 1996, the United Nations estimated that US $ 1 billion daily was involved in money laundering. The Commercial Crime Bureau of the international Chamber of Commerce believes this figure to be greatly understated.[405] With regard to terrorism alone, the amount of money involved is surprisingly large. As Deputy Secretary of the Treasury Kenneth Dam testified: "*Since September 11, the*

---

[401] See George J. Moscarino and Michael R. Shumaker, Beating the shell Game: Banking Secrecy laws and Their Impact on Civil Recovery in International Fraud Actions, *Journal of Money laundering Control*, Vol. 1 No. 1, 1997, p. 48.

[402] However, with international efforts against money laundering, these jurisdictions also have made efforts to establish and improve their anti-money laundering systems. For example, in 2000, a new regulation was introduced in Hong Kong, which requires banks to report suspicious transactions. There were 6,100 suspicious transactions report in 2000 and 95 percent of them were from banks. (http://www. hongkong. org/press/ny-021400. htm, 15 August 2001.) Another example, two anti-money laundering decrees were enacted in Panama on 3 October 2000, which provide that banks, cooperatives, stock exchanges and other financial institutions should take steps to fight money laundering. Anyone whose behavior violates the new decrees shall be sentenced to imprisonment of not less than five years but not more than 12 years, or shall be fined not less than $ 5,000 but not more than $ 1million. See *People's Police News*, 11 October 2000.

[403] See *Financial Action Task Force on Money Laundering Annual Report 1990*, at I (A).

[404] See *US Treasury Dept Financial Crimes Enforcement Network Assessment of US Money Laundering: Submission to the Financial Action Task Force 2 (1994)*.

[405] See International Chamber of Commerce, Guide to the Prevention of Money Laundering, *Journal of Commerce 4*, June 1998.

United States and other countries have frozen more than $ 80 million in terrorist—related assets."[406]

Money laundering activity attracts a great deal of attention at international level not only because of its growing rampancy, but also because of its potential damage to the whole society. It can undermine the integrity of financial institutions and thus undermine public confidence in the financial system. Money laundering can facilitate underlying crime to self-finance, diversify and grow by allowing criminal funds to be reinvested. Money laundering can also have a corrosive influence on economic development and political stability.

Money laundering is a serious crime, and it is therefore essential to understand where it is at its most vulnerable. At present criminals will tend to seek more sophisticated and complex techniques, as a result of strong anti-money laundering legislation, regulation and practices. However, the most common method of money laundering is through financial systems. This phenomenon, to a certain extent, is due to the increasing liberalization and integration of world financial markets, the removal of barriers to the free movement of capital. Apart from these reasons, it is obvious that banking secrecy is particularly exposed to money laundering offences. Banks that offer private banking service provide the greatest opportunities for money launderers.

Money laundering is an international crime and criminals often take advantage of differences between national jurisdictions and the existence of international boundaries. Therefore, enhancing cooperation between enforcement agencies, financial institutions and other competent authorities is critical. Since most money laundering activities take place for economic reasons, it is also important to make provisional measures and ultimate confiscation orders more effective in order to eliminate their main incentive and bring the criminals to book in a very firm way. In addition, money launderers often utilize advanced techniques and turn to professional knowledge. Money laundering schemes are not easily discovered. Therefore it is essential to establish perfect and sound preventive measures. This requires banks and other financial institutions to perform with due diligence in the course of business, such as customer identification, record keeping and suspicious transactions reporting. All these

---

[406] Financial War on Terrorism and Implementation of Money-Laundering Provisions in the USA Patriot Act: Hearing of the Senate Banking, *Housing and Urban Affairs Committee*', 107th Congress.

plus international cooperation, provisional measures and confiscation orders and the due diligence of financial institutions challenge the issue of banking secrecy. Herein lies the problem—which is more important, banking secrecy or the fight against money laundering?

8.1.4 The Lifting of Banking Secrecy

Although banking secrecy is an important part of individual privacy, which is highly valued and considered a performance of good faith, it is equally important to continue the fight against money laundering in order to ensure a safe and secure society. For this reason, it is widely accepted that banking secrecy is not absolute and in certain cases should be lifted. In fact, lifting banking secrecy has already been embodied in the most important international documents: the 1988 Vienna UN Convention, the 1990 Strasbourg Convention, the 2000 Palermo UN Convention, the EC Directive and the FATF 40 Recommendations.

Specifically, under the 1988 Vienna UN Convention, the 1990 Strasbourg Convention and the 2000 Palermo UN Convention, each country should empower the court or other authorities to order that bank, financial or commercial records be made available or be seized. A party cannot refuse to act on the grounds of banking secrecy.[407] In addition, when dealing with mutual legal assistance, each party cannot invoke banking secrecy as a ground for refusing cooperation.[408] These provisions are intended to prevent banking secrecy laws from obstructing either forfeiture proceedings or the investigation and prosecution of money laundering crimes.

Under the FATF Recommendations and the EC Directive, banking secrecy should also be lifted by the requirement that financial institutions "*get to know*" their customers, report large transactions, and make inquires into suspicious transactions. Specifically, in respect of customer identification, the FATF Recommendations provide that financial institutions should be required to identify and record the identity of

---

[407] See *United Nations Convention Against Illicit Traffic in Narcotic Drugs and Psychotropic Substances*, Article 5 (3); *1990 Council of Europe Convention on Laundering, Search, Seizure and Confiscation of the Proceeds from Crime*, Article 4 (1); *United Nations Convention against Transnational Organized Crime*, Article12 (6).

[408] See *United Nations Convention Against Illicit Traffic in Narcotic Drugs and Psychotropic Substances*, Article 7 (5); *1990 Council of Europe Convention on Laundering, Search, Seizure and Confiscation of the Proceeds from Crime*, Article 18 (7); *United Nations Convention against Transnational Organized Crime*, Article18 (8).

their clients, either occasionally or habitually, when establishing business relations or conducting transactions[409]. Similarly, the EC Directive also requires the identification of customers and beneficial owners when entering into business relations.[410] In respect of unusual transactions reporting, the FATF Recommendations instruct that financial institutions should pay special attention to all complex, unusual or large transactions, which have no apparent economic or visible lawful purpose. The background and purpose of such transactions should be examined, the findings established in writing, and be available to help supervisors, auditors and law enforcement agencies. If financial institutions suspect that funds stem from criminal activity, they should be required to report their suspicions promptly to the competent authorities.[411] In the same way, the EC Directive stipulates that financial institutions should cooperate fully with authorities by informing those authorities of any fact which might be an indication of money laundering, and by furnishing those authorities with all the necessary information.[412] In respect of record keeping, the FATF Recommendations stipulate that financial institutions should maintain all necessary records on transactions for at least five years, to enable them to comply with requests for information from competent authorities[413]. In like manner, the EC Directive provides that financial institutions must keep the identification material and transaction records for use as evidence in any investigation into money laundering for at least five years.[414]

From the above overview, it is clear where banking secrecy should be lifted in the fight against money laundering. In short, it should be lifted in two situations: one is under the Vienna UN Convention, the Strasbourg Convention and the Palermo UN Convention, that is in the course of confiscation and international cooperation procedures; the other is under the FATF Recommendations and the EC Directive, that is in the course of due diligence of financial institutions. The former is for the purpose

---

[409]　See *The FATF Recommendations on Money Laundering* (1996), Recommendation 10.

[410]　See *Council Directive of 10 June 1991 on Prevention of the Use of the Financial System for the Purpose of Money Laundering*, Article 3 (1).

[411]　See *The FATF Recommendations on Money Laundering* (1996), Recommendations 14, 15.

[412]　See *Council Directive of 10 June 1991 on Prevention of the Use of the Financial System for the Purpose of Money Laundering*, Article 6 (1).

[413]　See *The FATF Recommendations on Money Laundering* (1996), Recommendation 12.

[414]　See *Council Directive of 10 June 1991 on Prevention of the Use of the Financial System for the Purpose of Money Laundering*, Article 4.

of suppression, the latter for prevention. Both methods of lifting banking secrecy are accepted in many countries.

In the first situation, for example, even in Switzerland, which is usually considered to be "*secrecy heaven*", there are public law exceptions to banking secrecy. Both the Swiss Federal Code of Criminal Procedure and the Swiss Federal Code of Civil Procedure impose a public duty to testify as well as to produce documents, and neither law exempts bankers from its requirements.[415] This example demonstrates the fact that at the national level, the principle of banking secrecy should give way to law enforcement authorities in the performance of provisional measures, and the principle of banking secrecy should be overridden by the obligations to cooperate as required by procedure laws.

In the second situation, lifting banking secrecy in the course of due diligence by financial institutions is popular in many countries. Financial institutions in all EU member states are required to consider the origin of their customer's money, cooperate with law enforcement agencies on their own initiative, and expose suspicious transactions of their customers, without alerting them to this fact. China also adopted some rules concerning these requirements recently. It should be noted that these measures are revolutionary and innovative and remarkably different from traditional banking system. Traditionally, the relations between financial institutions and customers were based on the confidentiality of the relationship: the banker did not ask questions; the customer did not make disclosures. However, now the situation has changed, and the mindset of both bank directors and employees must change with it, as well as that of supervisory authorities.[416]

8.1.5 Banking Secrecy in China

In China, banking secrecy is provided under the Law on Commercial Banks, which was adopted at the 13th Meeting of the Standing Committee of the Eighth Na-

---

[415] However, the Swiss Federal law on Administrative Procedure allows banks to invoke the secrecy privilege to protect professional secrets. See Marc G. Corrado, The Supreme Court's Impact on Swiss Banking Secrecy: Socite Nationale Industrielle Aerospatiale V. United States District Court, *1988 the American University Law Review*, Spring, 1988.

[416] See Gil Galvao, Countering Money Laundering: The FATF, The European Union and the Portuguese Experiences, Past and Current Developments, *Work Product of the 117 International Seminar*.

tional People's Congress, and came into force as of 1 July 1995. It appears that banking secrecy in China is based on the principle of good faith and is contractual in nature.

Article 29 of the Law on Commercial Banks of China states: *"In handling savings deposits for individuals, commercial banks shall adhere to the principles of voluntary deposit, unimpeded withdrawal, interest payment on deposits and confidentiality for the depositors."* This means that bank secrecy concerns not only part of professional ethics, which financial institutions must comply with, but is also a legal obligation mandated by law. Moreover, commercial banks will assume civil liability if the property of depositors is damaged as a result of the commercial banks' failure to implement the obligation of banking secrecy.[417] Besides, commercial banks may be charged with the crime of infringement of business secrecy if they cause heavy losses to the obligee.[418]

But the principle of bank confidentiality has exceptions. Article 29 (2) under the Law on Commercial Banks states: *"Commercial banks shall have the right to refuse to answer the inquires into and to refuse to freeze, deduct or transfer an individual's savings deposits—as made or requested by any organization or individual, except where otherwise provided for by laws."* And Article 30 again states: *"Commercial banks shall have the right to refuse to answer the inquires into an organization's deposits by any other organization or individual, except where otherwise provided for by laws and administrative rules and regulations, and shall have the right to refuse to freeze, deduct or transfer an organization's deposits as requested by any other organization or individual, except where otherwise provided for by laws."* In addition, under the Rules for Anti-money Laundering by Financial Institutions, which came into force in March 2003, Article 6 states: *"Financial institutions shall assist the judiciary and/or law enforcement departments including the customs and tax authorities in combating money laundering in accordance to relevant laws and regulations through making inquiry of, freezing or suspending the transfer of suspicious customers' deposits."*

These articles announce two key points of the principle of banking secrecy: on the one hand, banking secrecy is not only a legal obligation of financial institutions to

---

[417] See *Law of the People's Republic of China on Commercial Banks*, Article 73.
[418] Ibid., Article 76; See also *Criminal Law of the People's Republic of China*, Article 219.

protect the rights of depositors, but also gives the legal right to refuse to answer illegal inquires into clients' savings deposits and to refuse to freeze, deduct or transfer clients' savings deposits by any other organization or individual; on the other hand, banking secrecy is not absolute but does have exceptions.

According to Chinese laws and regulations, there are 11 institutions that have the right to enquire into an individual's savings deposits. They are the People's Court, People's Procuratorate, Public Security Sector, State Security Organization, Army, Customs, Tax Authority, Auditing Office, Administrative Organization for Industry and Commerce, Supervisory Department and Notary Organization. And there are 12 institutions that hold the right to enquire into an organization's savings deposits. Apart from the above mentioned sectors, the Commission for Disciplinary Inspection also holds this right in terms of the Regulations on Inspecting Cases of Commission for Disciplinary Inspection of the Chinese Communist Party.[419] The institutions that hold the right to freeze the savings deposits of organizations or individuals are seven in number: the People's Court, Public Security Sector, State Security Organization, Army, Customs and Tax Authority. And there are three institutions that can transfer savings deposits: the People's Court, Customs and Tax Authority.[420]

The preceding description makes it clear that banking secrecy should be lifted in a suppression procedure. Apart from this, banking secrecy should also be lifted during a course of prevention. As stated in Chapter 5, in 2003, the PBC promulgated three rules, namely Rules for Anti-money Laundering by Financial Institutions, Administrative Rules for the Reporting of Large-Value and Suspicious RMB Payment Transactions, and Administrative Rules for the Reporting by Financial Institutions of Large-Value and Suspicious Foreign Exchange Transactions. These three rules draw fully on international experience for reference and provide guidance for Chinese financial institutions in the fight against money laundering. Under these rules, concrete obligations for financial institutions are formulated, such as customer identification, record keeping and large-value/suspicious transaction reporting. The measures should be effective in helping to lift bank secrecy, however, these obligations for financial institutions have arrived very recently in China, and it is as yet impossible to judge

---

[419] http://www.szptt.net.cn/9810jrzq/JRZS/012.htm, November 2001.
[420] http://www.shenyou.com.cn/jrzs/khck.htm/, November 2001.

the effectiveness of their implementation.

8.1.6 The Conflict between Banking Privacy and the Fight against Crime

It is evident that protecting banking privacy is in conflict with the fight against money laundering crime. In the modern world, every country that has sound and honest political, judicial and legal systems values the right of individual privacy and gives it a high priority. The level of respecting individual privacy is considered a norm when judging the level of democracy and rule of law of any country. However, at the same time, with the ever-growing gravity of drug trafficking, smuggling, the mafia, terrorism, money laundering and other serious crimes, governments have to adopt intrusive measures to strengthen the force of suppression, such as lifting banking secrecy under certain circumstances. Since *"crimes can't be totally stopped, the questions arises as to how far a country can or should go"*[421]? This leads to the question of balance. What is the proper balance between protecting banking privacy and fighting money laundering crimes? Finding the right balance between the two potentially competing interests is critical, although it also is very difficult.

It is interesting to note that, after the proposals concerning the Know Your Customer (KYC) principle[422] unveiled on 7 December 1998 in USA, the public reacted strongly to the perceived privacy concerns. Letters from customers carried similar themes such as *"I resent the government requiring banks to create a system to detect transactions they deem to be 'unusual' for me and then to investigate the circumstances of my transaction in order to determine whether the bank should report me as a possible criminal."* As of 8 March 1999, the banking agencies had received between them over

---

[421] Richard Parlour, *International Guide to Money Laundering, Law and Practice*, Butterworths, 1995, p. 138.

[422] The Know Your Customer program provides a system for: determining the identity of the bank's customers; determining the customer's sources of funds for transactions involving the bank; determining the particular customer's normal and expected transactions involving the bank; monitoring customer transactions to determine if such transactions are consistent with normal and expected transactions for that particular customer of for customers in the same or similar categories of classes, as established by the bank; identifying customer transactions that do not appear to be consistent with normal and expected transactions for that particular customer or for customers in the same or similar categories or classes, as established by the bank; and determining if a transaction is unusual or suspicious, in accordance with the agency's suspicious activity reporting regulations, and reporting accordingly.

250,000 letters of comment.[423] This example reflects the fact that, at that time, the public regarded individual privacy as more important than due efforts of crime fighting.

However, after the 11 September 2001, terrorist attacks on the USA, the situation changed substantially. When entering a government building, passing through the customs or getting on a plane, no matter how thorough the search is, the public considers it normal and understands the reason. Airlines or customs officials can examine bags at random, remove all material from baggage, and question people thoroughly and intrusively. In order to support the needs of law enforcement, providing blood samples, examples of handwriting and voiceprints is not viewed as an unconstitutional invasion of privacy.[424] After all, everyone knows that privacy interests are highly valued, so are safety and security.

These two adverse examples which took place in one country (the first occurred in the course of legislation, and the next in the process of law enforcement), suitably highlight the phenomenon that preserving privacy rights and fighting crime constitute an anomaly. It is interesting to note that the pendulum swings from one side to the other, along with the changing situations. Before 11 September 2001, the USA was the country that valued financial privacy and individual privacy more than any other country. However, after 11 September, the horror of terrorism has made the USA go too far in the other direction. The Excessive tension can be seen in the following remarks: "*government agencies and law enforcement officials need greater access to financial information to shore up our national security ... Perhaps the sacrifice is small considering we are a nation at war ...* " It was even said that, "*in the battle of security versus liberty, security is now winning ... Civil liberties will no longer be able to stand in the way of the war on terrorism.* "[425]

It should be noted that this problem cannot be understood in terms of winning or losing. On this issue, what should attract attention is not who is in the driver's seat and who is in a back seat, but where the proper balance is, between protecting indi-

---

[423] See John J. Byrne, Know Your Customer: What Happened and What Happened Next? *Journal of Money Laundering Control*, Vol. 3 No. 4, pp. 345—349.

[424] See Robert S. Pasley, Privacy Rights V. Anti-Money Laundering Enforcement, *2002 University of North Carolina School of Law Banking Institute*, North Carolina Banking Institute, April, 2002.

[425] Ibid.

vidual rights and fighting serious crimes. This balance, which should be sought by both lawmakers and law executors, must not go to extremes. It should do all that is possible to maximize benefits and should not fluctuate decisions based only on external events. Things tend to develop in the opposite direction when they become extreme.

8.1.7 Conclusions

It is true that the original intention of banking secrecy was to prevent people from arbitrary or unlawful interference. Unfortunately, it is also a fact that banking secrecy provides a safe harbor for money laundering activities and makes criminals launder money more audaciously. Since both suspicious transactions and legitimate transactions need financial secrecy, banking secrecy itself cannot be considered as good or bad, its nature lies in the hands of those who seek to take advantage of it.

With the increasing gravity of money laundering crime, countermeasures are getting much more intrusive. Thus there is tension between preserving privacy rights and enforcing a strong and effective anti-money laundering effort. This tension also reflects the tension between individual liberty and social order. Privacy interests are highly valued, but so are the interests of being safe and secure from money laundering and other serious crimes. Thus the overriding issue is where the balance should be. The balance should not be buffeted by external events alone.

8.2 Lawyers, Notaries, Accountants and Money Laundering

8.2.1 Introduction

The majority of countries have rules in place for financial institutions to fight against money laundering. However, many countries do not impose anti-money laundering obligations on lawyers, notaries and accountants. This section first describes a new trend of money laundering method, laundering money through professionals. Then it analyses the necessity and rationale of bringing professionals under the obligations of anti-money laundering and the currently legal situation will be introduced as well. And also it presents the contradiction between professional privilege and anti-money laundering obligations. Finally it tries to present a reasonable solution to this sensitive problem.

8.2.2 A New Trend of Money Laundering Methods: From Financial Institutions to Professionals

For a long time, criminals took advantage of financial institutions to conduct money laundering activities. Therefore, since the beginning of the fight against money laundering in the 1980s, the most important international documents on prevention of money laundering activities all considered that financial institutions should play a significant role in the field to prevent money laundering.[426] These documents all emphasize that financial institutions should assume such obligations as customer identification, record keeping and suspicious transaction reporting. Besides, the Wolfsberg Principles, the voluntary central code of conduct agreed to by 11 central banks, was adopted in 2000. These Principles state that banks should ascertain the identity of depositors and the origin of funds as well as should pay special attention to the clients from those countries or regions that have no effective anti-money laundering systems.[427]

As a result of the comparatively rigid and systemic measures adopted by financial institutions to prevent money laundering, criminals turned to expertise of professionals to start new methods for money laundering and minimize risks surrounding their criminal activities. Since the late nineties, the phenomenon that lawyers, notaries, accountants and other professionals became involved in money laundering schemes increased steadily.

Case One—In one country, an enquiry revealed how a lawyer could use a client

---

[426] As mentioned in the preceding chapters, these documents are as follows: the Recommendations on Measures Against the Transfer and Safekeeping of Funds of Criminal Origin (adopted by the Committee of Ministers of the Council of Europe on 27 June 1980), the Statement on Prevention of Criminal Use of the Banking System for the Purpose of Money-Laundering (adopted by the Basle Committee on Banking Regulations and Supervisory Practices in December 1988), the Recommendations of Financial Action Task Force, the Council Directive of 10 June 1991 on Prevention of the Use of the Financial System for the Purpose of Money Laundering, and its amendment, the Directive 2001/97/EC of 4 December 2001.

[427] http://www.dailynews.tyfo.com/news/itknowing/block/html/2000121100040html, 11 December 2000.

account to launder the proceeds from a credit fraud offence. The funds were paid into the lawyer's client account, and converted by him into checks drawn on a bank of another country which were subsequently cashed by a correspondent designated by the lawyer concerned.[428]

Case Two—In one country, a solicitor transferred funds to a colleague, explaining that they were the proceeds from a sale of assets bequeathed by an individual in his will. The second solicitor was not satisfied with this explanation and reported his suspicions. The subsequent enquiry confirmed these suspicions about the legitimacy of the purported asset transactions.[429]

Case Three—In one country, a prominent attorney performed services for a whole clientele of launderers. A client with $ 80 million, proceeds from an insurance fraud, used the lawyer to transfer the money to financial institutions in countries where there are few or no anti-laundering regulations. The attorney opened accounts in various banks under false names of individuals or corporations. The illegal funds were placed in the form of cash or checks in banks in the country in question, then wired to different accounts controlled by the attorney. It should be noted that because of his professional repute the domestic banks never considered it necessary to look more closely at the nature of the transactions in question.[430]

Case Four—Beginning in May 1994, two alleged narcotics traffickers used an accounting firm to launder criminal proceeds generated from amphetamine sales. The "clients" of the firm would on a regular basis hand their accountant cash in brown envelopes or shoe boxes for which no receipt was issued. The funds were then stored in the accountant's office until he decided how they could be introduced into the financial system and laundered. At any one time, there was between USD 38,000 and USD 63,000 stored in the accountant's office. The law enforcement agency investigating the matter found that the accountant established company and trust accounts on behalf of his clients and opened personal bank accounts in the names of relatives. He then made structured deposits to those accounts with the funds received from the al-

---

[428] See Financial Action Task Force on Money Laundering, *Report on Money Laundering Typologies* (*1996—1997*).

[429] See Financial Action Task Force on Money Laundering, *Report on Money Laundering Typologies* (*1997—1998*).

[430] Ibid.

leged traffickers. Additionally, he transferred approximately USD 114,000 overseas—again, using structured transactions—to purchase truck parts, which were later brought back into the country and sold at a profit, and also used some of the funds to purchase properties. The accountant and three of his colleagues (who were also implicated in the scheme) reportedly laundered approximately USD 633,900 and received a 10% commission for his services.[431]

The increasing number of cases involving lawyers, accountants, notaries and other professionals attracted high attention of international community. Just as the annual Typologies Reports of FATF stated: "*As regards money laundering techniques, the most noticeable trend is the continuing increase in the use by money launderers of non-bank financial institutions and non-financial businesses relative to banking institutions. This is believed to reflect the increased level of compliance by banks with anti-money laundering measures ... Money launderers continue to receive the assistance of professional facilitators, who assist in a range of ways to mask the origin and ownership of tainted funds.*"[432] Besides, the 1998 Report of the UN Office for Drug Control and Crime Prevention on financial havens, banking secrecy and money laundering also referred to the frequent misuse of lawyers and accounts to help criminal funds.[433]

In the case of criminals making full use of financial institutions to launder illicit proceeds from criminal activities, we enhanced the responsibility of the financial system to prevent money-laundering crime. Now with the evolution of money laundering schemes, we should make quick response to develop and update preventive measures. Therefore, under the current situation, it is of great significance to bring the lawyers, notaries, accountants and other professionals under the obligations of anti-money laundering.

---

[431] See Financial Action Task Force on Money Laundering, *Report on Money Laundering Typologies* (*1998—1999*).

[432] Financial Action Task Force on Money Laundering, *Report on Money Laundering Typologies* (*1996—1997*).

[433] See *Proposal for a European parliament and Council Directive amending Council Directive 91/308/EEC of the 10 June 1991 on Prevention of the Use of the Financial System for the Purpose of Money Laundering*, Explanatory memorandum.

8.2.3 The Necessity and Rationale of Bringing the Professionals under the Obligation of Anti-money Laundering

The fact that lawyers, notaries, accountants and other independent professionals are vulnerable to money laundering activities is really linked with the nature of their professions. That is to say, the nature of these professions indicates that some of these professionals will invariably be utilized by money launderers. The reasons are as follows:

First, money laundering is a high complex and professional industry, which is difficult for ordinary criminals to commit. Money laundering activities often touch upon complicated financial and legal systems, both national and international. Criminals have to turn to the expertise of lawyers, notaries, accountants and other professionals to aid them to minimize suspicion surrounding their criminal activities.

Second, lawyers, notaries, accountants and other professionals provide a wide range of services, and a large number of services are closely related to economic activities, such as creation of corporate vehicles, buying or selling of property, performing financial transactions and the like. All of these operations are considerably vulnerable to money laundering crimes. Even if the professionals are reluctant to aid criminals to launder money purposely, they may participate in the money laundering schemes unconsciously.

Third, lawyers, notaries, accountants and other independent professionals are highly regulated by professional ethics and discipline, and they have respectable social status. It is unlikely to be suspected if these professionals perform economic activities on behalf of their clients. For this reason, it will be more subtle and safer for these professionals to launder illicit proceeds.

Last, professional secrecy exists in almost all countries, although it varies from country to country. Therefore, clients needn't worry about that their criminal activities will be revealed by these professionals and these professionals may take advantage of the privilege to aid criminals to launder money. Owing to the inherent nature of these professionals, it is unavoidable that some professionals are infected by money launderers.

Lawyers, notaries, accountants and other professionals are vulnerable to money laundering activities on one hand, on the other hand, if these professionals undertake anti-money laundering obligations, they will exert a more distinct effect than financial institutions. As we already know, three main duties concerning customer identification, record keeping and reporting of suspicious transactions are imposed on financial institutions under many international documents and national regulations. But these three duties are insufficient, especially at present, when money-laundering schemes are getting increasingly complicated.

It should be noted that the Internet, electronic money and other new technology indeed promote economic growth, however these new technologies are utilized by money launderers at the same time. Internet banking and electronic transactions make it more difficult for financial institutions to identify customers' identity, let alone to keep records and report suspicious transactions. Even in face-to-face transactions, criminals easily circumvent relevant regulations through a practice called "*smurfing*", which means money launderers break up the whole transaction into parts to bring the transaction amount under the threshold, so that financial institutions will not suspect any illegal transactions. Furthermore, criminals can perform financial transactions in several different financial institutions so that each institution only knows of a single, isolated transaction of their customers. In addition, criminals may also invent the nature and amount of transactions through the way of making up contracts.

However, lawyers, notaries, and especially accountants, can know all transactions of their customers by examining all contracts, and inspecting venture capital and enterprise accounting report forms. The ability to see the entire picture, not just a single, isolated transaction puts these professionals in a much better position than financial institutions to detect and report money laundering activities.[434]

8.2.4 The Current Legal Situation of Professionals' Anti-money Laundering Obligations

Just as mentioned above, lawyers, notaries, accountants and other professional are vulnerable to money laundering, and also they are in a better position than finan-

---

[434] See Steven V. Melnik, The Inadequate Utilization of the Accounting Profession in the United States Government's Fight against Money Laundering, 2000 New York University School of Law Journal of Legislation and Public Policy, *Journal of Legislation and Public Policy*, New York University School of Law, 2000, p. 5.

cial institutions in the prevention of money laundering. For these reasons, more and more international documents stipulate that non-financial institutions (including lawyers, notaries and accountants) should assume anti-money laundering obligations. Under the 1996 Recommendations of FATF, it advised that the financial activities of non-financial businesses or professions should also be subject to the financial Recommendations.[435] The extended scope of *"financial activities of non-financial businesses of professions"* mirrored the mental attitude that the revised FATF Recommendations paid more attention to what is done rather than to the legal form of entities. Later under the 2003 revised Recommendations, lawyers, notaries, accountants and independent legal professions are definitely covered by the 40 Recommendations.[436] And under the 2001 amendment to the 1991 EC Directive, it is also very clear that anti-money laundering obligations are imposed on notaries and other independent legal professionals, as well as auditors, external accountants and advisors.[437] This stipulation will be sure to transform the domestic laws of the member states of the European Union.

Apart from these international documents, more and more national laws also impose anti-money laundering obligations on these professionals. In this regard, the European Union countries are good examples. Under the 1991 EC Directive, the Money Laundering Regulations in the United Kingdom, which came into force on 1 April 1994, already provides that notaries public, accountants, and solicitors are all required to comply with the identification and reporting procedures, although the legal community challenges these provisions as detrimental to the quality of their services. In the Netherlands, notaries have announced a voluntary scheme to report very suspicious transactions indicating serious cases of money laundering. Lawyers and accountants already have a similar arrangement.[438] In addition, Belgian notaries, bailiffs and certified accountants must report to the Belgian Financial Intelligence Unit (Cellule de Traitement des Informations Financieres) if within the framework of their profes-

---

[435] See *The FATF Recommendations on Money Laundering (1996)*, Recommendation 9.

[436] See *The FATF Recommendations on Money Laundering (2003)*, Recommendations 12 and 16.

[437] See *Directive 2001/97/EC of the European Parliament and of the Council of 4 December 2001, Amending Council Directive 91/308/EEC on Prevention of the Use of the Financial System for the Purpose of Money Laundering*, Article 2a-(3)-7.

[438] See *Second Commission Report to the European Parliament and the Council on the implementation of the Money Laundering Directive*, Annex 6.

sional role they are informed or come to suspect that money laundering is taking place. French notaries, bailiffs, and chartered auditors who, within the framework of their professional duties exercise, supervise or advise on an operation which results in capital flows must make a report to the public prosecutor if they have reason to suspect or believe that money laundering is taking place.[439] After the enactment of the 2001 amendment to the 1991 EC Directive, it is important to note that Germany enacted broad new money laundering legislation in June 2002. Under the new law, attorneys, accountants, real estate agents, tax advisors and notaries are required to comply with the obligations that banks and insurance companies must follow. These professionals together with financial institutions are required to obtain adequate identification from clients and report suspicious transactions to the German Financial Intelligence Unit, Zentralstelle fur Verdachtsanzeigen.[440]

8.2.5 The Perplexity of Professionals' Anti-money Laundering Obligations

Lawyers, notaries, accountants and other independent professionals could play a significant role in prevention of money laundering activities, however, imposing anti-money laundering obligations on these professionals is always a sensitive and puzzling topic and causes a lot of debate. The difficulty is linked with the following reasons.

First, compliance with anti-money laundering requirements may conflict with the privilege of confidentiality in communication between these professionals and their clients. Through the way of contract, lawyers, notaries, accountants and other independent professionals can touch the entire and secret information of the clients. Only in this way can the professionals provide sufficient legal aids, make an accurate financial report and work out objective and precise certification. Under the situation that these professionals assume the obligations of customer identification and record keeping, perhaps it does not substantially jeopardize the interests of clients. In the case of suspicious transactions reporting, however, it will do considerable damage to the confidential relationship between professionals and customers. And in the final analysis,

---

[439] See Helen Xanthaki, Lawyers' duties under the Draft EU Money Laundering Directive: Is Confidentiality a Thing of the Past? *Journal of Money Laundering Control*, Vol.5 No.2, 2001.

[440] http://www.moneylaundering.com/news.htm#Top, 20 June 2002.

it may seriously interfere with the individual right of privacy and the defendant's right to legal defense.

Second, imposing anti-money laundering obligations on lawyers, notaries and accountants may also pose serious risk to professionals who come into contact with "*dirty money*". With the enhancement of the fight against money laundering, several international documents and national regulations provide that the mens rea of money laundering can be both scienter and negligence.[441] Also, the behavior of money laundering comprises acquisition and possession illegal proceeds from criminal activities besides concealment and disguise of the illicit origin of property.[442] For such a wide scope of money laundering elements, these professionals may commit money laundering crime unknowingly when they perform their professional activities. For example, if lawyers, notaries or accountants fail to perform the obligation of customer identification and receive payments derived from criminal activities, these professionals may face the threat of being charged with money laundering crimes.

Third, facing the risk of committing money laundering crimes, these professionals are unwilling to know precise information about clients, such as the origin of funds, to protect themselves to avoid being charged. Thus, it certainly will have an ill effect on the professionals' fundamental right to exercise their professions. Specifically, it will impede lawyers to exercise a defensive right for clients as well as have a negative impact on normal legal proceedings. It will also influence the authenticity and accuracy of financial reports and notarial documents.

The above analysis shows that it is a double-sided sword for lawyers, notaries, accountants and other professionals to undertake the responsibility of anti-money laundering. On one side, it is beneficial to the fight against money laundering. On the other side, it may be harmful to fundamental rights both of clients and professionals

---

[441] At the international level, negligent laundering can be found in the Article 6 of the 1990 Convention on Laundering, Search, Seizure and Confiscation of the Proceeds from Crime and the Recommendation 6 of the Financial Action Task Force. At the national level, it can also be found in the domestic legislation of several European countries including the Netherlands, Norway and Sweden. See William C. Gilmore, *Dirty Money, The Evolution of Money Laundering Counter-measure*, Council of Europe Press, p. 142.

[442] Such provisions can be easily found in the 1988 United Nations Convention against Illicit Traffic in Narcotic Drugs and Psychotropic Substances, the 1990 Convention on Laundering, Search, Seizure and Confiscation of the Proceeds from Crime and the 1991 Council Directive on Prevention of the Use of the Financial System for the Purpose of Money Laundering.

as well as the quality of intermediary activities.

It is obvious that there is a conflict between the fight against money laundering and protection of professional secrecy or privilege. Since money laundering cannot be totally stopped and professional secrecy or privilege cannot be protected unconditionally, the key to the settlement of the question lies in seeking a proper balance between these conflicting interests.

8.2.6 The Solution to This Conflict

In order to solve this conflict, the professional activities provided by lawyers, notaries, accountants and other professionals should be analyzed. These professionals may perform legal proceedings on behalf of clients, such as providing legal advice for criminal suspects, carrying out advocacy for defendants, or taking part in lawsuits as an attorney. These professionals may also provide specific financial or company law activities, such as buying or selling property, performing financial transactions, creation of corporate vehicles and the like. It should be noted that the nature of the professional activities under these two situations are different. Under the former situation, these professionals are performing their traditional role of legal adviser or representative. It is necessary for them to be able to preserve the confidentiality of their clients. After all it is also important to pay close attention to human rights while putting stress on combating crimes. Under the latter case, the activities provided by these professionals are similar with the business performed by financial institutions. These activities are neither linked with professional confidentiality nor related to fundamental rights. For this reason, whether these professionals should assume anti-money laundering obligations depends on the nature of the activities performed by them.

It is commendable that the 2001 Amendment to the 1991 EC Directive touches this sensitive problem and resolves this knotty matter appropriately. The Amendment to the Directive provides that notaries, independent legal professionals, auditors, external accountants and tax advisors would be exempted from the obligation to report any information obtained either before, during or after judicial proceedings, or in the course of ascertaining the legal position for a client.[443] However, under two different situations notaries and other independent legal professionals should perform anti-money laundering obligations laid down in the Directive: *(1) when they assist in the planning or execution of certain transactions for their client (Specifically, the following activities are covered: buying and selling of real property or business entities; managing of client money, securities or other assets; opening or management of bank, savings or securities accounts; organization of contributions necessary for the creation, operation or management of companies; creation, operation or management of trusts, companies or similar structures.)*;[444] *(2) when they act on behalf of and for their client in any financial or real estate transaction.*

In addition, given the particular status of these professionals and the special relationship between these professionals and their clients, it is not appropriate for them to report their suspicions to enforcement authorities. To solve this problem, the Directive stipulates that, "*In the case of the notaries and independent legal professionals referred to in Article 2a (5), member states may designate an appropriate self-regulatory body of the profession concerned as the authority to be informed of the facts referred to in paragraph 1 (a)*[445] *and in such case shall lay down the appropriate forms of cooperation between that body and the authorities responsible for combating money laundering.*"[446] That is to say, in view of their particular status, member states are given the option of allowing these independent professionals to communicate their suspicions of money laundering not to the normal anti-money laundering authorities but to their bar associations or other self-regulatory bodies. In this case, the rules governing the treatment of such reports and their possible onward transmission to the authorities responsible for combating money laundering and the appropriate forms of cooperation between the bar associations or professional bodies and these authorities should be de-

---

[443] See *Directive 2001/97/EC of the European Parliament and of the Council of 4 December 2001, Amending Council Directive 91/308/EEC on Prevention of the Use of the Financial System for the Purpose of Money Laundering*, Article 6(3).

[444] Ibid., Article 2a-5.

[445] The obligation of informing authorities responsible for combating money laundering of any fact, which might be an indication of money laundering.

[446] *Directive 2001/97/EC of the European Parliament and of the Council of 4 December 2001, Amending Council Directive 91/308/EEC on Prevention of the Use of the Financial System for the Purpose of Money Laundering*, Article 6(3).

termined by the member states.[447]

8.2.7 Conclusions

The continuing efforts by financial institutions to combat money laundering have made the work of the money launderers more difficult. To circumvent relevant counter-measures, money launderers have had to develop more complex schemes. They turn to the expertise of lawyers, notaries, accountants and other professionals to aid them to minimize suspicion surrounding their criminal activities. The involvement of these professionals, to a certain degree, is linked with their professional characteristics. They have specialized professional expertise needed by money launderers. They perform a wide range of services in the economic sphere. They hold a respectable social status which leads to little suspicion of money laundering activities. Furthermore, professional confidentiality or privilege as a general principle exists in almost every country. For these reasons, it is sensible that these professions are vulnerable to money laundering schemes.

However, on the other hand, the role of anti-money laundering played by these professionals should not be underestimated. They are independent legal professionals and will not be controlled by any institutions and individuals. In economic activities, they are reliable *"watch dogs"* not only for clients but also for third parties as well as for public interests. They can know more complete and first-hand economic information about their clients and can distinguish false information from authentic more easily than financial institutions. In consideration of these facts, more and more international documents and national legislation bring these professionals under the obligations of anti-money laundering crime.

Nevertheless, lawyers, notaries, accountants and other independent professionals have a particular status and the relationship between these professionals and their clients are especially intimate. Imposing anti-money laundering obligations on these professionals is a sensitive matter and may interfere with individual interests, litigation right and the quality of intermediary activities. To solve this knotty problem, the proper solution is to make a distinction between their activities: when professional ac-

---

[447] Ibid., Preamble.

tivities are linked with judicial proceedings or in the course of ascertaining the legal position of clients, they would be exempted from the obligation of anti-money laundering. However they should assume anti-money laundering obligations when they perform financial or company law activities. Furthermore, they should report their suspicions of money laundering crime not to enforcement authorities but to self-regulatory bodies to respect the sensitive relationship between these professionals and their clients.

8.3 High Technology and Money Laundering
—A New Trend in Money Laundering: From the Real World to Cyberspace

8.3.1 Introduction

The development of high technology is a double-edged sword. It does raise people's living standards on the one hand; and on the other hand, it also provides great opportunity for criminals. This section first introduces the inconvenience of traditional methods of money laundering. It then describes the new challenges we are confronted with, as a result of high technology, such as electronic money, Internet banks and Internet casinos. Finally it presents some responses to this high technology laundering.

8.3.2 The Inconvenience of Traditional Methods

Due to its complicated characteristics, the methods of money laundering are destined to be diversified. Generally speaking, the common methods of money laundering, which are widely used by criminals, include smuggling currency, laundering money through financial institutions and non-financial institutions. With the enhancement of anti-money laundering measures, however, the drawbacks of the traditional approaches to money laundering are evident.

Currency smuggling means that money launderers transfer illegal proceeds in secret to another country or territory.[448] Currency smuggling, as one of the means of money laundering, has not been outdated because currency is still the primary form of illegal proceeds. Furthermore, once it is done successfully, it will be possible to conceal the criminal origin of these currencies and achieve what the criminal wishes. However, it is unlikely to be the best method at present, especially in the days of economic globalization and electronic finance. Currency smuggling runs a bigger risk of being discovered due to its limited face amount of traditional currency. The more the amount is, the bigger the space is. In addition, it must take the criminals considerable time and resource to take large amounts of money through customs and transfer them to other countries and territories.

The majority of money laundering schemes are to make use of visible intermediaries, such as banks, non-bank financial institutions or non-financial institutions. However, due to the ever-growing gravity of money laundering crime, the international community has put stress on the vulnerable institutions to assume the responsibility to fight against money laundering. The continuous effects of combating money laundering, such as sufficient implementation of client identification, record keeping and suspicious transactions reporting for vulnerable institutions, make laundering through intermediaries more difficult.

8.3.3 New Challenges to Existing Anti-money Laundering Counter-Measures

8.3.3.1 Electronic Money

Electronic money is not a new concept, however the definition of electronic money varies. One point of view considers electronic money, electronic cash, digital cash, digital currency and cyber-currency as synonyms for an electronic medium of

---

[448] For example, in May 1988, the inspectors of the Miami Airport in America found $ 30 million, which were demonstrated to be proceeds from drug trafficking, hidden in luggage, TV sets, deodorant cans and even in tennis balls. See Li Wei, The Research on Money Laundering Methods, *Criminal Law*, Vol. 1, 2002. Another example, in September 2001, Hong Kong uncovered the biggest trans-boundary money laundering criminal gang throughout its history, which involved 50 billion HK dollars. It is surprising that in almost 6 years money launderers every day carried suitcases filled with 10 million HK dollars from Luo Hu Custom in Shen Zhen to Hong Kong and then transferred these funds to 1300 accounts. Besides, money launderers three times a day transferred 29 kinds of currencies from Guang Zhou to Hong Kong by vans and sedans. The largest sum of dirty money transferred to Hong Kong in one day amounted to 50 million HK dollars.

exchange.[449] Another view regards electronic money as not the same as electronic cash, "*Electronic Money includes electronic cash, as well as the immense torrents of digital funds that zip through international and national payment networks (such as SWIFT and CHIPS).*"[450] In 1996, the Bank of International Settlement (BIS) defined electronic money as "*stored value*" or "*prepaid*" products in which a record of the funds or "*value*" available to a consumer is stored on an electronic device in the consumer's possession.[451]

Although the definition of electronic money varies, in sum, electronic money has the following common characteristics, which greatly attract money launderers and facilitate money-laundering activity:

First, the bulk of electronic money can be ignored. One smart card or computer can store uncountable electronic money. This character is largely different from traditional currency. A suitcase filled with $1 million worth of $20 bills weighs more than 100 lbs.[452]

Second, electronic money is easy to transfer quickly over long distance. With the help of Internet, electronic money can be conveyed to every corner in the world in a split second.[453]

Third, electronic money is much more anonymous than traditional currency. Traditional money has numbers which can be tracked. Besides, face-to-face transactions also influence the anonymity of traditional money. However, in the case of electronic money, the adoption of encryption techniques and the facility of remote transfer extraordinarily increase the anonymity of electronic money.

---

[449] See Wan Yixian, *The Legal Issues of Electronic Commerce*, Law Press, 2001. p.132.

[450] R. Mark Bernkopf, *Electronic Cash and Money Policy*, 1996, http://www.firstmonday.dk/issues/issue1/ecash/index.html.

[451] See Bank of International Settlement, *Implications for Central Banks of The Development of Electronic Money*, October 1996, http://www.bis.org/publ/bisp01.pdf.

[452] See R. Mark Bortner, *Cyberlaundering: Anonymous Digital Cash and Money Laundering*, Note 2. http://www.law.miami.edu/~froomkin/seminar/papers/bortner.

[453] See There are three major electronic funds transfers systems: (1) SWIFT: the Society for Worldwide Interbank Financial Telecommunication, is a Belgian-based association of banks that provides the communications network for a large number of international funds transfers, as well as intracountry transfers within the United States; (2) CHIPS: the Clearing House Interbank Payment System, is a funds settlement system operated by the New York Clearing House; and (3) Fedwire: the funds transfer system operated exclusively by the Federal Reserve System. See R. Mark Bortner, *Cyberlaundering: Anonymous Digital Cash and Money Laundering*, Note 14. http://www.law.miami.edu/~froomkin/seminar/papers/bortner.

The immateriality, anonymity and high transfer speed of electronic money not only offer great convenience to money launderers, but also bring much trouble to existing preventive and investigative measures combating money laundering. Existing anti-money laundering counter-measures mostly emphasize that vulnerable institutions should assume anti-money laundering obligations, such as customer identification, record keeping, suspicious transactions reporting and the like. These techniques were developed based on certain assumptions, such as the use of banks to make certain transactions, the ability of financial institutions to monitor its customers' activities and the use of physical currency.

E-money systems challenge not only these assumptions about the nature of banking but also the way in which investigations are conducted.[454] E-money reduces the need for currency smuggling. Simple keyboard operation replaces shipping containers or many suitcases. Vast amounts of money can be transmitted instantaneously and securely to every corner of the world, especially to countries or regions that don't have enough anti-money laundering measures or have no measures at all.

Furthermore electronic transactions don't have to rely on a physical intermediary. E-money systems might make it difficult to know your customer. "*On the Internet, the largest international conglomerate and the smallest garage business may be indistinguishable, and, in both cases, next to nothing may be revealed about the organization's actual activities.*"[455] As to record keeping measures, it is very difficult to centralize the information of electronic transactions. "*And even if technologically feasible, a record of each and every transaction would be cost prohibitive and provide huge masses of data of no commercial or law enforcement value.*"[456] Besides, detailed record-keeping touches upon the privacy right of customers. It is also a knotty issue on how to keep a balance between protecting privacy right and retaliating against money-laundering crime. It is difficult to implement these measures of client identification and record keeping, let alone to carry out the obligation of suspicious transaction reporting.

In addition, because electronic money is designed to operate internationally and in multiple currencies, the international financial borders are banished and "*the myth

---

[454] See Financial Action Task Force on Money Laundering, *Report on Money Laundering Typologies* (*1996—1997*), Annex 1.
[455] Ibid.
[456] Ibid.

that crimes stops at the border is dispelled"[457]. For this reason, electronic money also challenges the jurisdictional issue.

8.3.3.2　Internet Banks

The revolution of information technology represented by computers and the Internet has far-reaching impact on economic and social life. At the same time, it also provides scarce opportunity to criminals. When people gain access to the cyberspace created by computers and the Internet, money launderers also have a secure preventive screen.

At present, one of the new issues of anti-money laundering is how to prevent and control laundering through Internet banks. Internet banks also refer to virtual banks, which can offer all kinds of financial services anywhere and any time on the Internet. It has been reported that the number of financial institutions that provide Internet financial services appears to be growing, and so are the range of financial services available on the Internet. These financial services include direct payments, electronic funds transfers, issue of cheques, purchase of securities and opening/closing of accounts. It has been estimated that cyber-laundering is being carried out at $ 50 billion per year.[458]

Of course, "*these trends vary from one jurisdiction to another. In Hong Kong, for example, cash payments are the norm, and, although banks offer on-line banking services, the public currently favors the use of automated teller machine (ATMs) or direct contact with the financial institutions. In Finland on the other hand, almost half of the population has access to the Internet, and some 85% of retail payment orders are transmitted to banks electronically*"[459]. Another example, in America, almost 16% of families accept all sorts of financial services provided by Internet banks and this figure accounts for one third of all American Internet citizens. In China, however, less than 0.1% of families accept Internet banking services and this figure accounts for less

---

[457]　Jason Haines and Peter Johnstone, Global Cybercrime: New Toys for the Money Launderers, *Journal of Money Laundering Control*, Vol. 2 No. 4, p. 317.

[458]　See Steven Philippsohn, The Dangers of New Technology—Laundering on the Internet, *Journal of Money Laundering Control*, Vol. 5 No. 1, 2001, p. 87.

[459]　Financial Action Task Force on Money Laundering, *Report on Money Laundering Typologies (2000—2001)*.

than one tenth of all Chinese Internet citizens.[460]

The possibility of laundering through Internet banking is due to the features of the Internet. It is easy to access the Internet. The contact between the customer and the institution can be depersonalized. And electronic transactions through Internet banks are prompt and convenient. Furthermore, transnational financial services can be easily available through Internet banks. It is obvious that these features of Internet banking can improve efficiency and reduce the costs of financial services and extend operation scope as well. However, these features of Internet banks, access, speed, anonymity and capacity to extend beyond national borders are sure to make Internet banking become a launderer's paradise, because it is very difficult for Internet banks to identify clients, keep records and report suspicious transactions.[461]

As everyone knows, a potential risk exists at any first stage of the contact between a new customer and a financial institution. For this reason, current anti-money laundering measures in most countries focus on customer identification, as a minimum, when the business relationship is established.

"*In the case of Internet banking, the difficulties for the financial institutions are increased if the procedures for opening such as account are permitted to take place without face to face contact or without a link to an already existing traditional account.*"[462] Even if financial institutions have implemented client identification procedures at the time of opening an account, owing to lack of face to face contact in the following Internet transactions, the dealer on the Internet transaction may be not the one who has opened an account at the first stage. In fact, with an elimination of personal contact between customer and the institution, it is very difficult to know who is actually controlling the account and what constitutes normal business practices.

"*The financial institutions will routinely only be able to ascertain that a particular account was accessed at a particular time, the sum involved, and possibly the beneficiary (name or account number). The bank will only be able to assume that access took place by the nominal account holder and will have no way to verify the exact location*

---

[460] See *Wen Hui Newspaper*, 20 February 2002.

[461] See Steven Philippsohn, The Dangers of New Technology—Laundering on the Internet, *Journal of Money Laundering Control*, Vol. 5 No. 1, 2001, p. 87.

[462] Financial Action Task Force on Money Laundering, *Report on Money Laundering Typologies (2000—2001)*.

from which the customer made the transaction. This means that a single individual could ultimately control a number of accounts simultaneously without necessarily drawing the attention of the financial institution or institutions in which those accounts are maintained. "[463] Thus, financial institutions also have no way to suspect normal transactions and can't perform suspicious transactions reporting measures at all.

Another issue which is also troublesome is the regulatory or investigative jurisdiction that might be involved in detecting and ultimately pursuing potential money laundering violations. "*Internet banking, as with other on-line commercial activities, has already been promoted as having the potential to break down the barriers of national borders. A quick browse through lists of financial services available on the Internet shows a number of these that claim to offer their services regardless of the location of the account holder.*"[464] Internet money laundering is so complicated that it is difficult to decide where it occurs. Does is take place where the launderer is located, where the server is located or where the accounts are held?[465] And also it is very confusing to determine which authority has jurisdiction to investigate and prosecute the transnational crime.

8.3.3.3　Internet Casinos

Among the activities that launder money through non-financial institutions, cases of making use of casinos to commit money-laundering crime abounds. Some criminals buy chips with cash and then request repayment by check drawn on the casino's account. Some criminals have the receipt by casino clients of winner's checks make out in the name of third persons. Others make use of tokens for purchases of goods and services and for drug purchases.[466] In response to these cases, many countries have resorted to corresponding measures. Turkey closed casinos as of 10 February 1998 and anticipated the closing of casinos will be useful to anti-money laundering. In the

---

[463]　Financial Action Task Force on Money Laundering, *Report on Money Laundering Typologies (1999—2000)*.

[464]　Ibid.

[465]　A joint report in 2000 by the Bank of France and the French Banking Commission suggested that the accounts' location is where the transaction takes place. See Steven Philippsohn, The Dangers of New Technology—Laundering on the Internet, *Journal of Money Laundering Control*, Vol. 5 No. 1, 2001, p. 87.

[466]　See Financial Action Task Force on Money Laundering, *Report on Money Laundering Typologies (1997—1998)*.

Netherlands, casinos belong to a public establishment named Casinos of Holland. Casinos are covered by the anti-money laundering legislation, and only winnings from gambling are accepted for electronic transfer to a bank account. In the United Kingdom emphasis is being placed on the importance of client identification.[467] And in the 2001 EC Directive, casinos are specifically required to assume anti-money laundering obligations just as the financial institutions have already done.

Since traditional casinos are regulated to prevent being exploited for money laundering, Internet casinos may be good places for money launderers. At present, hundreds of casino websites are established in the Caribbean area, which is considered a *"tax heaven"*. Many of these websites are not regulated by a government at all. Some of them even don't enquire as to customers' identity. All these provide criminals with money laundering opportunities. With an account on the Internet website, criminals can transfer money freely. Many criminal gangs remit dirty money into their accounts on the Internet website, after several times of nominal gambling, they request repayment by cheque drawn on the Internet casinos' accounts. Thus, a large amount of dirty money has been laundered easily. It has been reported that these casinos' websites established in Caribbean area are threatening the traditional international financial system.[468]

As Internet gambling has been identified as a significant money laundering vulnerability, the members of the USA Congress have repeatedly attempted to pass legislation to prohibit Internet gambling. The first proposal targets individual gambler and the second one targets offshore Internet casino operators. Unfortunately, both of them failed. After the World Trade Center and Pentagon terrorist attacks of 11th September 2001, another legislative approach, which targets the payment mechanisms used by Internet gamblers, has surfaced. This approach prohibited payments for wagers to Internet gambling sites. The prohibited payment methods would have included credit cards, checks, or funds transferred electronically. The logic underlying this scheme was that if the flow of money to Internet gambling sites could be blocked, Internet gambling would be effectively prohibited. Thus, laundering through Internet gambling also would be controlled. However, the feasibility of this

[467] Ibid.
[468] http://www.dailynews.tyfo.com/news/itknowing/block/html/2000121100040html.

proposal met with suspicion, for Internet gambling has become a very popular activity within the USA. The number of gamblers located in the United States placing sports wagers or playing casino-style games at Internet websites is over one million per day. Internet gambling is too popular to be eliminated without great difficulties. Furthermore, other than credit cards, checks and wires transfer, alternative methods of payment for wagers would be exploited by money launderers, such as electronic money which is much more anonymous. Thus, Internet laundering with electronic money may be promoted and anti-money laundering enforcement may be much more troublesome.[469]

8.3.4 Responses to High Technology Laundering

It should be noted that the emergence of electronic money, Internet banks, Internet casinos and other neoformation has great influence on the methods of money laundering. Although experts are not yet able to provide many case examples of high technology laundering, the lack of such evidence was not considered a sign that laundering is not taking place with the help of high technology. Rather, some experts believe that adequate means of detecting this type of laundering activity have not yet been fully developed.[470]

The Finance Action Task Force has already recognized the lure from high technology for money laundering activities. Therefore, Recommendation 13 among the revised 40 Recommendations of 1996 states, *"Countries should pay special attention to money laundering threats inherent in new or developing technologies that might favor anonymity, and take measures, if needed, to prevent their use in money schemes."*

In 1997, Recommendation 26 (f) of the Action Plan to Combat Organized Crime of the European Union also addressed the issue of money laundering on the Internet and via electronic money products and required that a message be sent giving details of the originator and the beneficiary in electronic payment and message system.

---

[469] See Mark D. Schopper, Internet Gambling, Electronic Cash & Money Laundering: The Unintended Consequences of a Money Control Scheme, *Chapman Law Review*, Spring, 2002.

[470] See Financial Action Task Force on Money Laundering, *Report on Money Laundering Typologies* (2000—2001).

In addition, under the 2001 EC Anti-Money Laundering Directive, Article 3 (11) also makes a mention of laundering through non-face to face transactions. It provides, "*Member States shall, in any case, ensure that the institutions and persons subject to this Directive take specific and adequate measures necessary to compensate for the greater risk of money laundering which arises when establishing business relations or entering into a transaction with a customer who has not been physically present for identification purposes (non-face to face operations).*" Furthermore, also under this article, several measures are enumerated, "*Such measures shall ensure that the customer's identity is established, for example, by requiring additional documentary evidence, or supplementary measures to verify or certify the documents supplied, or confirmatory certification by an institution subject to this Directive, or by requiring that the first payment of the operation is carried out through an account opened in the customer's name with a credit institution subject to this Directive.*" It is evident that the above-mentioned documents all address the issue of high technology laundering, though they don't specify concrete counter-measures.

It is commendable that FATF has made a positive response to high technology laundering to limit the vulnerability to money laundering. In respect of measures that prevent criminals from making use of electronic money to launder money, several measures are put forward by the FATF typology reports. These counter-measures are as follows:[471]

—*Limiting the functions and capacity of smart cards (including maximum value and turnover limits, as well as number of smart cards per customer)*;

—*Linking new payment technology to financial institutions and bank accounts*;

—*Requiring standard record keeping procedures for these systems to enable the examination, documentation, and seizure of relevant records by investigating authorities*;

—*Establishing international standards for these measures.*

In regard to laundering through Internet banking, the experts of FATF consider

---

[471] See Financial Action Task Force on Money Laundering, *Report on Money Laundering Typologies* (1998—1999).

that whether customer identification is carried out is of great importance for controlling money-laundering crime, especially when a business relationship is established. They stated that customer identification measures would also apply for on-line accounts. "*For instance, in Japan, on-line transactions may only be conducted for accounts that have been opened in a traditional, face-to-face manner. In Belgium, anti-money laundering legislation makes no distinction on whether the initiation of the business relationship takes place in person or by letter, fax, e-mail or Internet. The financial institution must in each case establish the identity of the client by means of a probative document, a copy of which must be maintained by the institution. In the United States, the opening of an account may be initiated on-line; however, the customer must provide identification numbers that are subject to verification by the financial institution. This procedure is no different from that which would apply for opening a bank account by mail.*"[472]

Except for focusing on customer identification, a few specific suggestions also were offered in the FATF Typology Report to deal with the potential vulnerability of on-line banking to money laundering:[473]

　　—*Establishing new procedures that will facilitate the ability of financial institutions to truly know their customers over the life of the business relationship;*

　　—*Working toward uniformity of standards among jurisdictions;*

　　—*Developing new information technology capabilities that will permit both the detection of suspicious on-line transactions and verification of the customer;*

　　—*Limiting the types of permitted on-line services or the amount of such transaction;*

　　—*Restricting on-line transactions only to those accounts that have been established in a traditional manner (i. e. , with face-to-face contact between customer and financial institution);*

　　—*Prohibiting financial institutions not licensed in a particular jurisdiction form offering their services in that jurisdiction on-line;*

　　—*Ultimately, oversight must be exercised by both the jurisdiction chartering*

---

[472] Financial Action Task Force on Money Laundering, *Report on Money Laundering Typologies* (1999—2000).

[473] Ibid.

the Internet bank and by those jurisdictions where the Internet banks have clients.

As regards to Internet casinos and other services provides through the Internet, considering the difficulties of following Internet links between possible criminal proceeds and the individual attempting to launder them, the experts of FATF offered the following suggestions:[474]

——*Requiring Internet service providers (ISPs) to maintain reliable subscriber resisters with appropriate identification information*;
——*Requiring ISPs to establish log files with traffic data relating Internet-protocol number to subscriber and to telephone number used in the connection*;
——*Requiring that this information be maintained for a reasonable period (6 months to a year)*;
——*Ensuring that this information may be made available internationally in a timely manner when conducting criminal investigations.*

8.3.5 Conclusions

It is noted that criminals try every possible means to launder money. Dirty money is moved by smuggling cash, through various money transfer mechanisms of financial institutions, by the way of purchasing cars, precious metal, valuable jewelry and antiques, and by means of operating restaurants, hotels, shops and casinos. However, with the continuous and intensive efforts of combating money laundering both at the national level and the international level, these traditional methods of money laundering are confronted with more and more difficulties.

To circumvent existing counter-measures against money laundering, money launderers try to move their activities from physical world to cyberspace with the help of electronic money, Internet banks and Internet casinos. Given these new challenges, existing preventive and repressive measures against money laundering should be modified.

Woefully little has been done in regard to the new challenge posed by new tech-

---

[474] See Financial Action Task Force on Money Laundering, *Report on Money Laundering Typologies* (2000—2001).

nology both at the national level and the international level. What is a consolation is the experts of FATF have put forward some suggestions. However suggestions are only suggestions, it is important to carry out these suggestions and try to find out whether they are able to be implemented and how to improve them so that we can efficiently control high technology laundering.

Chapter 9

Summary and Conclusions

9.1 The Issue of Money Laundering

In the modern world, drug trafficking, smuggling, Mafia, extortion and other forms of organized crime generate a large amount of wealth. However, it is hard to spend, transfer and circulate the funds derived from these criminal activities because of the rigid system of finance and taxation. Criminals need to disguise their money so that they can use it freely. Thus a special crime, money laundering, in modern times came into existence.

With the advancement of modern technology and prosperity of economy, grand scale, extensive scope and modernization of means are the characteristics of organized crime. Money laundering, simultaneously, is getting increasingly rampant. Money laundering poses significant risks to society. Money laundering disguises the original source of dirty money and impedes the investigation exercised by competent authorities. Money laundering damages the credibility of public confidence in the financial system in general and banks in particular. Money laundering sabotages the fair and competitive order of the market economy and tends to lead to financial crisis. Furthermore, there is the risk that further criminal activities can be developed by allowing criminal funds to be reinvested.

Although money laundering has been widely accepted as a term at both the international level and the national level, the precise meaning varies from country to country and from region to region. Many problems concerning the money laundering definition need to be discussed to get unanimous. Should money laundering only be regarded as drug-related laundering or should the definition be expanded to non-drug related laundering? Should money laundering only qualify as an offence in cases where the offender actually knew that he was dealing with the funds from crimes or should it qualify as an offence in cases where the offender ought to have assumed that the property was illegal proceeds? Should money laundering be considered only as fencing, which means a sort of favor or should it become an independent and autonomous crime?

The most general meaning of money laundering contains the following elements: First, money laundering depends upon the existence of an underlying crime that has generated proceeds, whether it is a drug-related crime or not. Second, money launderers already know or ought to have assumed that they are dealing with the property from a crime, "*property shall means assets of every kind, whether corporeal or incorporeal, movable or immovable, tangible or intangible, and legal documents or instruments evidencing title to, or interest in, such assets.*"[475] Third, a money launderer could be an individual or an organization, whether he is the owner of the dirty money or not. Fourth, the behavioral patterns of money laundering could include the conversion or transfer of the property, the concealment or disguise of the true nature, source of the property, the acquisition, possession or use of the property.

As current anti-money laundering legislation all emphasize that money-laundering crime has an implied or specific predicate offence that generates financial reward, while terrorism may not results in profits but will use funds that may be legally or illegally earned, the act of terrorists hidden the revenue generating process and gain access to their funds cannot be considered as "*money laundering*" but as "*terrorism financing*".

9.2 Common Efforts in the World

Money laundering is an international problem. Therefore common efforts in the world are needed if it is to be combated effectively. In the last two decades, all kinds

---

[475] *United Nations Convention against Transnational Organization Crime*, Article 2 (d). *United Nations Convention Against Illicit Traffic in Narcotic Drugs and Psychotropic Substances*, Article 1-(17).

of institutions expressed their common awareness of the growing gravity of money laundering and showed their resolve and capability to deal with this problem in every possible way. Conventions, statements, suggestions, resolutions, directives and other kinds of formats, came into existence one after another. Generally speaking, these instruments can be divided into two different categories: suppressive instruments and preventive instruments. The 1988 Vienna UN Convention, the 2000 Palermo UN Convention, the 1990 Strasbourg Convention fall into the first category, while the Council of Europe Recommendations, the Basel Committee Statement of Principles, the 40 Recommendations of the FATF, and the European Community Directives fall into the second one.

Suppressive measures and preventive measures, as two parallel measures against money laundering crimes, have respective advantages and disadvantages. Suppressive measures are indispensable to deal with crimes and they have more deterrence. They are *"essentially offensive in nature and intent"*[476]. Of course, they also have high cost. Criminal law making, investigation, prosecution, conviction and tracing, freezing and ultimately confiscation of proceeds, all involve a large amount of resources. Preventive measures stress more on defense rather than punishment. Preventive measures implicate the notion that combating money laundering can't be the sole responsibility of government authorities, but also of private sectors. It should be noted that the ultimate goal of criminal mechanism is not punishment but prevention. For this reason, *Cesare Beccaria*, a world famous scholar of criminal law in Italy said two hundred years ago: "*Prevention is better than punishment. Prevention is the major purpose of all excellent legislations.* "[477]

9.2.1 Suppression

As a suppressive instrument, the 1988 Vienna UN Convention for the first time created the obligation for member states to criminalize drug-related laundering at the international level. And it put stress on the confiscation of proceeds derived from crimes, which not only can prevent criminals from unjust enrichment but also can e-

---

[476] William C. Gilmore, *Dirty Money*, *The evolution of money laundering counter-measures*, Council of Europe Press, 1995 p. 223.

[477] Cesare Beccaria, *Crime and Punishment*, Chinese Encyclopedia Press, 1996, p. 104.

liminate the main incentive for profit-oriented wrongdoings. Besides, it also promoted international cooperation by requiring member states to provide the widest measure of mutual legal assistance in criminal matters and administration of justice as well. The Vienna UN Convention is considered as the foundation of the international legal regime in the area of combating money laundering, though only drug-related laundering is specified under this Convention.

The 1990 Strasbourg Convention, as a multilateral treaty to specify the obligations under the 1988 Vienna Convention, lays stress upon two issues: requiring states to criminalize the offence of money laundering and providing states the means to confiscate proceeds from crime both at the national level and the international level. In the first regard, the 1990 Strasbourg Convention requires states to enlarge the scope of predicate offences, thus overcoming the 1988 Vienna Convention's biggest flaw, restricting predicate offences to drug-related offences. In the second regard, the Convention provides a complete set of rules, covering all the stages of the procedure from investigation to confiscation and international cooperation as well, thus makes the Vienna Convention more effective.

The 2000 Palermo UN Convention represents a major step forward in the fight against transnational organized crime. The Convention deals with the fight against organized crime and some of the major activities that related to transnational organized crime, such as money laundering. As to money laundering measures, it goes beyond drug-related laundering for the first time at the international level. In addition, legal persons become liable for taking part in money laundering activities. Legal liability may be criminal, civil or administrative. It provides criminal, financial and administrative measures to control transnational organized crime in general and money laundering in particular, to eliminate differences among national legal systems and to set standards for domestic laws.

9.2.2 Prevention

As the earliest preventive instrument, the Council of Europe Recommendation for the first time recognized the fact that banking systems not only can play a preventive role in the fight against money laundering but also can assistant the judicial authorities and the police to repress such activities. However the Council of Europe

Recommendation was neither widely accepted nor implemented in practice.

The Basel Committee Statement of Principles, like the Council of Europe Recommendation, is not a legal document and has no binding legal effect, however, it not only had profound impacts on members of the Basel Committee, but also had far-reaching influence beyond its scope. It emphasized the notion, provided first by the Council of Europe Recommendation, that financial institutions are the linchpin to effective money laundering prevention and detection, which has been widely adopted in subsequent national regulations and international instruments.

The FATF, as an international body specializing in the fight against money laundering, plays a particular role in this area. It establishes an international standard for effective money laundering control. Its Recommendations have international recognition and application. More importantly, the FATF not only put forward Recommendations but also urged members to implement its Recommendations in practice by the way of self-exercise and mutual evaluation process. Furthermore, the FATF measures evolve constantly with the development of money laundering techniques. With the original 1990 Forty Recommendations, the 1990—1995 Interpretive Notes, the 1996 Revised Recommendations, and the 2003 Revised Recommendations, every stage goes a further step to establish stricter obligations for membership. However, the Recommendations of FATF also have no legal constraining force.

The 1991 European Community Directive and the 2001 Amendment to the 1991 Directive are landmarks in the international efforts against money laundering in different stages of history. The 1991 Directive primarily focuses on money laundering prevention and detection by financial institutions. It imposes a number of specific obligations on financial institutions, such as customer identification, record keeping, obligatory suspicious transaction reporting[478] and internal control procedures and training programs. *"The issuance of the Directive marks the EC's adoption of the strictest anti-money laundering standards in the world."*[479] Because the money laundering threat and the response to that threat have evolved a lot since the issue of the 1991 Direc-

---

[478] Under the original 40 Recommendations of the FATF, financial institutions are merely permitted to report suspicious transactions, while the 1991 Directive makes such reporting mandatory. For this reason, the 1991 Directive is considered a step forward from the original 40 Recommendations.

[479] Kern Alexander, The International Anti-Money-Laundering Regime: The Role of the Financial Action Task Force, *Journal of Money Laundering Control*, Vol. 4 No. 3, p. 239.

tive, the 2001 Amendment to the 1991 Directive emerges. The 2001 Amendment addresses the most sensitive issues in the fight against money laundering, that is the expanded scope of predicate offences, the coverage of non-financial professions and activities, the solution to the contradiction between professional privilege and anti-money laundering obligations, and the new challenges created by high technology. The 2001 Amendment continues to be a leading international instrument in the fight against money laundering.

9.3　China's Anti-money Laundering Efforts and the Gaps between the EU and China

The efforts to combat money laundering in China resulted from international requirements and national necessity. At the international level, it is apparent that with the ever-growing gravity of money laundering activities, the international community has paid due attention to the money laundering problem since the 1980s. Conventions, Recommendations, Principles of anti-money laundering have been shaping up and constantly updated. All the member states of the United Nations are required to pay indispensable attention to fight and prevent money laundering by means of setting up a comprehensive system. In order to conform to the obligations proposed by the international community, China should make a quick response to money laundering. At the national level, with the transition of the economic system from planned economy to market economy, and with the booming economy providing greater opportunities for investment, money laundering is a true problem in China. Domestic and foreign criminal gangs try every possible means to launder money in China. However, the mechanism to combat money laundering in China was insufficient or even completely absent.

It was in the 1990s that the Chinese government started the campaign of combating money laundering. The initial action was the issue of the *"Decision on Suppressing of Drug Dealing"*, under which drug-related money laundering was stipulated. Afterwards, money laundering offence was formulated under the 1997 Criminal Code, which extends well beyond drug-related laundering. After the terrorist attacks on New York and Washington on 11 September 2001, the third set of amendments to the Chinese Criminal Code were adopted, where terrorism is put on the list of predicate offences.

For quite a long time, Chinese criminal law was the only weapon cracking down on money laundering. It is not logical that only "*red warning*" is put in place while no preceding "*yellow warning*" has been established to prevent money laundering. Chinese preventive measures against money laundering didn't emerge until January 2003, when three administrative rules were adopted, namely, the Rules for Anti-money Laundering by Financial Institutions, the Administrative Rules for the Reporting of Large-Value and Suspicious RMB Payment Transactions, and the Administrative Rules for the Reporting by Financial Institutions of Large-Value and Suspicious Foreign Exchange Transactions. These three rules fully draw on international experience for reference and formulate concrete obligations for financial institutions in the fight against money laundering, such as customer identification, record keeping, and large-value/suspicious transaction reporting.

In sum, with the fight against money laundering deepening in the international community, China has made significant progress in combating and preventing money laundering in recent years. In other words, it has established a money laundering offence for several serious crimes; it already has a confiscation system not only for money laundering crime but also for other crimes; it has established identification requirements for customers and it has established a mandatory large-value/suspicious transaction reporting system. However, compared with the standards set up in the EU countries, the gaps between the EU and China are obvious, which can be concluded as follows:

9.3.1 Suppressive Measures

In respect of the constitutional elements of money laundering, the scope of predicate offences needs to be widened. In China, the scope of the predicate offence is confined to four kinds of crimes: drug-related crimes, organizational crime of the underworld, smuggling and terrorism. In fact, money laundering is associated with all types of crimes. It is not appropriate to limit money-laundering offences to drug-trafficking proceeds; neither is suitable to limit it to any type of criminal offence. As to the mental element of money laundering crime, the Chinese Criminal Code doesn't provide for negligent laundering but merely for willful laundering. Taking the experience of some EU countries for reference, negligent money laundering should also be taken into account by legislators.

In regard to the confiscation system, the existing confiscation system of China still has substantial room for improvement, compared with the EU countries. Since the general confiscation system is not enough to cope with these extraordinarily sophisticated crimes, it will be more desirable to enact a special confiscation law dedicated to dealing with money laundering crime. Value confiscation system should be set up to prevent criminals from escaping confiscation measures simply by converting the proceeds into other property or intermingling the proceeds with property acquired from legitimate sources. More importantly, the mechanism of confiscated assets sharing should be put in place in China to contribute confiscated property to intergovernmental bodies specializing in the fight against money laundering crimes or to share confiscated property with other states.

9.3.2 Preventive Measures

The biggest shortcoming of the Chinese preventive measures against money laundering is that anti-money laundering obligations are only imposed on financial institutions. Compared with the situation in the EU, not only banks, non-bank financial institutions, but also non-financial persons or entities, such as auditors, external accountants and advisors, real estate agents, notaries and other independent legal professionals, dealers in high-value goods, and casinos are covered by anti-money laundering legislation.

Besides, an FIU has not been established in China. From the experience in the EU, it can be concluded that an operational FIU is a necessary part of a suspicious transaction reporting system. The effectiveness of the reporting system will be severely limited by the lack of FIU. The next step of anti-money laundering effort in China should consider what kind of FIU, administrative body, police authority or judicial authority should be established.

Furthermore, since the preventive measures against money laundering came into existence only a couple of years ago in China, a *"culture"* of conducting customer identification, record keeping and large-value/suspicious transactions reporting is still at the initial stages. Some troublesome issues, such as how to control smurfing practices, how to implement customer identification measures in case of non-face to face contact, whether to report attempted money laundering, how to keep suspicious transactions reporting confidential and to protect their staff, and how to make feedback for suspicious transactions reporting sufficient, all haven't attracted much attention of Chinese legislators as well as law-executors.

9.4 Banking Secrecy, Professional Privilege and High Technology

9.4.1 Banking Secrecy

The original intention of banking secrecy is to prevent persons from arbitrary or unlawful interference. Unfortunately, it is a fact that banking secrecy provides a safe harbor for money laundering activities and allows criminals to launder money more easily.

According to the legal practice, banking secrecy should be lifted under two situations: one is during the law enforcement process or international cooperation procedure, which means that the principle of banking secrecy should give way to the law enforcement authority performing provisional measures, and also, the principle of banking secrecy should be overridden by international cooperation obligations. The other is in the procedure of due diligence of financial institutions, which means that financial institutions should care about the origin of their customer's money, cooperate with law enforcement agencies on their own initiative, and expose suspicious transactions of their customers, without alerting them to this fact. In short, the former exists in the suppression course, while the latter happens in the prevention course.

Undoubtedly, anti-money laundering measures are getting much more intrusive. Thus there is a strong tension between preserving privacy rights and enforcing a strong and effective anti-money laundering effort. This tension also reflects the tension between individual liberty and social order. Privacy interests are highly valued, so are the interests of being safe and secure from money laundering and other serious crimes. Thus the overriding issue is where the balance should be. This balance should be made to maximize benefit and should not swing based merely on external events.

9.4.2 Professional Privilege

The continuing efforts by financial institutions to combat money laundering have made the work of money launderers more difficult. To circumvent relevant countermeasures, money launderers have to develop more complex schemes. They turn to the expertise of lawyers, notaries, accountants and other professionals to aid them to minimize suspicion surrounding their criminal activities. To deal with this problem, more and more international documents and national legislation bring these professionals under the obligations of anti-money laundering crime.

Nevertheless, lawyers, notaries, accountants and other independent professionals have particular status and the relationship between these professionals and their clients are especially intimate. Imposing anti-money laundering obligations on these professionals is a sensitive matter and may interfere with the individual interests, litigation rights and the quality of intermediary activities. Thus the problem of how to strike a balance between protecting professional privilege and fighting against money laundering arises. The proper settlement is to make a difference between their activities: when professional activities are linked with judicial proceedings or in the course of ascertaining the legal position of clients, they would be exempted from the obligation of anti-money laundering. However they should assume anti-money laundering obligations when they perform financial or company law activities. Furthermore they should report their suspicion of money laundering crime not to enforcement authorities but to self-regulatory bodies in order to acknowledge the sensitive relationship between these professionals and their clients.

9.4.3 High Technology

The inconvenience of traditional laundering, such as currency smuggling, laundering through financial institutions or non-financial institutions, is obvious. The reasons are twofold. First, traditional laundering often links with traditional currency. Traditional currency has limited face amounts. The bigger the amount is, the bigger the space needed to store it. Besides, the counting of traditional currency is troublesome and takes much time, thus lowering the speed of transactions and raising the risk of money launderers being detected. Second, traditional laundering also links with traditional intermediaries, financial institutions or non-financial institutions. With the continuous and intensive efforts carried out by these intermediaries, traditional launderers are confronted with more and more difficulties.

The development of high technology is a double-edged sword. It raises people's living standards on the one side; and on the other side, it also provides great opportunities for criminals. The immateriality, anonymity and high speed of electronic money can offer money launderers great convenience. Internet banks and Internet casinos are likely to be a launderers' paradise, because it is very difficult for them to identify a client, keep records and report suspicious transactions. Therefore, with the emergence of electronic money, Internet banks and Internet casinos, there is every probability that money launderers move their activities from the physical world to cyberspace.

Existing anti-money laundering measures were developed based on certain assumptions, such as the use of banks to make certain transactions, the ability of financial institutions to monitor its customers' activities and the use of physical currency. However, the above-mentioned neoformations challenge these assumptions as well as the existing money laundering countermeasures. Given this new challenge, existing measures need to be modified. Woefully little has been done in regard to the new challenge posed by new technology both at the national level and the international level. Although some experts have put forward some suggestions, suggestions are only suggestions. What is more important is to carry out these suggestions and try to find out whether they are capable of being implemented and how to improve them so that we can efficiently control high technology laundering.

9.5 Final Remarks

With the ever-growing gravity of money laundering activities, unprecedented actions have been taken to control money laundering by the international community and the EU countries. China, has also made great efforts to respond to this problem. However, it is a fact that in general the deterrence of money laundering in China is just at the initial stage. China still has a long way to go. Moreover, with the new trends of money laundering schemes, efforts to combat laundering should be similarly dynamic not only for China but also for all the other countries.

Appendix

Appendix 1 《中华人民共和国刑法修正案(六)》对洗钱罪的修改

2006年6月29日第十届全国人民代表大会常务委员会第二十二次会议通过了《中华人民共和国刑法修正案(六)》。

《修正案》第16条将刑法第191条第1款修改为:"明知是毒品犯罪、黑社会性质的组织犯罪、恐怖活动犯罪、走私犯罪、贪污贿赂犯罪、破坏金融管理秩序犯罪、金融诈骗犯罪的所得及其产生的收益,为掩饰、隐瞒其来源和性质,有下列行为之一的,没收实施以上犯罪的所得及其产生的收益,处五年以下有期徒刑或者拘役,并处或者单处洗钱数额百分之五以上百分之二十以下罚金;情节严重的,处五年以上十年以下有期徒刑,并处洗钱数额百分之五以上百分之二十以下罚金:

(一)提供资金账户的;
(二)协助将财产转换为现金、金融票据、有价证券的;
(三)通过转账或者其他结算方式协助资金转移的;
(四)协助将资金汇往境外的;
(五)以其他方法掩饰、隐瞒犯罪所得及其收益的来源和性质的。"

《修正案》对原有的洗钱犯罪作了两个方面的修改:第一,将洗钱罪的上游犯罪进一步扩大。在1997年《刑法》与2001年刑法修正案中,洗钱罪的上游犯罪为毒品犯罪、黑社会性质的组织犯罪、恐怖活动犯罪、走私犯罪,而本次修正又将洗钱罪上游犯罪的范围扩大到贪污贿赂犯罪、破坏金融管理秩序罪和金融诈骗犯罪。由于这些上游犯罪都是类罪名,包括了一系列的具体罪名,因此,洗钱罪的上游犯罪的具体罪名目前已达七十多个,其中毒品犯罪有12个,黑社会性质的组织犯罪有1个,恐怖活动犯罪有2个,走私犯罪有10个,贪污贿赂犯罪有12个,破坏金融管理秩序罪有30个(包括洗钱罪),金融诈骗犯罪有8个。这七十多个犯罪中,大部分犯罪能直接产生犯罪收益,如所有的走私犯罪,大部分毒品犯罪、贪污罪、受贿罪以及证券、期货犯罪等等;但是,也有一些犯罪不能直接产生收益,如组织、领导、参加恐怖组织罪,资助恐怖活动罪,行贿罪,单位行贿罪,介绍贿赂罪,强迫他人吸毒罪,容留他人吸毒罪,引诱、教唆、欺骗他人吸毒罪,包庇毒品犯罪分子罪等等。但是根据联合国的《反腐败公约》和《打击跨国有组织犯罪公约》的规定,"犯罪所得"系指通过实施犯罪而直接或间接产生或者获得的任何财产。从理论上说,所有犯罪都有可能间接地获得犯罪收益,因此把以上犯罪都规定为洗钱犯罪的上游犯罪是与国际社会的立法宗旨相符的。第二,对洗钱罪的行为方式作了细小的调整。在原有的刑法规定中,洗钱罪的第二种行为方式是"协助将财产转换为现金、金融票据的",而新的刑法修正案修改为:"协助将财产转换为现金、金融票据、有价证券的"。金融票据一般是指汇票、本票和支票,而有价证券则包括股票、债券、国库券等等。

尽管《修正案》再此扩大了洗钱罪的上游犯罪,但是根据联合国《打击跨国有组织犯罪公约》的规定,所有的严重犯罪,即最高刑为4年以上自由刑的犯罪都可以构成洗钱犯罪的上游犯罪。与此国际公约相比,我国的洗钱罪范围还不够宽。但是,除了洗钱罪之外,我国刑法还规定了窝藏、转移、收购、销售赃物罪,刑法第312条的规定:"对明知是犯罪所得而予以窝藏、转移、收购或者代为销售的,处三年以下有期徒刑、拘役或者管制,并处或者单处罚金。"为了进一步明确法律界限,以利于打击对其他犯罪的违法所得予以掩饰、隐瞒的严重违法行为,《修正案》第19条将《刑法》第312条修改为:"明知是犯罪所得及其产生的收益而予以窝藏、转移、收购、代为销售或者以其他方法掩饰、隐瞒的,处三年以下有期徒刑、拘役或者管制,并处或者单处罚金;情节严重的,处三年以上七年以下有期徒刑,并处罚金。"即对洗钱罪上游犯罪以外的犯罪的违法所得进行掩饰和隐瞒的,虽然不构成洗钱罪,但可以构成第312条规定的犯罪。

Appendix 2　Rules for Anti-money Laundering by Financial Institutions

Article 1　These rules are formulated in line with the Law of the People's Republic of China on the People's Bank of China and other relevant laws, administrative rules and regulations to combat money laundering by criminals so as to safeguard the healthy operation of the financial industry.

Article 2　These rules are applicable to all financial institutions involved in combating money laundering.

Financial institutions hereunder refer to institutions legally established and engaged in financial business within the territory of the People's Republic of China, including policy banks, commercial banks, credit cooperatives, postal savings institutions, finance companies, trust and investment companies, financial leasing companies and foreign-funded financial institutions etc.

Article 3　Money laundering in these rules refers to any action that legalize the ill-gotten income and yields generated from criminal activities like drug trafficking, gang violence, terrorist act, smuggling or other crimes through various means in which the source and origin of such income and yields are disguised.

Article 4　Financial institutions and their employees shall abide by these rules to fulfill their due obligation to combat money laundering activities in real earnest and identify suspicious transactions on a prudent basis, and shall not engage in any unfair competition that may run counter to their anti-money laundering obligations.

Article 5　Financial institutions and their employees shall abide by relevant rules and regulations to and refrain from disclosing any information on anti-money laundering activities to their customers and/or other personnel.

Article 6　Financial institutions shall assist the judiciary and/or law enforcement departments including the customs and taxation authorities in combating money laundering in accordance to relevant laws and regulations through making inquiry of, freezing or suspending the transfer of suspicious customers' deposits.

Overseas branch offices of the Chinese financial institutions shall abide by anti-money laundering laws and regulations of their host countries or regions and provide assistance to departments involved in anti-money laundering operation in these countries or regions.

Article 7 The People's Bank of China is the supervisory authority for anti-money laundering operation by financial institutions.

The People's Bank of China shall establish a leading group supervising the work of anti-money laundering by the financial institutions, which shall perform the following responsibilities:

(1) Supervising and coordinating anti-money laundering activities of financial institutions;

(2) Conducting research and formulating strategies, working plans and policies on anti-money laundering for financial institutions, establishing working mechanisms for anti-money laundering operation and reporting system for large-value and/or suspicious RMB fund transactions;

(3) Establishing a monitoring system to scrutinize payment transactions;

(4) Working out proper solutions to major difficulties encountered by financial institutions in combating money laundering;

(5) Participating in international anti-money laundering cooperation and providing guidance for international exchange in the areas of anti-money laundering by financial institutions; and

(6) Other anti-money laundering functions of the People's Bank of China.

The Sate Administration of Foreign Exchange is responsible for supervising reporting of large-value and/or suspicious foreign exchange transactions and shall establish a reporting arrangement to monitor such transactions.

Article 8 Financial institutions shall establish and improve their internal anti-money laundering mechanisms and report such mechanisms to the People's Bank of China for record as required by the People's Bank of China.

Article 9 Financial institutions shall establish or designate relevant internal departments to specialize in anti-money laundering efforts and equip these departments with managers and working staff as needed.

Pursuant to concrete needs, financial institutions shall establish relevant departments or designate certain personnel in their branch offices to specialize in anti-money laundering activities, and shall conduct supervision over implementation of these rules and establishment of internal anti-money laundering mechanisms in their branch offices.

Effective anti-money laundering measures shall be made when new financial institutions are incorporated or financial institutions set up new branch offices.

Article 10　Financial institutions shall establish a customers' identity registry system to verify the identities of customers who process financial business including deposits and settlement with them.

Financial institutions shall not be allowed to open anonymous accounts or accounts in obviously fictitious names for their customers, and/or provide financial services including deposits and settlement for customers whose identities are yet to be clarified.

Article 11　When opening deposit accounts or providing settlement service for individual customers, financial institutions shall verify the customers' IDs and record the names and ID numbers. If a customer is represented by another person to open personal deposit account with a financial institution, the financial institution shall verify both the representative's and principal's IDs and record the names and ID numbers thereof.

Financial institutions shall not open deposit accounts for customers who decline to show IDs or do not use names appeared in their IDs.

Article 12　When opening accounts or providing financial services including deposits and settlement for institutional customers, financial institutions shall abide by relevant rules of the People's Bank of China and ask the customers to show valid documents for verification and recording.

Financial institutions shall not provide financial services including deposits and settlement for institutional customers who fail to show valid documents as required by relevant rules.

Article 13　Financial institutions shall abide by relevant rules and report to the People's Bank of China and/or the State Administration of Foreign Exchange of any large-value transactions detected in the process of providing financial services to customers.

Classification of large-value transactions shall be determined in line with relevant rules made by the People's Bank of China and the State Administration of Foreign Exchange on reporting of fund transactions.

Article 14　Financial institutions shall abide by relevant rules and report to the People's Bank of China and/or the State Administration of Foreign Exchange of any suspicious transactions detected in the process of providing financial services to customers.

Reporting of suspicious transactions shall be determined in line with relevant rules made by the People's Bank of China and the State Administration of Foreign Exchange on reporting of fund transactions.

Article 15　Branch offices of financial institutions shall report large-value and/or suspicious transactions to the local branch offices of the People's Bank of China or the State Administration of Foreign Exchange in line with relevant rules made by the People's Bank of China and the State Administration of Foreign Exchange on procedures of reporting of fund transactions, and at the same time keep their superior units informed of such transactions.

Article 16　Financial institutions shall carry out examination and analysis on large-value and/or suspicious transactions, and shall report to the local public security departments if criminal activities are detected.

Article 17　Financial institutions shall keep records on account information and transaction records of the customers in accordance with the following prescription:

(1) Records of account information shall be kept for five years at minimum from the date of closing the account;

(2) Transaction records shall be kept for five years at minimum from the date of booking the transaction.

Transaction records in item (2) include information on the ownership of the account, amount of deposit or withdrawal effected through the account, time of transaction, source and destination of funds and the means of fund transfer etc.

Account information and transaction records shall be kept in line with relevant state rules on management of accounting files.

Article 18　The People's Bank of China or the State Administration of Foreign Exchange shall hand over the report and other related materials on large-value and/or suspicious transactions submitted by financial institutions to the judiciary departments in accordance with procedures laid by the Rules for Administrative Departments in Transferring Suspected Criminal Cases if criminal activities are suspected after conducting review of such report and related materials, and shall not disclose contents of the report to the customers of the financial institutions and other people.

Article 19 The People's Bank of China shall provide guidance and organize training activities on the subject of anti-money laundering for financial institutions.

Financial institutions shall launch anti-money laundering publicity among their customers and provide training for their staff on anti-money laundering so as to familiarize them with laws, administrative rule and regulations on anti-money laundering and strengthen their competence in combating money laundering activities.

Article 20 The People's Bank of China shall issue a warning to and order a financial institution committing any of the following irregularities in violation of these rules to take remedial actions within a specified period of time, and if the financial institution fails to make corrections within the specified period of time, a fine of no more than RMB30,000 yuan may be imposed and its senior executives immediately accountable for such misconduct may be disqualified from holding any positions in the financial industry if the circumstances are serious:

(1) failing to establish an internal anti-money laundering mechanism as required;

(2) failing to establish or designate relevant departments to specialize in anti-money laundering efforts as required;

(3) failing to ask institutional customers to show valid documents and other related materials for verification and recording as required;

(4) failing to keep account information and transaction records of customers as required;

(5) leaking anti-money laundering information to customers and other people in violation of rules; or

(6) failing to report to the authorities of large-value and/or suspicious transactions as required.

Article 21 When a financial institution engaged in foreign exchange operation fails to report on a timely basis to authorities of abnormal foreign exchange transactions such as purchase of foreign exchange in large value and/or high frequency and move of large amount of foreign currency cash in and out of account, it shall be penalized in line with Article 25 of the Rules on Penalizing Financial Irregularities.

Article 22 Where a financial institution, in violation of relevant laws and administrative rules and regulations, engages in unfair competition which hampers the fulfillment of its anti-money laundering obligation, it shall be penalized in line with relevant provisions of the Rules on Penalizing Financial Irregularities. A disciplinary warning shall be issued for its staff held immediately accountable for such misconduct and the senior executives directly responsible for the misconduct shall be disqualified from holding any positions in the financial industry if the circumstances are serious.

Article 23 Where a financial institution opens accounts for customers who have declined to show their personal IDs or use the names appeared in the personal IDs in opening bank accounts, the People's Bank of China shall give it a warning and impose concurrently a fine of not less than RMB1000 yuan but not more than RMB5000 yuan. If the circumstances are serious, its senior executives held immediately accountable for such misconduct shall be disqualified from holding any positions in the financial industry.

Article 24 The China's Association of Banks, China's Association of Finance Companies and other self-regulatory organizations in the financial industry may formulate their own anti-money laundering work guidance in line with these rules.

Article 25 These rules shall enter into effect on March 1, 2003.

Appendix 3 Administrative Rules for the Reporting of Large-Value and Suspicious RMB Payment Transactions

Article 1   These Rules are formulated in accordance with Law of the People's Republic of China on the People's Bank of China and other laws and regulations in order to strengthen supervision over RMB payment transactions, regulate RMB payment transaction reporting activities and prevent bank payment and settlement from being misused for money laundering and other law-violating and criminal activities.

Article 2   RMB payment transactions referred to in these Rules are RMB-denominated monetary payment made by institutions and individuals through bills, bank cards, remittance, entrusted collection, custodian acceptance, online payment and cash and its clearing transactions.

Large-value payment transactions refer to any RMB payment transaction whose value is above the specified threshold.

Suspicious payment transactions refer to those RMB payment transactions with abnormality in amount, frequency, direction, use or nature.

Article 3   Policy banks, commercial banks, urban and rural credit cooperatives and their unions, postal savings institutions (hereinafter referred to as financial institutions) licensed by the People's Bank of China and established within the territory of the People's Republic of China shall abide by these Rules when handling payment transactions.

Article 4   The People's Bank of China and its branch offices shall be charged with supervising and administering reporting of payment transactions.

Article 5   The People's Bank of China shall establish a payment transaction monitoring system.

Article 6   Financial institutions shall create specialized anti-money laundering posts in their operational offices, specify their responsibilities, and have specified staff record, analyze and report large-value payment transactions and suspicious payment transactions.

Article 7　The following transaction payments constitute large-value transaction payments:

(1) Any single credit transfer above RMB one million yuan between legal persons, other organizations and firms created by self-employed persons (hereinafter referred to as institutions);

(2) Any single cash transaction above RMB 200,000 yuan, including cash deposit, cash withdrawal, cash remittance, cash draft, cash promissory note payment.

(3) Fund transfer above RMB200,000 yuan among individual bank settlement accounts, and between individual bank settlement account and corporate bank settlement account.

Article 8　The following payment transactions constitute suspicious payment transactions:

(1) Fund being moved out in large quantities after coming into a financial institution in small amounts and in many batches within a short period of time or vice versa;

(2) The frequency and amount of fund movement apparently not commensurate with the magnitude of an enterprise's business operation;

(3) Direction of fund movement apparently not commensurate with the range of business operation of an enterprise;

(4) Current fund movement apparently not commensurate with the features of an enterprise's business operation;

(5) Regular occurrence of frequent fund movement apparently not commensurate with the nature and business operation of an enterprise;

(6) Frequent fund movement within a short period of time between the same receiving party and the same paying party;

(7) Sudden and frequent fund movement in and out of an account that has been dormant for a long time;

(8) An enterprise frequently receiving individual remittance that is obviously unrelated to its range of business within a short period of time;

(9) Cash deposit and withdrawal whose amount, frequency and use are apparently different from the normal fund movement of a customer;

(10) The accumulated cash movement through an individual bank settlement account exceeding RMB one million yuan within a short period of time;

(11) Frequent fund transfer within a short period of time to and from customers located in regions with serious drug-trafficking, smuggling and terrorist activities;

(12) Accounts being opened and closed frequently, and experiencing large fund movement before being closed;

(13) Breaking large-value fund movement up into small amounts deliberately in order to escape large-value payment transaction monitoring;

(14) Other suspicious payment transaction defined by the People's Bank of China; or

(15) Other suspicious payment transaction identified by a financial institution.

"A short period of time" referred to in this Article is 10 or less than 10 business days.

Article 9 When a depositor applies for opening a bank settlement account, the financial institution should examine the authenticity, completeness and legality of the documents submitted by the depositor.

Article 10 A financial institution shall create depositor's database to record information of holders of bank settlement accounts, including, in the case of a corporate customer, the title of the institution, name of legal representative or person-in-charge and name and number of his/her valid ID, supporting documents for opening the account, organization registration code, address, registered capital, range of business, major parties of fund movement, average size of daily fund movement of the account, and in the case of an individual customer, the name of the customer, name and number of his/her ID, address and other information.

Article 11 When a financial institution discovers from its customer any occurrence as listed in Article 8 in the processing of payment and settlement business, it shall record, analyze the suspicious payment transaction, and fill in the Suspicious Payment Transaction Reporting Form before reporting the case.

Article 12 When a financial institution finds it necessary to further verify a case of suspicious payment transaction, it shall report to the People's Bank of China in a timely manner.

When the People's Bank of China inquires about a case of suspicious payment transaction, the inquired financial institution shall find out the truth, reply promptly and record the case in the file.

Article 13   A financial institution shall keep the record of payment transactions in accordance with the regulations on bank accounting files.

Article 14   A financial institution shall formulate internal rules and operational procedures for payment transaction reporting in line with these Rules, and report the rules and procedures to the People's Bank of China.

A financial institution shall supervise and examine the implementation of these rules and procedures by its branch offices.

Article 15   Large-value fund transfer from accounts shall be reported by the financial institution through connecting its system with the payment transaction monitoring system.

Large-value cash transfer shall be reported by the financial institution through its business processing system or by writing.

Suspicious payment transaction shall be examined by the financial institution at the counter and reported in writing or other forms.

Article 16   When a financial institution processes a large-value fund transfer, it shall report to the head office of the People's Bank of China within the next business day after the day of the transaction's occurrence.

When a financial institution processes a large-value cash transfer, the financial institution shall report within the next business day after the day of the transaction's occurrence to the local branch office of the People's Bank of China, who shall in turn report to head office of the People's Bank of China.

Article 17   When an operational office of a policy bank, a wholly state-owned commercial bank, or a joint-stock commercial bank discovers a suspicious payment transaction, it shall fill in the Suspicious Payment Transaction Reporting Form and report to the tier-one branch of the bank, who shall report, within the next business day after receiving the Form, to the regional branch, operations office and provincial capital sub-branch of the People's Bank of China, and at the same time report to its superior branch.

When an operational office of a city commercial bank, a rural commercial bank, a rural or urban credit cooperative or its union, a wholly foreign-funded bank, a sino-foreign joint-equity bank or a foreign bank's branch discovers a suspicious payment transaction, it shall fill in a Suspicious Payment Transaction Reporting Form and report to the local branch office, operations office, provincial capital sub-branch or prefecture sub-branch of the People's Bank of China. When a prefecture sub-branch of the People's Bank of China receives such a report, it shall report, within the next business day after receipt, to the branch, operations office or provincial capital sub-branch of the People's Bank of China.

Article 18 When an operational office of a financial institution finds, after analyzing a case of RMB payment transaction, the need for immediate criminal investigation against the suspect, it shall report to the local public security authority immediately and its superior branch at the same time.

Article 19 Branches, operation offices and provincial capital sub-branches of the People's Bank of China shall analyze the Suspicious Payment Transaction Reporting Forms submitted by financial institutions. When it is necessary for the reporting financial institution to provide additional material or further explanation, the said financial institution shall be informed immediately.

Article 20 Each branch, operation office and provincial capital sub-branch of the People's Bank of China shall make a weekly summary of the Suspicious Payment Transaction Reporting Forms submitted by financial institutions and report to the head office of the People's Bank of China on the first business day of every week. The payment transaction shall be reported to the head office of the People's Bank of China immediately after its discovery if the case is serious.

Article 22 The People's Bank of China and financial institutions shall not disclose to any institution or individual information about suspicious payment transactions, unless otherwise stipulated by laws.

Article 23 When a financial institution fails to examine the document submitted for opening accounts in accordance with relevant regulations and opens a settlement account for an individual, the People's Bank of China shall issue a warning and concurrently impose on it a fine between RMB1,000 yuan and RMB5,000 yuan. In a serious case, its senior executives directly responsible for such misconduct shall be banned from taking any senior position in the financial industry.

Article 24 In the case of any of the following misconduct by a financial institution, the People's Bank of China shall issue a warning and order the financial institution to take remedial action within a specified period of time, and if the financial institution fails to do so within the specified time limit, a fine up to RMB30,000 yuan may be imposed.

(1) Opening account without examining the submitted materials according to relevant regulations that leads to the opening of a falsified institutional bank settlement account;

(2) Failing to create depositor's databank or having incomplete depositor's information;

(3) Failing to keep customer transactions record as stipulated;

(4) Failing to examine and report payment transactions in accordance with these Rules;

(5) Failing to report any known suspicious payment transaction or a suspicious payment transaction that should have been reported;

(6) Disclosing suspicious payment transaction information in violation of Article Twenty-One.

Article 25   Disciplinary penalty shall be imposed on the staff of a financial institution who is/are involved in falsifying account-opening materials to open bank settlement account(s) for individual(s) and facilitate money-laundering activities; when the misconduct constitutes a violation of the criminal law, the case shall be transferred to judiciary authorities.

Article 26   When a financial institution seriously violates these Rules, the People's Bank of China shall cease its approval for the institution to open basic deposit account, suspend or terminate part or all of its payment and settlement business and ban the senior executives directly responsible for such violations from taking any senior management position in the industry.

Article 27   Staff of the People's Bank of China shall be imposed an administrative penalty in accordance with laws for any violation of Article 21 of these Rules.

Article 28   When "above", "between" and "up to" are used to indicate a threshold number, a floor or a ceiling, the number that ensues any of them is also included.

Article 29   These Rules shall enter into effect as of March 1, 2003.

Appendix 4 Administrative Rules for the Reporting by Financial Institutions of Large-Value and Suspicious Foreign Exchange Transactions

Article 1 These Rules are formulated in accordance with Regulations of the People's Republic of China on Foreign Exchange Administration and other regulations in order to monitor large-value and suspicious foreign exchange transactions.

Article 2 Financial institutions located in the territory of China that run foreign exchange business (hereinafter referred to as financial institutions) shall report, in accordance with these Rules, to foreign exchange administration authorities large-value and suspicious foreign exchange transactions.

Large-value foreign exchange transaction refers to foreign exchange transactions above a specified amount made by transactions parties in any form of settlement through financial institutions.

Suspicious foreign exchange transaction refers to foreign exchange transaction with abnormal amount, frequency, source, direction, use or any other such nature.

Article 3 State Administration of Foreign Exchange and its branches (hereinafter referred to as SAFE) are responsible for supervising and administering the reporting of large-value and suspicious foreign exchange transactions.

Article 4 When opening foreign exchange accounts for customers, financial institutions shall abide by Rules on Using Real Name for Opening Individual Deposit Account and Rules on Administration of Foreign Exchange Account within the Territory of People's Republic of China and shall not open anonymous foreign exchange accounts or accounts in obviously fictitious names for their customers.

When processing foreign exchange transactions for customers, financial institutions shall verify information about the customer's real identity, including the name of work unit, name of the legal representative or person-in-charge, ID and its number, supporting documents for account opening, organization registration code, address, registered capital, business scope, size of business operation, average daily transaction volume of the account and in the case of an individual customer, name of the depositor, ID and its number, address, occupation, household income and other information about the customer's family.

Article 5　Financial institutions shall record all large-value and suspicious foreign exchange fund transactions and keep the record for a minimum of five years as of the day of transaction.

Article 6　Financial institutions shall establish and improve internal anti-money laundering post responsibility system, formulate internal anti-money laundering procedure and, have specified staff record, analyze and report large-value and suspicious foreign exchange transactions.

Article 7　Financial institutions shall not disclose to any agency or individual information about large-value and suspicious foreign exchange transactions, unless otherwise provided for by laws.

Article 8　The following foreign exchange transactions constitute large-value foreign exchange transactions:

(1) Any single deposit, withdrawal, purchase or sale of foreign exchange cash above US $ 10,000 or its equivalent, or the accumulated amount of multiple deposit, withdrawal, purchase or sale transactions of foreign exchange within one day above US $ 10,000 or its equivalent;

(2) Foreign exchange non-cash receipt and payment transactions made through transfer, bills, bank card, telephone-banking, internet banking or other electronic transactions or other new financial instruments in which a single transaction volume or accumulated transaction volume within one day exceeding US $ 100,000 or its equivalent by individual customers, and in the case of corporate customers, a single transaction volume or accumulated transaction volume within one day exceeding US $ 500,000 or its equivalent.

Article 9　The following foreign exchange transactions constitute suspicious foreign exchange cash transactions:

(1) Frequent deposit and/or withdrawal of large amount of foreign exchange cash from an individual bankcard or individual deposit account that are apparently not commensurate with the identity of or use of fund by the cardholder or account owner;

(2) An individual resident transferring to or withdrawing cash in large amount in a foreign country after depositing large amount of foreign exchange cash in a bankcard

in China;

(3) Frequent depositing, withdrawal or sale of foreign exchange through an individual foreign exchange cash account below the SAFE validated threshold;

(4) Non-resident individual requiring banks to open traveler's check or draft to convert large amount of foreign exchange cash he/she has brought into China in order to take the fund out of China;

(5) Frequently depositing large amount of foreign exchange cash in a bankcard held by non-resident individual;

(6) Frequent and large-amount fund movement through a corporate foreign exchange account not commensurate with the business activities of the account owner;

(7) Regular and large-amount cash deposit into a corporate foreign exchange account without withdrawal of large amount of cash from the said account;

(8) An enterprise frequently receiving export proceeds in cash that is apparently not commensurate with the range and size of its business;

(9) The RMB fund that an enterprise uses to buy foreign exchange for overseas investment is mostly in cash or has been transferred from a bank account not belonging to the said enterprise;

(10) The RMB fund that a foreign-funded enterprise uses to buy foreign exchange for repatriation of profit is mostly in cash or has been transferred from a bank account not belonging to the said enterprise;

(11) A foreign-funded enterprise making investment in foreign exchange cash.

Article 10   The following foreign exchange transactions constitute suspicious foreign exchange non-cash transactions:

(1) Foreign exchange account of an individual resident frequently receiving fund from domestic accounts that are not under the same name;

(2) An individual resident frequently receiving large amount of foreign exchange remittance from abroad before remitting the total amount out in the original denomination, or frequently remitting foreign exchange fund of the same denomination that is transferred from abroad in large amount;

(3) Non-resident individual frequently receiving remittance in large amount from abroad, especially from countries (regions) with serious problems of narcotics production and trafficking;

(4) Foreign exchange account of a resident or non-resident individual with a

regular pattern of receiving large amount of fund which is withdrawn in several transactions the next day, and then receiving large amount of fund again which is withdrawn in several transactions the next day;

(5) An enterprise making frequent and large advance payment for import and commission under trade account below the SAFE validated threshold through its foreign exchange account;

(6) An enterprise frequently receiving, through its foreign exchange account, export payment in bills (such as check, draft and promissory note) in large amount;

(7) Dormant foreign exchange accounts or foreign exchange accounts usually with no large fund movement suddenly receiving abnormal foreign exchange fund inflow, and the inflow gradually becoming larger in a short period of time;

(8) An enterprise having frequent and large amount fund transactions through its foreign exchange account not commensurate with the nature and size of its business operation;

(9) The foreign exchange account of an enterprise becoming inactive abruptly following frequent and large amount inflow and outflow of fund;

(10) Frequent fund movement through the foreign exchange account of an enterprise in amounts divisible by thousand;

(11) Rapid inflow and outflow of fund through the foreign exchange account of an enterprise, the amount of which is big within one day but the outstanding balance of the account is very small or nil;

(12) The foreign exchange account of an enterprise remitting abroad the bulk of balance received in multiple small amount electronic transfers, check or draft deposits;

(13) A domestic enterprise opening an offshore account in the name of an overseas legal person or natural person, and the said offshore account experiencing regular fund movement;

(14) An enterprise remitting fund to many domestic residents through an offshore account and surrendering foreign exchange to banks in the name of donation, the transfer of fund and foreign exchange sales all done by one person or few persons;

(15) The annual expatriation of profit by a foreign-funded enterprise exceeding the amount of originally invested equity by a large margin and obviously not commensurate with its business operation;

(16) A foreign-funded enterprise rapidly moving the fund abroad in a short period of time after receiving the investment, which is not commensurate with the payment demand of its business operation;

(17) Offsetting deposit and loan transactions with affiliates or connected companies of financial institutions located in regions with serious smuggling, drug trafficking or terrorist activities or other crimes;

(18) Securities institutions ordering banks to transfer foreign exchange fund not for the purpose of securities dealing or settlement;

(19) Securities institutions that engages in B share trading business frequently borrowing large amount of foreign exchange fund through banks; and

(20) Insurance institutions frequently making compensation payment in large amount to or discharging insurance in large amount for the same overseas policy holder through banks.

Article 11　Financial institutions shall report the large-value or suspicious foreign exchange fund transactions as defined by Articles 8, 9 and 10 monthly in hard copy as well as in electronic copy.

Article 12　Financial institutions shall examine the following foreign exchange cash transactions and report promptly any discovery of suspected money laundering in hard copy with relevant documents attached.

(1) Amount of expenditure of foreign exchange account roughly tallying with the amount of deposit in the previous day;

(2) Depositing foreign exchange or RMB cash in many transactions in the foreign exchange deposit accounts of other individuals and receiving at the same time RMB or foreign exchange of equivalent amount;

(3) An enterprise frequently purchasing foreign exchange with RMB cash.

Article 13　Financial institutions shall conduct verification over the following non-cash foreign exchange transactions, and shall promptly report any discovering of suspected money laundering activity and attach related files to the superior authorities:

(1) An individual resident frequently switching from one denomination to another when conducting foreign exchange transactions apparently with no profit-seeking purpose;

(2) An individual resident asking a bank to issue traveler's check or draft after

frequently receiving foreign exchange remittance from abroad;

(3) A non-resident individual frequently ordering traveler's check or cashing traveler's check or draft in large amount through foreign exchange account;

(4) When opening foreign exchange account, an enterprise declining to provide supporting documents or general information on different occasions;

(5) An enterprise group making internal foreign exchange fund transfer exceeding the volume of actual business operation;

(6) An enterprise providing incomplete documents when surrendering to or purchasing foreign exchange from a bank, or the amount of buying or selling suddenly expanding, selling and buying becoming more frequent, or the amount of foreign exchange sold to the bank apparently exceeding the normal level of its business operation;

(7) When entering an item of export revenue into an account in a bank, an enterprise failing to provide valid documents but frequently collecting foreign exchange sales statement (for verification purpose), or rejecting to provide valid documents but frequently collecting foreign exchange sales statement (for verification purpose);

(8) An enterprise frequently receiving foreign exchange, making foreign exchange payment or frequently selling foreign exchange to banks, all in large amount, for the purpose of donation, advertising, sponsoring conference or exhibition, which is apparently not commensurate with its range of business;

(9) An enterprise frequently receiving foreign exchange, making foreign exchange payment, or frequently selling foreign exchange to banks, all in large amount, for the purchase of buying or selling technology or trade mark right or other intangible assets, which is apparently not commensurate with its range of business;

(10) Freight, premium and commission paid by an enterprise apparently not commensurate with its import and export trade;

(11) An enterprise often depositing traveler's check or foreign exchange draft, especially those issued abroad and not commensurate with its business operation;

(12) An enterprise suddenly paying its overdue foreign exchange loan in full with fund whose source is unspecified or not commensurate with the background of the said enterprise;

(13) An enterprise applying for a loan guaranteed by assets or credit belonging

to itself or a third party, the source of which is unspecified or not commensurate with the background of the customer;

(14) Raising fund abroad through letter of credit with no foreign trade background or other means;

(15) An enterprise knowingly conducting loss-making sales or purchase of foreign exchange;

(16) An enterprise seeking to conduct a swap between the local currency and foreign currency for a fund whose source and use is unspecified;

(17) The capital invested by the foreign partner of a foreign-funded enterprise exceeding the approved amount or direct external borrowing of a foreign-funded enterprise being remitted from a third country where there is no connected enterprise;

(18) Local currency fund converted from capital invested by the foreign partner of a foreign-funded enterprise or external borrowing being diverted to bank accounts for securities and other investment, which is not commensurate with its business operation;

(19) Fund movement in and out of the foreign exchange cash account of a financial institution apparently not commensurate with the size of the deposit in the account, or the fluctuation of fund movement apparently exceeding the change in the size of deposit;

(20) Fund movement of the internal foreign exchange transaction accounts of a financial institution apparently not commensurate with its daily business operation;

(21) Fund movement of the inter-bank foreign exchange transaction account, onshore and offshore business transaction account, or account for transactions with overseas affiliates apparently not commensurate with the daily business operation of the financial institution;

(22) Foreign exchange credit or settlement between a financial institution and its connected enterprises fluctuating by a large margin within a short period of time;

(23) A financial institution buying an insurance policy with large value foreign currency cash; and

(24) Any foreign exchange fund transaction being suspected with proper reasons by the staff of a bank or other financial institutions as money laundering.

Article 14　Tier-one branches located in provincial capital, capital of autonomous region and municipality directly under the central government of a financial institution shall act as the major reporting unit and the head office of the financial institution shall designate a major reporting unit if there is no such branch in these places.

Sub-branches and offices of a financial institution shall report, within the first five work days of every month, large-value and suspicious foreign exchange fund transactions of the preceding month through their superior office to the major reporting unit and at the same time to the local branch office of SAFE.

Each major reporting unit shall summarize large-value and suspicious foreign exchange fund transactions that take place in the province, autonomous region or municipality directly under central government in the preceding month and report, within the first 15 work days of every month, to the local branch office of SAFE.

The head office of each financial institution shall report, within the first five days of every month, large-value and suspicious foreign exchange fund transactions that take place within the head office in the preceding month to the local branch office of SAFE.

Article 15 When a financial institution discovers suspected crime during the examination and analysis of large-value and suspicious foreign exchange fund transactions, it shall report to the local public security authority and local SAFE office within three work days as of the day of discovery.

Article 16 SAFE branch offices in every province, autonomous region, and municipality directly under the central government shall summarize large-value and suspicious foreign exchange fund transactions reported by financial institutes and report to SAFE head office within the first 20 work days of every month; when a foreign exchange transaction is suspected as crime, the case shall be transferred promptly to local public security authority and to the SAFE head office.

Article 17 In the case of any of the following misconduct by a financial institution, the SAFE shall issue a warning, order the financial institution to take remedial action, and impose a fine between RMB10,000 yuan to RMB30,000 yuan.

(1) Failing to report, according to relevant rules and regulations, large-value or suspicious foreign exchange fund transactions;

(2) Failing to keep large-value or suspicious foreign exchange transactions in record as stipulated by relevant rules and regulations;

(3) Disclosing large-value or suspicious foreign exchange fund transactions in

violation of relevant rules and regulations; and

(4) Opening foreign exchange account without examining account-opening document.

Article 18 When a financial institution opens a foreign exchange account for an individual customer without examining account-opening documents, the SAFE shall issue a warning, order it to take remedial action and may impose a fine between RMB1,000 yuan and RMB5,000 yuan.

Article 19 When a financial institution brings about grave loss as a result of its serious violation of these Rules, the SAFE may cease or revoke its approval for foreign exchange purchase and sales business in part or in full.

Article 20 Disciplinary penalty shall be imposed on the staff of a financial institution who provides assistance to money-laundering activities; when the misconduct constitutes a violation of the criminal law, the case shall be transferred to judiciary authorities.

Article 21 "Frequent" in these Rules means foreign exchange fund transactions occurring at least three times each day or occurring daily for at least five days in a row.

"Large amount" in these Rules refers to amount close to the threshold amount for reporting as a large-value foreign exchange transaction.

"A short period of time" in these Rules means within 10 business days.

When "above", "between" and "up to" are used to indicate a threshold number, a floor or a ceiling, the number that ensues any of them is also included.

Article 22 These Rules shall enter into effect as of March 1, 2003.

Appendix 5   The Forty Recommendations (2003)

Introduction

Money laundering methods and techniques change in response to developing counter-measures. In recent years, the Financial Action Task Force (FATF) has noted increasingly sophisticated combinations of techniques, such as the increased use of legal persons to disguise the true ownership and control of illegal proceeds, and an increased use of professionals to provide advice and assistance in laundering criminal funds. These factors, combined with the experience gained through the FATF's Non-Cooperative Countries and Territories process, and a number of national and international initiatives, led the FATF to review and revise the Forty Recommendations into a new comprehensive framework for combating money laundering and terrorist financing. The FATF now calls upon all countries to take the necessary steps to bring their national systems for combating money laundering and terrorist financing into compliance with the new FATF Recommendations, and to effectively implement these measures.

The review process for revising the Forty Recommendations was an extensive one, open to FATF members, non-members, observers, financial and other affected sectors and interested parties. This consultation process provided a wide range of input, all of which was considered in the review process.

The revised Forty Recommendations now apply not only to money laundering but also to terrorist financing, and when combined with the Eight Special Recommendations on Terrorist Financing provide an enhanced, comprehensive and consistent framework of measures for combating money laundering and terrorist financing. The FATF recognizes that countries have diverse legal and financial systems and so all cannot take identical measures to achieve the common objective, especially over matters of detail. The Recommendations therefore set minimum standards for action for countries to implement the detail according to their particular circumstances and constitutional frameworks. The Recommendations cover all the measures that national systems should have in place within their criminal justice and regulatory systems; the preventive measures to be taken by financial institutions and certain other businesses and professions; and international co-operation.

The original FATF Forty Recommendations were drawn up in 1990 as an initiative to combat the misuse of financial systems by persons laundering drug money. In 1996 the Recommendations were revised for the first time to reflect evolving money laundering typologies. The 1996 Forty Recommendations have been endorsed by more than 130 countries and are the international anti-money laundering standard.

In October 2001 the FATF expanded its mandate to deal with the issue of the financing of terrorism, and took the important step of creating the Eight Special Recommendations on Terrorist Financing. These Recommendations contain a set of measures aimed at combating the funding of terrorist acts and terrorist organizations, and are complementary to the Forty Recommendations.

A key element in the fight against money laundering and the financing of terrorism is the need for countries systems to be monitored and evaluated, with respect to these international standards. The mutual evaluations conducted by the FATF and FATF-style regional bodies, as well as the assessments conducted by the IMF and World Bank, are a vital mechanism for ensuring that the FATF Recommendations are effectively implemented by all countries.

LEGAL SYSTEMS

Scope of the criminal offence of money laundering

- **Recommendation 1**

    Countries should criminalize money laundering on the basis of United Nations Convention against Illicit Traffic in Narcotic Drugs and Psychotropic Substances, 1988 (the Vienna Convention and United Nations Convention against Transnational Organized Crime, 2000 (the Palermo Convention).

    Countries should apply the crime of money laundering to all serious offences, with a view to including the widest range of predicate offences. Predicate offences may be described by reference to all offences, or to a threshold linked either to a category of serious offences or to the penalty of imprisonment applicable to the predicate offence (threshold approach), or to a list of predicate offences, or a combination of these approaches.

Where countries apply a threshold approach, predicate offences should at a minimum comprise all offences that fall within the category of serious offences under their national law or should include offences which are punishable by a maximum penalty of more than one year's imprisonment or for those countries that have a minimum threshold for offences in their legal system, predicate offences should comprise all offences, which are punished by a minimum penalty of more than six months imprisonment.

Whichever approach is adopted, each country should at a minimum include a range of offences within each of the designated categories of offences.

Predicate offences for money laundering should extend to conduct that occurred in another country, which constitutes an offence in that country, and which would have constituted a predicate offence had it occurred domestically. Countries may provide that the only prerequisite is that the conduct would have constituted a predicate offence had it occurred domestically.

Countries may provide that the offence of money laundering does not apply to persons who committed the predicate offence, where this is required by fundamental principles of their domestic law.

- **Recommendation 2**

    Countries should ensure that:

    a) The intent and knowledge required to prove the offence of money laundering is consistent with the standards set forth in the Vienna and Palermo Conventions, including the concept that such mental state may be inferred from objective factual circumstances.

    b) Criminal liability, and, where that is not possible, civil or administrative liability, should apply to legal persons. This should not preclude parallel criminal, civil or administrative proceedings with respect to legal persons in countries in which such forms of liability are available. Legal persons should be subject to effective, proportionate and dissuasive sanctions. Such measures should be without prejudice to the criminal liability of individuals.

Provisional measures and confiscation

- **Recommendation 3**

Countries should adopt measures similar to those set forth in the Vienna and Palermo Conventions, including legislative measures, to enable their competent authorities to confiscate property laundered, proceeds from money laundering or predicate offences, instrumentalities used in or intended for use in the commission of these offences, or property of corresponding value, without prejudicing the rights of bona fide third parties.

Such measures should include the authority to: (a) identify, trace and evaluate property which is subject to confiscation; (b) carry out provisional measures, such as freezing and seizing, to prevent any dealing, transfer or disposal of such property; (c) take steps that will prevent or void actions that prejudice the State's ability to recover property that is subject to confiscation; and (d) take any appropriate investigative measures.

Countries may consider adopting measures that allow such proceeds or instrumentalities to be confiscated without requiring a criminal conviction, or which require an offender to demonstrate the lawful origin of the property alleged to be liable to confiscation, to the extent that such a requirement is consistent with the principles of their domestic law.

MEASURES TO BE TAKEN BY FINANCIAL INSTITUTIONS AND NON-FINANCIAL BUSINESSES AND PROFESSIONS TO PREVENT MONEY LAUNDERING AND TERRORIST FINANCING

- **Recommendation 4**

Countries should ensure that financial institution secrecy laws do not inhibit implementation of the FATF Recommendations.

Customer due diligence and record-keeping

- **Recommendation 5**

Financial institutions should not keep anonymous accounts or accounts in obviously fictitious names.

Financial institutions should undertake customer due diligence measures, including identifying and verifying the identity of their customers, when:

- establishing business relations;
- carrying out occasional transactions: (i) above the applicable designated threshold; or (ii) that are wire transfers in the circumstances covered by the Interpretative Note to Special Recommendation VII;
- there is a suspicion of money laundering or terrorist financing; or
- the financial institution has doubts about the veracity or adequacy of previously obtained customer identification data.

The customer due diligence (CDD) measures to be taken are as follows:

a) Identifying the customer and verifying that customer's identity using reliable, independent source documents, data or information.

b) Identifying the beneficial owner, and taking reasonable measures to verify the identity of the beneficial owner such that the financial institution is satisfied that it knows who the beneficial owner is. For legal persons and arrangements this should include financial institutions taking reasonable measures to understand the ownership and control structure of the customer.

c) Obtaining information on the purpose and intended nature of the business relationship.

d) Conducting ongoing due diligence on the business relationship and scrutiny of transactions undertaken throughout the course of that relationship to ensure that the transactions being conducted are consistent with the institution's knowledge of the customer, their business and risk profile, including, where necessary, the source of funds.

Financial institutions should apply each of the CDD measures under (a) to (d) above, but may determine the extent of such measures on a risk sensitive basis depending on the type of customer, business relationship or transaction. The measures that are taken should be consistent with any guidelines issued by competent authorities. For higher risk categories, financial institutions should perform enhanced due diligence. In certain circumstances, where there are low risks, countries may decide that financial institutions can apply reduced or simplified measures.

Financial institutions should verify the identity of the customer and beneficial owner before or during the course of establishing a business relationship or conducting transactions for occasional customers. Countries may permit financial institutions to complete the verification as soon as reasonably practicable following the establishment of the relationship, where the money laundering risks are effectively managed and where this is essential not to interrupt the normal conduct of business.

Where the financial institution is unable to comply with paragraphs (a) to (c) above, it should not open the account, commence business relations or perform the transaction; or should terminate the business relationship; and should consider making a suspicious transactions report in relation to the customer.

These requirements should apply to all new customers, though financial institutions should also apply this Recommendation to existing customers on the basis of materiality and risk, and should conduct due diligence on such existing relationships at appropriate times.

(See Interpretative Notes: Recommendation 5 and Recommendations 5, 12 and 16)

- **Recommendation 6**

Financial institutions should, in relation to politically exposed persons, in addition to performing normal due diligence measures:

a) Have appropriate risk management systems to determine whether the customer is a politically exposed person.

b) Obtain senior management approval for establishing business relationships with such customers.

c) Take reasonable measures to establish the source of wealth and source of funds.

Conduct enhanced ongoing monitoring of the business relationship.

- **Recommendation 7**

Financial institutions should, in relation to cross-border correspondent banking and other similar relationships, in addition to performing normal due diligence measures:

a) Gather sufficient information about a respondent institution to understand fully the nature of the respondent's business and to determine from publicly available information the reputation of the institution and the quality of supervision, including whether it has been subject to a money laundering or terrorist financing investigation or regulatory action.

b) Assess the respondent institution's anti-money laundering and terrorist financing controls.

c) Obtain approval from senior management before establishing new correspondent relationships.

d) Document the respective responsibilities of each institution.

e) With respect to "payable-through accounts", be satisfied that the respondent bank has verified the identity of and performed on-going due diligence on the customers having direct access to accounts of the correspondent and that it is able to provide relevant customer identification data upon request to the correspondent bank.

- **Recommendation 8**

Financial institutions should pay special attention to any money laundering threats that may arise from new or developing technologies that might favour anonymity, and take measures, if needed, to prevent their use in money laundering schemes. In particular, financial institutions should have policies and procedures in place to address any specific risks associated with non-face to face business relationships or transactions.

- **Recommendation 9**

Countries may permit financial institutions to rely on intermediaries or other third parties to perform elements (a) (c) of the CDD process or to introduce business, provided that the criteria set out below are met. Where such reliance is permitted, the ultimate responsibility for customer identification and verification remains with the financial institution relying on the third party.

The criteria that should be met are as follows:

a) A financial institution relying upon a third party should immediately obtain the necessary information concerning elements (a) (c) of the CDD process. Financial institutions should take adequate steps to satisfy themselves that copies of identification data and other relevant documentation relating to the CDD requirements will be made available from the third party upon request without delay.

b) The financial institution should satisfy itself that the third party is regulated and supervised for, and has measures in place to comply with CDD requirements in line with Recommendations 5 and 10.

It is left to each country to determine in which countries the third party that meets the conditions can be based, having regard to information available on countries that do not or do not adequately apply the FATF Recommendations.

- **Recommendation 10**

Financial institutions should maintain, for at least five years, all necessary records on transactions, both domestic or international, to enable them to comply swiftly with information requests from the competent authorities. Such records must be sufficient to permit reconstruction of individual transactions (including the amounts and types of currency involved if any) so as to provide, if necessary, evidence for prosecution of criminal activity.

Financial institutions should keep records on the identification data obtained through the customer due diligence process (e. g. copies or records of official identification documents like passports, identity cards, driving licenses or similar documents), account files and business correspondence for at least five years after the business relationship is ended.

The identification data and transaction records should be available to domestic competent authorities upon appropriate authority.

- **Recommendation 11**

Financial institutions should pay special attention to all complex, unusual large transactions, and all unusual patterns of transactions, which have no apparent economic or visible lawful purpose. The background and purpose of such transactions should, as far as possible, be examined, the findings established in writing, and be available to help competent authorities and auditors.

- **Recommendation 12**

The customer due diligence and record-keeping requirements set out in Recommendations 5, 6, and 8 to 11 apply to designated non-financial businesses and professions in the following situations:

a) Casinos when customers engage in financial transactions equal to or above the applicable designated threshold.

b) Real estate agents - when they are involved in transactions for their client concerning the buying and selling of real estate.

c) Dealers in precious metals and dealers in precious stones - when they engage in any cash transaction with a customer equal to or above the applicable designated threshold.

d) Lawyers, notaries, other independent legal professionals and accountants when they prepare for or carry out transactions for their client concerning the following activities:

- buying and selling of real estate;
- managing of client money, securities or other assets;
- management of bank, savings or securities accounts;
- organisation of contributions for the creation, operation or management of companies;
- creation, operation or management of legal persons or arrangements, and buying and selling of business entities.

e) Trust and company service providers when they prepare for or carry out transactions for a client concerning the activities listed in the definition in the Glossary.

Reporting of suspicious transactions and compliance

- **Recommendation 13**

If a financial institution suspects or has reasonable grounds to suspect that funds are the proceeds of a criminal activity, or are related to terrorist financing, it should be required, directly by law or regulation, to report promptly its suspicions to the financial intelligence unit (FIU).

- **Recommendation 14**

Financial institutions, their directors, officers and employees should be:

a) Protected by legal provisions from criminal and civil liability for breach of any restriction on disclosure of information imposed by contract or by any legislative, regulatory or administrative provision, if they report their suspicions in good faith to the FIU, even if they did not know precisely what the underlying criminal activity was, and regardless of whether illegal activity actually occurred.

b) Prohibited by law from disclosing the fact that a suspicious transaction report (STR) or related information is being reported to the FIU.

- **Recommendation 15**

Financial institutions should develop programmes against money laundering and terrorist financing. These programmes should include:

a) The development of internal policies, procedures and controls, including appropriate compliance management arrangements, and adequate screening procedures to ensure high standards when hiring employees.

b) An ongoing employee training programme.

c) An audit function to test the system.

- **Recommendation 16**

The requirements set out in Recommendations 13 to 15, and 21 apply to all designated non-financial businesses and professions, subject to the following qualifications:

a) Lawyers, notaries, other independent legal professionals and accountants should be required to report suspicious transactions when, on behalf of or for a client, they engage in a financial transaction in relation to the activities described in Recommendation 12(d). Countries are strongly encouraged to extend the reporting requirement to the rest of the professional activities of accountants, including auditing.

b) Dealers in precious metals and dealers in precious stones should be required to report suspicious transactions when they engage in any cash transaction with a customer equal to or above the applicable designated threshold.

c) Trust and company service providers should be required to report suspicious transactions for a client when, on behalf of or for a client, they engage in a transaction in relation to the activities referred to Recommendation 12(e).

Lawyers, notaries, other independent legal professionals, and accountants acting as independent legal professionals, are not required to report their suspicions if the relevant information was obtained in circumstances where they are subject to professional secrecy or legal professional privilege.

Other measures to deter money laundering and terrorist financing

- **Recommendation 17**

    Countries should ensure that effective, proportionate and dissuasive sanctions, whether criminal, civil or administrative, are available to deal with natural or legal persons covered by these Recommendations that fail to comply with anti-money laundering or terrorist financing requirements.

- **Recommendation 18**

    Countries should not approve the establishment or accept the continued operation of shell banks. Financial institutions should refuse to enter into, or continue, a correspondent banking relationship with shell banks. Financial institutions should also guard against establishing relations with respondent foreign financial institutions that permit their accounts to be used by shell banks.

- **Recommendation 19**

    Countries should consider:

    a) Implementing feasible measures to detect or monitor the physical cross-border transportation of currency and bearer negotiable instruments, subject to strict safeguards to ensure proper use of information and without impeding in any way the freedom of capital movements.

    b) The feasibility and utility of a system where banks and other financial institutions and intermediaries would report all domestic and international currency transactions above a fixed amount, to a national central agency with a computerized data base, available to competent authorities for use in money laundering or terrorist financing cases, subject to strict safeguards to ensure proper use of the information.

- **Recommendation 20**

    Countries should consider applying the FATF Recommendations to businesses and professions, other than designated non-financial businesses and professions, that pose a money laundering or terrorist financing risk.

    Countries should further encourage the development of modern and secure techniques of money management that are less vulnerable to money laundering.

Appendix

Measures to be taken with respect to countries that do not or insufficiently comply with the FATF Recommendations

- **Recommendation 21**

   Financial institutions should give special attention to business relationships and transactions with persons, including companies and financial institutions, from countries which do not or insufficiently apply the FATF Recommendations. Whenever these transactions have no apparent economic or visible lawful purpose, their background and purpose should, as far as possible, be examined, the findings established in writing, and be available to help competent authorities. Where such a country continues not to apply or insufficiently applies the FATF Recommendations, countries should be able to apply appropriate countermeasures.

- **Recommendation 22**

   Financial institutions should ensure that the principles applicable to financial institutions, which are mentioned above are also applied to branches and majority owned subsidiaries located abroad, especially in countries which do not or insufficiently apply the FATF Recommendations, to the extent that local applicable laws and regulations permit. When local applicable laws and regulations prohibit this implementation, competent authorities in the country of the parent institution should be informed by the financial institutions that they cannot apply the FATF Recommendations.

Regulation and supervision

- **Recommendation 23**

   Countries should ensure that financial institutions are subject to adequate regulation and supervision and are effectively implementing the FATF Recommendations. Competent authorities should take the necessary legal or regulatory measures to prevent criminals or their associates from holding or being the beneficial owner of a significant or controlling interest or holding a management function in a financial institution.

   For financial institutions subject to the Core Principles, the regulatory and supervisory measures that apply for prudential purposes and which are also relevant to money laundering, should apply in a similar manner for anti-money laundering and terrorist financing purposes.

Other financial institutions should be licensed or registered and appropriately regulated, and subject to supervision or oversight for anti-money laundering purposes, having regard to the risk of money laundering or terrorist financing in that sector. At a minimum, businesses providing a service of money or value transfer, or of money or currency changing should be licensed or registered, and subject to effective systems for monitoring and ensuring compliance with national requirements to combat money laundering and terrorist financing.

- **Recommendation 24**

Designated non-financial businesses and professions should be subject to regulatory and supervisory measures as set out below.

a) Casinos should be subject to a comprehensive regulatory and supervisory regime that ensures that they have effectively implemented the necessary anti-money laundering and terrorist-financing measures. At a minimum:
- casinos should be licensed;
- competent authorities should take the necessary legal or regulatory measures to prevent criminals or their associates from holding or being the beneficial owner of a significant or controlling interest, holding a management function in, or being an operator of a casino
- competent authorities should ensure that casinos are effectively supervised for compliance with requirements to combat money laundering and terrorist financing.

b) Countries should ensure that the other categories of designated non-financial businesses and professions are subject to effective systems for monitoring and ensuring their compliance with requirements to combat money laundering and terrorist financing. This should be performed on a risk-sensitive basis. This may be performed by a government authority or by an appropriate self-regulatory organisation, provided that such an organisation can ensure that its members comply with their obligations to combat money laundering and terrorist financing.

- **Recommendation 25**

The competent authorities should establish guidelines, and provide feedback which will assist financial institutions and designated non-financial businesses and professions in applying national measures to combat money laundering and terrorist financing, and in particular, in detecting and reporting suspicious transactions.

INSTITUTIONAL AND OTHER MEASURES NECESSARY IN SYSTEMS FOR COMBATING MONEY LAUNDERING AND TERRORIST FINANCING

Competent authorities, their powers and resources

- **Recommendation 26**

Countries should establish a FIU that serves as a national centre for the receiving (and, as permitted, requesting), analysis and dissemination of STR and other information regarding potential money laundering or terrorist financing. The FIU should have access, directly or indirectly, on a timely basis to the financial, administrative and law enforcement information that it requires to properly undertake its functions, including the analysis of STR.

- **Recommendation 27**

Countries should ensure that designated law enforcement authorities have responsibility for money laundering and terrorist financing investigations. Countries are encouraged to support and develop, as far as possible, special investigative techniques suitable for the investigation of money laundering, such as controlled delivery, undercover operations and other relevant techniques. Countries are also encouraged to use other effective mechanisms such as the use of permanent or temporary groups specialised in asset investigation, and co-operative investigations with appropriate competent authorities in other countries.

- **Recommendation 28**

When conducting investigations of money laundering and underlying predicate offences, competent authorities should be able to obtain documents and information for use in those investigations, and in prosecutions and related actions. This should include powers to use compulsory measures for the production of records held by financial institutions and other persons, for the search of persons and premises, and for the seizure and obtaining of evidence.

- **Recommendation 29**

    Supervisors should have adequate powers to monitor and ensure compliance by financial institutions with requirements to combat money laundering and terrorist financing, including the authority to conduct inspections. They should be authorised to compel production of any information from financial institutions that is relevant to monitoring such compliance, and to impose adequate administrative sanctions for failure to comply with such requirements.

- **Recommendation 30**

    Countries should provide their competent authorities involved in combating money laundering and terrorist financing with adequate financial, human and technical resources. Countries should have in place processes to ensure that the staff of those authorities are of high integrity.

- **Recommendation 31**

    Countries should ensure that policy makers, the FIU, law enforcement and supervisors have effective mechanisms in place which enable them to co-operate, and where appropriate co-ordinate domestically with each other concerning the development and implementation of policies and activities to combat money laundering and terrorist financing.

- **Recommendation 32**

    Countries should ensure that their competent authorities can review the effectiveness of their systems to combat money laundering and terrorist financing systems by maintaining comprehensive statistics on matters relevant to the effectiveness and efficiency of such systems. This should include statistics on the STR received and disseminated; on money laundering and terrorist financing investigations, prosecutions and convictions; on property frozen, seized and confiscated; and on mutual legal assistance or other international requests for co-operation.

Transparency of legal persons and arrangements

- **Recommendation 33**

Countries should take measures to prevent the unlawful use of legal persons by money launderers. Countries should ensure that there is adequate, accurate and timely information on the beneficial ownership and control of legal persons that can be obtained or accessed in a timely fashion by competent authorities. In particular, countries that have legal persons that are able to issue bearer shares should take appropriate measures to ensure that they are not misused for money laundering and be able to demonstrate the adequacy of those measures. Countries could consider measures to facilitate access to beneficial ownership and control information to financial institutions undertaking the requirements set out in Recommendation 5.

- **Recommendation 34**

Countries should take measures to prevent the unlawful use of legal arrangements by money launderers. In particular, countries should ensure that there is adequate, accurate and timely information on express trusts, including information on the settlor, trustee and beneficiaries, that can be obtained or accessed in a timely fashion by competent authorities. Countries could consider measures to facilitate access to beneficial ownership and control information to financial institutions undertaking the requirements set out in Recommendation 5.

INTERNATIONAL CO-OPERATION

- **Recommendation 35**

Countries should take immediate steps to become party to and implement fully the Vienna Convention, the Palermo Convention, and the 1999 United Nations International Convention for the Suppression of the Financing of Terrorism. Countries are also encouraged to ratify and implement other relevant international conventions, such as the 1990 Council of Europe Convention on Laundering, Search, Seizure and Confiscation of the Proceeds from Crime and the 2002 Inter-American Convention against Terrorism.

Mutual legal assistance and extradition

- **Recommendation 36**

   Countries should rapidly, constructively and effectively provide the widest possible range of mutual legal assistance in relation to money laundering and terrorist financing investigations, prosecutions, and related proceedings. In particular, countries should:

   a) Not prohibit or place unreasonable or unduly restrictive conditions on the provision of mutual legal assistance.

   b) Ensure that they have clear and efficient processes for the execution of mutual legal assistance requests.

   c) Not refuse to execute a request for mutual legal assistance on the sole ground that the offence is also considered to involve fiscal matters.

   d) Not refuse to execute a request for mutual legal assistance on the grounds that laws require financial institutions to maintain secrecy or confidentiality.

   Countries should ensure that the powers of their competent authorities required under Recommendation 28 are also available for use in response to requests for mutual legal assistance, and if consistent with their domestic framework, in response to direct requests from foreign judicial or law enforcement authorities to domestic counterparts.

   To avoid conflicts of jurisdiction, consideration should be given to devising and applying mechanisms for determining the best venue for prosecution of defendants in the interests of justice in cases that are subject to prosecution in more than one country.

- **Recommendation 37**

   Countries should, to the greatest extent possible, render mutual legal assistance notwithstanding the absence of dual criminality.

   Where dual criminality is required for mutual legal assistance or extradition, that requirement should be deeme to be satisfied regardless of whether both countries place the offence within the same category of offence or denominate the offence by the same terminology, provided that both countries criminalise the conduct underlying the offence.

- **Recommendation 38**

    There should be authority to take expeditious action in response to requests by foreign countries to identify, freeze, seize and confiscate property laundered, proceeds from money laundering or predicate offences, instrumentalities used in or intended for use in the commission of these offences, or property of corresponding value. There should also be arrangements for co-ordinating seizure and confiscation proceedings, which may include the sharing of confiscated assets.

- **Recommendation 39**

    Countries should recognize money laundering as an extraditable offence. Each country should either extradite its own nationals, or where a country does not do so solely on the grounds of nationality, that country should, at the request of the country seeking extradition, submit the case without undue delay to its competent authorities for the purpose of prosecution of the offences set forth in the request. Those authorities should take their decision and conduct their proceedings in the same manner as in the case of any other offence of a serious nature under the domestic law of that country. The countries concerned should cooperate with each other, in particular on procedural and evidentiary aspects, to ensure the efficiency of such prosecutions.

    Subject to their legal frameworks, countries may consider simplifying extradition by allowing direct transmission of extradition requests between appropriate ministries, extraditing persons based only on warrants of arrests or judgments, and/or introducing a simplified extradition of consenting persons who waive formal extradition proceedings.

Other forms of co-operation

- **Recommendation 40**

    Countries should ensure that their competent authorities provide the widest possible range of international co-operation to their foreign counterparts. There should be clear and effective gateways to facilitate the prompt and constructive exchange directly between counterparts, either spontaneously or upon request, of information relating to both money laundering and the underlying predicate offences. Exchanges should be permitted without unduly restrictive conditions. In particular:

a) Competent authorities should not refuse a request for assistance on the sole ground that the request is also considered to involve fiscal matters.

b) Countries should not invoke laws that require financial institutions to maintain secrecy or confidentiality as a ground for refusing to provide co-operation.

c) Competent authorities should be able to conduct inquiries; and where possible, investigations; on behalf of foreign counterparts.

Where the ability to obtain information sought by a foreign competent authority is not within the mandate of its counterpart, countries are also encouraged to permit a prompt and constructive exchange of information with non-counterparts. Co-operation with foreign authorities other than counterparts could occur directly or indirectly. When uncertain about the appropriate avenue to follow, competent authorities should first contact their foreign counterparts for assistance.

Countries should establish controls and safeguards to ensure that information exchanged by competent authorities is used only in an authorized manner, consistent with their obligations concerning privacy and data protection.

Appendix 6 Council Directive on Prevention of the Use of the Financial System for the Purpose of Money Laundering (2001)

Article 1

For the purpose of this Directive:

(A) Credit institution means a credit institution, as defined in Article 1(1) first subparagraph of Directive 2000/12/EC(9) and includes branches within the meaning of Article 1(3) of that Directive and located in the Community, of credit institutions having their head offices inside or outside the Community;

(B) "Financial institution" means:

1. an undertaking other than a credit institution whose principal activity is to carry out one or more of the operations included in numbers 2 to 12 and number 14 of the list set out in Annex I to Directive 2000/12/EC; these include the activities of currency exchange offices (bureaux de change) and of money transmission/remittance offices;

2. an insurance company duly authorised in accordance with Directive 79/267/EEC(10), insofar as it carries out activities covered by that Directive;

3. an investment firm as defined in Article 1(2) of Directive 93/22/EEC(11);

4. a collective investment undertaking marketing its units or shares.

This definition of financial institution includes branches located in the Community of financial institutions, whose head offices are inside or outside the Community,

(C) "Money laundering" means the following conduct when committed intentionally:

• the conversion or transfer of property, knowing that such property is derived from criminal activity or from an act of participation in such activity, for the purpose of concealing or disguising the illicit origin of the property or of assisting any person who is involved in the commission of such activity to evade the legal consequences of his action;

• the concealment or disguise of the true nature, source, location, disposition, movement, rights with respect to, or ownership of property, knowing that such property is derived from criminal activity or from an act of participation in such activity;

• the acquisition, possession or use of property, knowing, at the time of receipt, that such property was derived from criminal activity or from an act of participation in such activity;

• participation in, association to commit, attempts to commit and aiding, abetting, facilitating and counselling the commission of any of the actions mentioned in the foregoing indents.

Knowledge, intent or purpose required as an element of the abovementioned activities may be inferred from objective factual circumstances.

Money laundering shall be regarded as such even where the activities which generated the property to be laundered were carried out in the territory of another Member State or in that of a third country.

(D) "Property" means assets of every kind, whether corporeal or incorporeal, movable or immovable, tangible or intangible, and legal documents or instruments evidencing title to or interests in such assets.

(E) "Criminal activity" means any kind of criminal involvement in the commission of a serious crime.

Serious crimes are, at least:

• any of the offences defined in Article 3(1)(a) of the Vienna Convention;

• the activities of criminal organisations as defined in Article 1 of Joint Action 98/733/JHA(12);

• fraud, at least serious, as defined in Article 1(1) and Article 2 of the Convention on the protection of the European Communities' financial interests(13);

• corruption;

• an offence which may generate substantial proceeds and which is punishable by a severe sentence of imprisonment in accordance with the penal law of the Member State.

Member States shall before 15 December 2004 amend the definition provided for in this indent in order to bring this definition into line with the definition of serious crime of Joint Action 98/699/JHA. The Council invites the Commission to present before 15 December 2004 a proposal for a Directive amending in that respect this Directive.

Member States may designate any other offence as a criminal activity for the purposes of this Directive.

(F) "Competent authorities" means the national authorities empowered by law or regulation to supervise the activity of any of the institutions or persons subject to this Directive.

Article 2

(A) Member States shall ensure that the obligations laid down in this Directive are imposed on the following institutions:

1. credit institutions as defined in point A of Article 1;
2. financial institutions as defined in point B of Article 1;

and on the following legal or natural persons acting in the exercise of their professional activities:

3. auditors, external accountants and tax advisors;
4. real estate agents;
5. notaries and other independent legal professionals, when they participate, whether:

(a) by assisting in the planning or execution of transactions for their client concerning the

(i) buying and selling of real property or business entities;

(ii) managing of client money, securities or other assets;

(iii) opening or management of bank, savings or securities accounts;

(iv) organisation of contributions necessary for the creation, operation or management of companies;

(v) creation, operation or management of trusts, companies or similar structures;

(b) or by acting on behalf of and for their client in any financial or real estate transaction;

6. dealers in high-value goods, such as precious stones or metals, or works of art, auctioneers, whenever payment is made in cash, and in an amount of EUR 15000 or more;
7. casinos.

(B) Member States shall ensure that money laundering as defined in this Directive is prohibited.

Article 3

1. Member States shall ensure that the institutions and persons subject to this Directive require identification of their customers by means of supporting evidence when entering into business relations, particularly, in the case of the institutions, when opening an account or savings accounts, or when offering safe custody facilities.

2. The identification requirement shall also apply for any transaction with customers other than those referred to in paragraph 1, involving a sum amounting to EUR 15000 or more, whether the transaction is carried out in a single operation or in several operations which seem to be linked. Where the sum is not known at the time when the transaction is undertaken, the institution or person concerned shall proceed with identification as soon as it or he is apprised of the sum and establishes that the threshold has been reached.

3. By way of derogation from the preceding paragraphs, the identification requirements with regard to insurance policies written by insurance undertakings within the meaning of Council Directive 92/96/EEC of 10 November 1992 on the coordination of laws, regulations and administrative provisions relating to direct life assurance (third life assurance Directive) (14), where they perform activities which fall within the scope of that Directive shall not be required where the periodic premium amount or amounts to be paid in any given year does or do not exceed EUR 1000 or where a single premium is paid amounting to EUR 2500 or less. If the periodic premium amount or amounts to be paid in any given year is or are increased so as to exceed the EUR 1000 threshold, identification shall be required.

4. Member States may provide that the identification requirement is not compulsory for insurance policies in respect of pension schemes taken out by virtue of a contract of employment or the insured's occupation, provided that such policies contain no surrender clause and may not be used as collateral for a loan.

5. By way of derogation from the preceding paragraphs, all casino customers shall be identified if they purchase or sell gambling chips with a value of EUR 1000 or more.

6. Casinos subject to State supervision shall be deemed in any event to have complied with the identification requirement laid down in this Directive if they register and identify their customers immediately on entry, regardless of the number of gam-

bling chips purchased.

7. In the event of doubt as to whether the customers referred to in the above paragraphs are acting on their own behalf, or where it is certain that they are not acting on their own behalf, the institutions and persons subject to this Directive shall take reasonable measures to obtain information as to the real identity of the persons on whose behalf those customers are acting.

8. The institutions and persons subject to this Directive shall carry out such identification, even where the amount of the transaction is lower than the threshold laid down, wherever there is suspicion of money laundering.

9. The institutions and persons subject to this Directive shall not be subject to the identification requirements provided for in this Article where the customer is a credit or financial institution covered by this Directive or a credit or financial institution situated in a third country which imposes, in the opinion of the relevant Member States, equivalent requirements to those laid down by this Directive.

10. Member States may provide that the identification requirements regarding transactions referred to in paragraphs 3 and 4 are fulfilled when it is established that the payment for the transaction is to be debited from an account opened in the customer's name with a credit institution subject to this Directive according to the requirements of paragraph 1.

11. Member States shall, in any case, ensure that the institutions and persons subject to this Directive take specific and adequate measures necessary to compensate for the greater risk of money laundering which arises when establishing business relations or entering into a transaction with a customer who has not been physically present for identification purposes ("non-face to face" operations). Such measures shall ensure that the customer's identity is established, for example, by requiring additional documentary evidence, or supplementary measures to verify or certify the documents supplied, or confirmatory certification by an institution subject to this Directive, or by requiring that the first payment of the operations is carried out through an account opened in the customer's name with a credit institution subject to this Directive. The internal control procedures laid down in Article 11(1) shall take specific account of these measures.

Article 4

Member States shall ensure that the institutions and persons subject to this Directive keep the following for use as evidence in any investigation into money laundering:

- in the case of identification, a copy or the references of the evidence required, for a period of at least five years after the relationship with their customer has ended,
- in the case of transactions, the supporting evidence and records, consisting of the original documents or copies admissible in court proceedings under the applicable national legislation for a period of at least five years following execution of the transactions.

Article 5

Member States shall ensure that the institutions and persons subject to this Directive examine with special attention any transaction which they regard as particularly likely, by its nature, to be related to money laundering.

Article 6

1. Member States shall ensure that the institutions and persons subject to this Directive and their directors and employees cooperate fully with the authorities responsible for combating money laundering:

(a) by informing those authorities, on their own initiative, of any fact which might be an indication of money laundering;

(a) by furnishing those authorities, at their request, with all necessary information, in accordance with the procedures established by the applicable legislation.

2. The information referred to in paragraph 1 shall be forwarded to the authorities responsible for combating money laundering of the Member State in whose territory the institution or person forwarding the information is situated. The person or persons designated by the institutions and persons in accordance with the procedures provided for in Article 11(1)(a) shall normally forward the information.

3. In the case of the notaries and independent legal professionals referred to in Article 2a(5), Member States may designate an appropriate self-regulatory body of the profession concerned as the authority to be informed of the facts referred to in paragraph 1(a) and in such case shall lay down the appropriate forms of cooperation between that body and the authorities responsible for combating money laundering.

Member States shall not be obliged to apply the obligations laid down in paragraph 1 to notaries, independent legal professionals, auditors, external accountants and tax advisors with regard to information they receive from or obtain on one of their clients, in the course of ascertaining the legal position for their client or performing their task of defending or representing that client in, or concerning judicial proceedings, including advice on instituting or avoiding proceedings, whether such information is received or obtained before, during or after such proceedings.

Article 7

Member States shall ensure that the institutions and persons subject to this Directive refrain from carrying out transactions which they know or suspect to be related to money laundering until they have apprised the authorities referred to in Article 6. Those authorities may, under conditions determined by their national legislation, give instructions not to execute the operation. Where such a transaction is suspected of giving rise to money laundering and where to refrain in such manner is impossible or is likely to frustrate efforts to pursue the beneficiaries of a suspected money-laundering operation, the institutions and persons concerned shall apprise the authorities immediately afterwards.

Article 8

1. The institutions and persons subject to this Directive and their directors and employees shall not disclose to the customer concerned nor to other third persons that information has been transmitted to the authorities in accordance with Articles 6 and 7 or that a money laundering investigation is being carried out.

2. Member States shall not be obliged under this Directive to apply the obligation laid down in paragraph 1 to the professions mentioned in the second paragraph of Article 6(3).

Article 9

The disclosure in good faith to the authorities responsible for combating money laundering by an institution or person subject to this Directive or by an employee or director of such an institution or person of the information referred to in Articles 6 and 7 shall not constitute a breach of any restriction on disclosure of information imposed by contract or by any legislative, regulatory or administrative provision, and shall not involve the institution or person or its directors or employees in liability of any kind.

Article 10

Member States shall ensure that if, in the course of inspections carried out in the institutions or persons subject to this Directive by the competent authorities, or in any other way, those authorities discover facts that could constitute evidence of money laundering, they inform the authorities responsible for combating money laundering.

Member States shall ensure that supervisory bodies empowered by law or regulation to oversee the stock, foreign exchange and financial derivatives markets inform the authorities responsible for combating money laundering if they discover facts that could constitute evidence of money laundering.

Article 11

1. Member States shall ensure that the institutions and persons subject to this Directive:

(a) establish adequate procedures of internal control and communication in order to forestall and prevent operations related to money laundering;

(b) take appropriate measures so that their employees are aware of the provisions contained in this Directive. These measures shall include participation of their relevant employees in special training programmes to help them recognise operations which may be related to money laundering as well as to instruct them as to how to proceed in such cases.

Where a natural person falling within any of Article 2a(3) to (7) undertakes his professional activities as an employee of a legal person, the obligations in this Article shall apply to that legal person rather than to the natural person.

2. Member States shall ensure that the institutions and persons subject to this Directive have access to up-to-date information on the practices of money launderers and on indications leading to the recognition of suspicious transactions.

Article 12

Member States shall ensure that the provisions of this Directive are extended in whole or in part to professions and to categories of undertakings, other than the institutions and persons referred to in Article 2a, which engage in activities which are particularly likely to be used for money-laundering purposes.

Bibliography

Books

William C. Gilmore, *Dirty Money, The Evolution of Money Laundering Counter-measures*, Council of Europe Press, 1995.

Ernesto U. Savona, *Responding to Money Laundering, International Perspectives*, Harwood Academic Publishers, 1997.

George Square, Money Laundering, *Hume Papers on Public Policy*, Vol. 1 No. 2, Edinburgh University Press 22, 1993.

William C. Gilmore, International Efforts to Combat Money Laundering, *Cambridge International Document Series*, Volume 4, 1992.

Vincent. Mul, *Banken en witwassen* (Dutch), sanders instituut, Gouda Quint, 1999.

Gao Mingxuan, Zhao Bingzhi, *Collected Review of Criminal Law*, Law Press, 1999.

Xin Cunying, *Chinese Legal System and Current Legal Reform*, Law Press, 1999.

Gao Mingxuan, Wang Zuofu, *The Dictionary of Chinese Criminal Law*, Xue Lin Press, 1989.

Zhao Bingzhi, *The Strategy on Confused Problems in Crimes of Undermining the Order of the Socialist Market Economy*, Ji Lin People's Press, 2000.

Ma Kechang, Bao Suixian: The Current Situation, Reasons and Countermeasures of Drug Crimes in China. *The Theory and Practice of Suppression of Drug Crimes*, Publishing House of the China University of Political Science and Law, 1993.

Ruan Fang-ming, *Comparative Study on Money Laundering*, Press of the Chinese University of Political Science and Law, 2002.

Richard Parlour, *International Guide to Money Laundering, Law and Practice*, Butterworths, 1995.

Wan Yixian, *The Legal Issues of Electronic Commerce*, Law Press, 2001.

Cesare Beccaria, Crime and Punishment, Chinese Encyclopedia Press, 1996.

Shao Shaping, *Legal Control on Transnational Money Laundering*, Wu Han University Press, 1998.

Zhen Jinxin, *Money Laundering and the Counter-measures*, East Press, 2000.

Articles

Hans de Doelder, Vincent Mul, Marije van den Enden, Regulation of Financial Markets With Particular Reference to Market Abuse: A Perspective From the Netherlands, *Netherlands reports to the Fifteenth International Congress of Comparative law*, Bristol 1998.

He Ping, Chinese Criminal Law concerning Money Laundering, *Journal of Money Laundering Control*, Vol. 6 No. 4, 2003.

Zhu Lifang and He Ping, The Chinese Financial Institution Campaign against Money Laundering, *Journal of Money Laundering Control*, Vol. 7 No. 2, 2003.

He Ping, Banking Secrecy and Money Laundering, *Journal of Money Laundering Control*, Vol. 7 No. 4, 2004.

He Ping, New Trends in Money Laundering—From the Real World to Cyberspace, *Journal of Money Laundering Control*, Vol. 8 No. 1, 2004.

He Ping, Money Laundering and High Technology, *Science of Law*, 2nd Issue, 2003.

He Ping, Suspicious Transaction Reporting System, *Learned Journal of East China University of Politics and Law*, 1st Issue, 2003.

He Ping, Administrative Counter-measures Against Money Laundering in China, *the Study of Crime*, 3rd Issue, 2002.

He Ping, The New Weapon of Combating Money Laundering: the 2001 Amendment to the 1991 EC Directive, *the Study of Crime*, 1st Issue, 2003.

He Ping, Money Laundering and Banking Secrecy, *Shanghai Prosecutorial Theories Research*, 5th Issue, 2003.

Jackie Johnson, 11th September, 2001: Will it Make a Difference to the Global Anti-Money Laundering Movement? *Journal of Money Laundering Control*, Vol. 6 No. 1.

International Chamber of Commerce, Guide to the Prevention of Money Laundering, *Journal of Commerce 4*, June 1998.

Financial War on Terrorism and Implementation of Money-Laundering Provisions in the USA Patriot Act: Hearing of the Senate Banking, *Housing and Urban Affairs Comm.* 107th Cong.

Petrus C. Van Duyne, Money-Laundering: Estimates in Fog, *the Journal of Asset Protection and Financial Crime*, Vol. 2 No. 1, 1994.

Kern Alexander, The International Anti-Money-Laundering Regime: The Role of the Financial Action Task Force, *Journal of Money Laundering Control*, Vol. 4 No. 3.

Tom Sherman, International Efforts to combat Money Laundering: The Role of the Financial Action Task Force, *Money Laundering*, *Hume Papers on Public policy*, Vol. 1 No. 2, 1993.

Kern Alexander, The International Anti-Money-Laundering Regime: The Role of the Financial Action Task Force, *Journal of Money Laundering Control*, Vol. 4. No. 3.

Gil Galvao, Countering Money Laundering: The FATF, The European Union and The Portuguese Experiences, Past and Current Developments, *Work Product of the 117th International Seminar*.

Bibliography

Kern Alexander, The International Anti-Money-Laundering Regime: The Role of the Financial Action Task Force, *Journal of Money Laundering Control*, Vol. 4 No. 3.

Constantin Stefanou and Helen Xanthaki, The New EU Draft Money Laundering Directive: A Case of Inter-Institutional Synergy, *Journal of Money Laundering Control*, Vol. 3 No. 4.

Feng Zhaokui, We Welcome Foreign Capital—The Relation Between Introducing Foreign Capital and developing National Industry, *World Knowledge*, Vol. 13, 1997.

Gao Degui, The Achievement and future of the Financial Reform in China, *People's Daily*, Dec. 11, 1997.

Guo Weicheng, Observing Trend from the Lu-jia-zhui, *People's Daily*, Dec. 2, 1997.

Zhao Zuojun, Research on Money Laundering, *Law Science*, Volume 5, 1997.

Petrus C. Van Duyne, Money Laundering: Estimate in Fog, *The Journal of Asset Protection and financial crime*, Vol. 2 No. 1, 1994.

Liu Jie, Chinese Banking Business: the Storm of Anti-Money Laundering Is Ongoing, *Reform and Theory*, July 2000.

Shao Shaping, The New Criminal Law and Control on Money Laundering, *Front Edge of Law*, Vol. 1, Law Press 1997.

Barry A. K. Rider, The Control of Money Laundering Crime, *Peking University Law Journal*, Volume 5, 1999.

Ding Muying, The Research on Money Laundering, *Chinese Criminal Law Journal*, Vol. 38. 1998.

Wang Deqing, The Present Conditions of Money Laundering Crime and Preventive Counter-measures in China, *Tian Jing Politics Science and Law*, Vol. 4, 1997.

Jacqueline E. Ross, Tradeoffs in Undercover Investigations: A Comparative Perspective, *University of Chicago Law Review*, Summer, 2002.

Bert Ravenstijn, The Netherlands: Anti Money-Laundering Programes—The Case of ING, *Journal of Money Laundering Control*, Vol. 3 No. 4, 2000.

Michael Levi, New Frontiers of Criminal Liability: Money Laundering and Proceeds of Crime, *Journal of Money Laundering Control*, Vol. 3 No. 3, 2000.

Paolo Clarotti, EU: The Perspective of the European Commission, *Journal of Money Laundering Control*, Vol. 2 No. 2.

Valsamis Mitsilegas, New Forms of Transnational Policing: The Emergence of Financial Intelligence Units in the European Union and the Challenge for Human Rights: Part 1, *Journal of Money Laundering Control*, Vol. 3 No. 2, 1999.

George J. Moscarino and Michael R. Shumaker, Beating the shell Game: Banking Secrecy laws and Their Impact on Civil Recovery in International Fraud Actions, *Journal of Money Laundering Control* Vol. 1 No. 1, 1997.

Robert S. Pasley, Privacy Rights V. Anti-Money Laundering Enforcement, *University of North*

Carolina School of Law Banking Institute, *North Carolina Banking Institute*, April, 2002.

Peter Maynard, Bahamas: Civil Liberties and privacy—The Questions of Balance, *Journal of Money Laundering Control*, Vol. 1 No. 2.

George J. Moscarino and Michael R. Shumaker, Beating the shell Game: Banking Secrecy laws and Their Impact on Civil Recovery in International Fraud Actions, *Journal of Money Laundering Control*, Vol. 1 No. 1, 1997.

John J. Byrne, Know Your Customer: What Happened and What Happens Next, *Journal of Money Laundering Control*, Vol. 3 No. 4, 2000.

Marc G. Corrado, The Supreme Court's Impact on Swiss Banking Secrecy: Societe Nationale Industrielle Aerospatiale v. United States District Count, *the American University Law Review*, Spring, 1988.

Steven V. Melnik, The Inadequate Utilization of the Accounting Profession in the United States Government's Fight against Money Laundering, *2000 New York University School of Law Journal of Legislation and public Policy*.

Helen Xanthaki, Lawyers' Duties under the Draft EU Money Laundering Directive: Is Confidentiality a Thing of the Past? *Journal of Money Laundering Control*, Vol. 5 No. 2, 2001.

Mark D. Schopper, Internet Gambling, Electronic Cash & Money Laundering: The Unintended Consequences of a Money Control Scheme, *Chapman Law Review*, Spring 2002.

Steven Philippsohn, The Dangers of New Technology—Laundering on the Internet, *Journal of Money Laundering Control*, Vol. 5 No. 1, 2001.

Jason Haines and Peter Johnstone, Global Cybercrime: New Toys for the Money Launderiers, *Journal of Money Laundering Control*, Vol. 2 No. 4.

R. Mark Bortner, *Cyberlaundering: Anonymous Digital Cash and Money Laundering*, http://www.law.miami.edu/~froomkin/seminar/papers/bortner.

R. Mark Bernkopf, *Electronic Cash and Money Policy*, 1996. http://www.firstmonday.dk/issues/issuel/ecash/index.html.

Bank of International Settlement, *Implications for Central Banks of the Development of Electronic Money*, October 1996. http://www.bis.org/publ/bisp01.pdf.

Documents and Reports

United Nations Convention against Transnational Organization Crime.

United Nations Convention Against Illicit Traffic in Narcotic Drugs and Psychotropic Substances.

Basle Committee on Banking Regulations and Supervisory Practices December 1988 Statement on Prevention of Criminal Use of the Banking System for the Purpose of Money-Laundering.

The Single Convention on Narcotic Drugs, 1961.

The 1971 Convention on Psychotropic Substance.

UN Security Council Resolutions: S/RES/1267 (1999), S/RES/1269 (1999), S/RES/1333 (2000), S/RES/1373(2001) and S/RES/1390(2001).

Constitution of the Interpol.

1990 Council of Europe Convention on Laundering, Search, Seizure, and Confiscation of the proceeds from Crime.

Council Directive of 10 June 1991 on Prevention of the Use of the Financial System for the Purpose of Money laundering.

Directive 2001/97/EC of the European Parliament and of the Council of 4 December 2001 Amending Council Directive 91/308/EEC on Prevention of the Use of the Financial System for the Purpose of Money Laundering.

Action Plan to Combat Organized Crime.

Convention Based on Article K.3 of the Treaty on European Union, On the Establishment of European Police Office.

Special Action Against Money Laundering, Presidency Conclusion, Tampere European Council, 15 and 16 October 1999.

Rules for Anti-money Laundering by Financial Institutions.

Administrative Rules for the Reporting of Large-value and Suspicious RMB Payment Transactions.

Administrative Rules for the Reporting by Financial Institutions of Large-value and Suspicious Foreign Exchange Transactions.

Proposal for a European Parliament and Council Directive Amending Council Directive 91/308/EEC of the 10 June 1991 on Prevention of the Use of the Financial System for the Purpose of Money Laundering, Explanatory memorandum.

US Treasury Dept Financial Crimes Enforcement Network Assessment of US Money Laundering: Submission to the Financial Action Task Force 2 (1994).

Political Declaration and Action Plan against Money Laundering, New York, 10 June, 1988.

Second Commission Report to the European Parliament and the Council on the Implementation of the Money Laundering Directive.

Proposal for a European Parliament and Council Directive Amending Council Directive 91/308/EEC of the 10 June 1991 on Prevention of the Use of the Financial System for the Purpose of Money Laundering, Explanatory memorandum.

Second Protocol to the Convention on the Prevention of the European Communities' Financial Interests (1997) Article 1 (e).

Joint Action of 3 December 1998 adopted by the Council on the basis of Article K.3 of the Treaty on European Union, on Money Laundering, the Identification, Tracing, Freezing, Seizing and Confiscation of Instrumentalities and proceeds from crime.

2003 Europe Information Service European Report, June 28, 2003.

Justice and Home Affaires: Europol Shifts to Operational Side, Europe Information Service, European Report, May 14, 2003.

EU/US: Agreement on Transfer of Personal Data with Europol Imminent, Copyright 2002 Europe Information Service, European Report, Nov. 16, 2002.

Europe Information Service European Report, May 14, 2003.

Europe Information Service European Report, May 29, 2002.

The Bulletin of the Supreme People's Court On the meeting of the Fifth Session of the Ninth People's Congress on March 11, 2002.

The Work Section Points of the Supreme People's Court on Trying Drug Cases in Twelve Provinces, December 17, 1991.

Law Yearbook of China, Press of law yearbook of China, 1999, 2000.

Financial Action Task Force on Money Laundering 1990 Forty Recommendations.

Financial Action Task Force on Money Laundering 1996 Forty Recommendations.

Financial Action Task Force on Money Laundering 2003 Forty Recommendations.

Financial Action Task on Money Laundering Report of 6 February 1990.

Financial Action Task Force on Money Laundering Annual Report 2001-2002.

Financial Action Task Force on Money Laundering, Review of FATF Anti-Money laundering Systems and Mutual Evaluation Procedures 1992-1999, 16 February 2001.

Financial Action Task Force on Money Laundering Annual Report 1995-1996.

Financial Action Task Force on Money Laundering Annual Report 1999-2000.

Financial Action Task Force on Money Laundering, Report on Non-Cooperative Countries and Territories, 14 February 2000.

Financial Action Task Force on Money Laundering, Review to Identify Non-Cooperative Countries or Territories: Increasing The World-Wide Effectiveness of Anti-Money Laundering Measures, 21 June 2002.

Financial Action Task Force 1998-1999 Annual Report, 2 July 1999.

Financial Action Task Force 1996-1997 Annual Report, June 1997.

Financial Action Task Force on Money Laundering, 1996-1997 Report on Money Laundering Typologies, February 1997.

Financial Action Task Force on Money Laundering, The 1996 Forty Recommendations, 28 June 1996.

Financial Action Task Force on Money Laundering, The 2003 Forty Recommendations, 20 June 2003.

Financial Action Task Force 2000-2001 Typology Report.

Financial Action Task Force 1996-1997 Typology Report.